D1738949

The Descent of Darwin

The Descent of

Darwin

The Popularization of Darwinism

in Germany, 1860–1914

by Alfred Kelly

The University of North Carolina Press *Chapel Hill*

To JOYCE

for all her love and help

© 1981 The University of North Carolina Press

All rights reserved

Manufactured in the United States of America

Library of Congress Cataloging in Publication Data

Kelly, Alfred, 1947–
  The Descent of Darwin

  Bibliography: p.
  Includes index.
    1. Germany—Intellectual life. 2. Darwin,
Charles Robert, 1809–1882—Influence. 3. Philosophy,
German—19th century. 4. Social Darwinism—History
I. Title.
DD67.K4   001.1′0943   80-19445
ISBN 0-8078-1460-1

Contents

The Descent of Darwin

Chapter 1

The Question of

Popularization

THIS book studies the popularization in Germany of one of the great ideas of modern Western culture. If the proposal has a somewhat unfamiliar air, it is because intellectual historians (particularly in America) have traditionally neglected the thorny problem of how ideas move through a society. Most historians have confined themselves to an examination of high culture or "big intellectual guns"; those who have studied popular culture and ideas have tended to see them as subintellectual history, self-contained and detached from elites. As one prominent writer puts it, one can deal with either a "higher" or "lower" level of thought, and the "lower" level "is characteristically supposed to represent what has 'seeped down' from the first level after a generation or two of 'cultural lag': in this new setting ideas nearly invariably figure in vulgarized or distorted form."[1] Or, in the words of another historian: "The new ideas of a handful of men in one generation become the fashionable thoughts of the upper class in the next, and the common beliefs of the common man in the third."[2]

One could hardly argue with these pronouncements; they are too vague to merit vehement opposition. To say that ideas "seep down" after a "cultural lag" leaves hanging a number of important questions: What exactly is the relation between higher and lower levels of thought? How in fact do ideas originally limited to a tiny coterie of seminal minds move downward to become common currency? Who spreads ideas? Why? What kinds of changes occur on the way down? There must be concrete answers to these questions before historians can move beyond a mere description of intraintellectual dialogues and trace the social effects of ideas. Not until we understand the dynamics of popularization can the standard clichés of intellectual history, be they "climate of opinion," Zeitgeist, or mentalité, begin to acquire real substance.

This is not to suggest that all popularly held ideas necessarily move downward from tiny elites; that would be a crude distortion. In a mass society there are very complex exchanges between intellectual elites and the rest of society. Radio, television, and widespread higher education have combined to muddle greatly the question of just who is influencing whom. Still, these qualifications should not obscure the simple fact that many important and widely held ideas can be traced back to one, or at most a handful, of men. The ideas of Newton, Marx, Darwin, Nietzsche, Freud, and Einstein, as well as such philosophies as laissez-faire liberalism, positivism, and existentialism, come to mind as obvious examples among many. But of these we know something about the popularization only of Newton's ideas; and the reason is instructive. The popularizers of Newton, the philosophes, have merited attention mainly because they were also "serious thinkers." As for the other ideas, their paths into the minds of millions remain largely uncharted. It is misleading to object that the millions have only vague or wrong impressions of great ideas, for distortion may have consequences as momentous as precise understanding. Never mind that no seminal thinker ever said without qualification that, say, man was a beast or that science could solve all problems. A society in which the majority affirms these beliefs—with varying degrees of sophistication—is nonetheless profoundly different from one in which the majority denies them.

Certainly the history of education has something to say on the subject of popularization. But most learning, for adults at least, takes place outside of formal educational institutions. Studies of textbooks, curricula, and teacher education are useful, but can take us only so far. To find the sources of many popular beliefs we are forced to look elsewhere. In an age of mass literacy—though before radio and television—an obvious place to begin is with those self-appointed uplifters of the people, the successful popularizers. These were writers (a few of them important thinkers in their own right) who sought to break down the growing barriers between the increasingly complex world of scholarship and an ever-expanding reading public. Such efforts are traceable back to the seventeenth century; but it was only in the late nineteenth century, with the advent of mass literacy and the first impact of science on daily life, that the popularizer fully emerged as a cultural type, above all in Germany. Recent years have witnessed extensive studies of popular fiction, as well as the sociology of publishing and reading—all subjects that touch upon the question of popularization.[3] But too few historians have taken the trouble to analyze the contents of popular nonfiction books and magazines.

This study of German popular Darwinism should be seen in this larger context. It explores the process by which Darwinism reached beyond the scholars to the German general public. It asks who the popularizers were, what their motives were, what they said, to whom they said it, how they changed Darwin's ideas, and what their impact was on German society. But why Darwinism, and why Germany? The answers are simple: Darwinism lends itself to such a study because it attracted a plethora of popularizers. Indeed, Darwinism was a popularizer's dream. It had enormous philosophical, religious, political, and even emotional implications beyond the narrow realm of biology; further, it was, at least in simplified form, easy for the layman to understand. Darwin was probably the last of the great amateur scientists, and he often used a personalized, anecdotal technique that fared very well in popularized form. Then, too, Darwin's *The Origin of Species* came at a good time for popularization. The late nineteenth century was the great age of reading. Popular works could ride the crest of increasing literacy and the new mass circulation of books, newspapers, and magazines. Probably never before or since was the prestige of science so high and the interest of the layman in the meaning of science so great. Had Darwin's ideas appeared earlier in the nineteenth century, they could have been known by only a few; had they come in our century they might well have been lost in the trivial chatter of the so-called media. The leisurely reading of a century ago was the perfect setting for the spread of serious ideas.

Moreover, Darwinism became a kind of popular philosophy in Germany more than in any other country, even England. Darwinism caught on rapidly in the German scientific community; indeed, Germany, rather than England, was the main center of biological research in the late nineteenth century. This professional activity attracted large numbers of popularizers, who took advantage of the vast and unusually receptive reading public. For not only was Germany the most literate of the major European countries, it also offered the richest environment for Darwinism to expand beyond the confines of science. Political liberalism had been thwarted in Germany in 1848, and Darwinism became a pseudopolitical ideological weapon for the progressive segments of the middle class. Science commanded respect as an unstoppable form of progress. By the 1880s, as liberalism weakened, Darwinism found a new expression among the working class as popular Marxism in disguise—a simple faith in the triumph of justice. In both the quantity and quality of its popular Darwinism, Germany was unmatched.

To be sure, the direct influence of Darwin himself, whose works were translated but scarcely read, was small. Nor did the secondary schools play any direct role, for Darwin was largely excluded from the classroom. Instead, Darwin's thought was mediated by a host of scientific popularizers, who, from the 1860s on, produced a flood of lectures, magazine articles, and best-selling books. Of these men, only Ernst Haeckel is well known today. Few remember Friedrich Ratzel, Carl Vogt, Ludwig Büchner, C. Bock, E. A. Rossmässler, Alfred Brehm, Otto Zacharias, Carus Sterne, Wilhelm Preyer, Arnold Dodel, Oswald Köhler, Edward Aveling, Rudolf Bommeli, and Wilhelm Bölsche. But all of these authors were well known in their time, and their books and articles were widely read. Their combined efforts shaped the German people's view of Darwinism. Although Haeckel's role was significant, he by no means deserves the almost exclusive credit he is usually given for bringing Darwinism to the German public. If anyone merits the star role as *the* popularizer it is Haeckel's forgotten friend, the novelist turned science popularizer, Wilhelm Bölsche. The combined circulation of Bölsche's works was far greater than that of Haeckel's; and it was he who, beginning in the 1890s, brought German popular Darwinism to a climax. Of all the popularizers, he was the most eloquent and sensitive interpreter of the meaning of Darwinism, and his books were deservedly the most loved. Indeed Bölsche was the single bestselling nonfiction author in the German language before 1933. His ideas will therefore loom large in our story.

But there were hundreds of German books on Darwinism. How, then, can we define popular Darwinism? Surprisingly, this presents relatively little problem. Popular books say that they are popular books, and they stand out strikingly against the vast array of specialized studies. If this seems an overly facile answer to the question, it should be kept in mind that by the 1860s German popular science had developed an acute self-consciousness of its special role. A popular science book customarily began with an aggressive declaration of the need to spread knowledge beyond the scientific elite. This was true even of popular books written by members of the scientific elite. The same man who turned out an abstruse treatise for a few colleagues might also try his hand at popularization. But he would never confuse the two kinds of writings, and there is no reason to do so today. The division between popular and scholarly magazines was often less explicitly stated but equally sharp. A popular article differed both in style and content from its scholarly counterpart.

Of course, it is one thing to write in a popular style and quite another to achieve popularity. The true popular book was not only understandable, but also widely read, although just how widely read cannot be determined with any precision because circulation figures for nineteenth-century books are notoriously hard to come by. We do know how many editions a book went through and how often it was referred to in newspapers, magazines, or other books. And from such information it is possible to infer a book's popularity. Usually the impressions gained in this way dovetail very nicely with hard circulation figures when they are available. Numbers, however, do not necessarily reflect a book's influence. Not only do we not know how many people actually read each copy, but, more important, we do not know whether they understood it, agreed with it, or even thought it worth thinking about seriously. (Consider, for example, the millions of Bibles lying about unread and unheeded.)

Here we come up against the great barrier to any reliable social history of ideas. It is possible to analyze in detail the content of popular books, but to assess the effect of those books requires a leap of faith. We are forced to assume—without any real evidence—that popularity translates into widespread influence. This conclusion seems to be the height of good sense, especially if we find obvious relationships between those books and other popular expressions of opinion. Yet we are still trapped by vagueness and conjecture because we cannot demonstrate anything more than coincidence. There is always the danger that we may trace back to Darwinism beliefs or actions that actually resulted from other, even unrelated, causes.[4]

The study of the effects of popular Darwinism is particularly vulnerable to this problem because Darwinism could appear in so many different guises. On its way to the public via the popularizers, Darwinism changed and fragmented a great deal, mixing in very complex ways with other cultural and social forces. Darwin's theory of organic evolution through natural and sexual selection tended to lose its original narrowly scientific and empirical character and to become a loose cluster of popular philosophies or Weltanschauungen. Perhaps it is more accurate to speak of several popular Darwinisms than of one unified system of ideas. Almost anyone could and did appeal to Darwin's authority. Materialists, idealists, aristocrats, democrats, conservatives, liberals, and socialists, as well as protagonists of virtually every shade of religious opinion, all staked out their claims in Darwinian territory. The master's own regal silence on the larger implications of his ideas only added to the intellectual clutter that the term Darwinism suggested. As time passed, this diversity became ever greater, and there comes a point—about World War I—when it is no longer possible to find Darwinisms as separate strands of the cultural fabric. It should be stressed that the vagueness invoked here is not an evasion of historical responsibility. There was genuine confusion surrounding Darwinism, even on the most sophisticated levels of thought. On a popular level the situation was, if anything, worse, not so much because the popularizers distorted any more than anyone else, but rather because a certain superficiality is inherent in the reading of popular works. The popularizers should not be overanalyzed; what counts is the impression they must have given to the typical casual reader.

Despite the confusion, it is possible to sort out a number of themes. Broadly speaking, German popular Darwinism was a continuation of the old eighteenth-century Enlightenment tradition. German Darwinists sought to crush superstition, to inform, to liberate, and, indirectly, to democratize. In a more narrow sense, popular Darwinism may profitably be viewed as a cultural extension of the radical democratic spirit of 1848—a spirit that was suppressed in the political arena but could live on in less threatening nonpolitical guises. Thus Darwinism in the 1860s and 1870s was a weapon against such bastions of the conservative establishment as the churches and public education, and later it became a popular prop for Marxist socialism. Granted, the form of Social Darwinism peddled by both aristocratic and bourgeois apologists does not fit this pattern, but, as will become clear, Social Darwinism's popularity, influence, and indeed its actual dependence on Darwin have been exaggerated. The much touted Social Darwinism of Ernst Haeckel, for example, was scarcely in evidence in most of his really popular books. Not that popular Darwinism had a single developmental line; it tended to be at once diffuse and static. A book, for example, of 1870 might be little different from one of 1910. Nonetheless, it is safe to say that the bulk of popular Darwinism's influence was on the left half of the political, cultural, and social spectrum.

Surely Darwin himself would not have recognized a good deal of what was said in his name in Germany. But in diverging from Darwin the popularizers were doing no more than the so-called serious thinkers. Everyone took the liberty to use Darwin as he pleased, and the popularizers were no different. Contrary to what is often said, the popularizers usually did a fairly accurate job of representing Darwin. Some simplification was inevitable and necessary—few could follow Darwin's often tortuous qualifications—but charges that the popularizers vulgarized or sensationalized come from those who have labeled without bothering to read. These charges do not stand up to close scrutiny. If the popularizers changed Darwinism—and they did—they did so by going beyond Darwin's works to philosophize on their own. When Darwinism evolved into new Weltanschauungen in Germany, it usually did so on a sound factual basis; it was just that the facts often appeared in a context foreign to Darwin's own more limited perspective.

Our approach, then, will be twofold: first, to describe and analyze the content of the popular Darwinian literature; and, second, to attempt to weave that literature into an intelligible historical and social context by describing its relation to education, religion, and politics. As has been suggested, this second step presents the greater difficulties. The evidence, though provocative, is usually haphazard and ambiguous. Indeed, what does not happen may be indirectly as significant as what does happen. Thus the very absence of Darwinism in the schools not only illuminates social values but also gives the whole genre of popular Darwinism added importance. And the failure of popular authors to endorse Social Darwinism helps to relegate that ideology to the political sidelines. We know that at least into the 1880s most readers of popular Darwinism were middle class. But given the diversity of the middle-class reading public and the great variety of influences on it, it is well nigh impossible to make anything but the most general statements about Darwin's influence. Fortunately, in the case of the working class we are on much surer ground, for this was a relatively self-contained subculture whose reading and self-education tended to be focused and predictable.

Yet even where popular Darwinism's influence and effects are obvious, our conclusions must still be modest and tentative. As time went on, Darwinism was burdened with an increasing load of intellectual, ideological, religious, and emotional associations. Deciding what is Darwinism and what is not (to say nothing of deciding what are effects of Darwinism and what are not) requires ever finer distinctions. What begins as a task of clarification can easily end in hairsplitting and confusion. Still, these risks must be accepted if we are to give any substance to terms such as "The Age of Darwin" or "The Darwinian Revolution." What follows does not pretend to be exhaustive, but merely a charting of some unfamiliar or cliché-ridden territories.

Chapter 2

Darwinism and the

Popular Science Tradition

T H E origins of popular Darwinism lie deep within the broader tradition of popular science. Regrettably, popular science has yet to find its historian. The reasons for this lack are fairly obvious. To begin with, popular science is not a clearly defined genre. (It is no accident that none of the standard English or German encyclopedias has an entry under the term.) Prior to the mid-nineteenth century, its history tends to get lost among a host of other genres, especially the lexicon, the calendar or almanac, the travel report, and the newspaper feuilleton. In an age when knowledge was less compartmentalized, popular science might masquerade as moral philosophy, medical advice, or agricultural improvement. Moreover, as Walter Wetzels points out in one of the few articles on the subject, little real historical development is perceptible in those works that can clearly be identified as self-conscious attempts to popularize science. All the essential ingredients are present in the very earliest popular science, he believes, and thus a "history" of popular science would consist of no more than a chronological listing of works, each one scarcely different from the preceding.[1] Though, as we shall see, this is somewhat of an exaggeration, it is still evident that when talking of the popularization of science we have to cast our net very wide, lest the problem be defined out of existence. The best approach is probably to view popular science in the larger context of the growth of a mass reading public, whose taste includes not only belles lettres, but also various kinds of educational nonfiction.

In spite of these difficulties, it is clear that the rise of popular science is inextricably intertwined with the spirit of the European Enlightenment. Before the eighteenth century, most books, with the exception of popular religious tracts, miracle books, and the like, were written for a tiny elite of scholars. Popularization became an issue only when a middle class, bent on self-improvement through rational knowledge, found itself stymied in the face of the increasing complexity, specialization, and hence inaccessibility of science. In response to this new need, the popularizer stepped in to perform a hitherto undemanded, indeed unperceived, function as mediator between the world of learning and the educated layman. *Sapere audi!* Dare to know, was the way Kant summarized the desire of his contemporaries to throw off the shackles of oppressive traditional authority. Progress toward freedom depended upon the eradication of ignorance and superstition, which meant, in effect, the democratization of knowledge. Kant believed that only a few men would have the courage and ability to dare to know; but if there were true freedom of expression, those few could slowly spread the spirit of enlightenment to others. He remarked in his essay *What is the Enlightenment?* (1784): "For there will always be some independent thinkers, even among the established guardians of the great masses, who, after throwing off the yoke of tutelage from their own shoulders, will disseminate the spirit of the rational appreciation of both their own worth and every man's vocation for thinking for himself."[2] Though not intended as such, these lines of Kant could well serve as a definition of the popularizer—"a disseminator of the spirit of rational appreciation." Popular science has always borne the mark of its Enlightenment heritage. It has always tended to glorify reason and progress, while ridiculing the forces of reaction and superstition.

Wetzels considers Fontenelle's *Entretiens sur la pluralité des mondes* (*Conversations on the Plurality of Worlds*, 1686; German translation, 1725) the first piece of real popular science. The choice is arbitrary but instructive, because Fontenelle used many of the techniques that were to become the stock-in-trade of the popularizer down to the present day. These included conversational style, casual digressions, indirect social criticism, and anecdotes about famous scientists. Strictly logical and systematic development of an abstract argument was generally avoided in favor of a vivid sequence of images or comparisons to everyday experience that involved the reader on a highly personal level. Fontenelle attempted to bring the layman up-to-date on the latest in astronomy by relating in letter form a series of hypothetical conversations he had had with a countess while walking with her in her park. Naive but provocative questions from the countess were the catalyst for Fontenelle's discourse. Typical of his style of personal engagement was a remark he made on the fifth evening walk, comparing mathematical reasoning to love: "Here, Madam, answered I, because we are in the humor always to mix the little follies of gallantry with our most serious discourses; we reason in mathematics as we reason in love; you know that if you grant even so little to a lover, you must soon grant him much more, see in the end how far he goes; a great way. In the same manner, grant but the least principle to a mathematician, he will then proceed, and drawing a consequence or conclusion from it, you must grant him that also."[3] Such a mix of the lighthearted and personal would become a standard of popular science. Evoking noble feelings and fantasy was as important as getting the "facts" across. As Alexander von Humboldt put it in the preface to his *Ansichten der Natur* (*Views of Nature*, 1807), descriptions of nature were always on the verge of breaking into poetry. Nature, for Humboldt and many who followed, was a path to moral and spiritual uplift.[4]

The encyclopedia, a characteristic product of the Enlightenment mentality, may also be considered an ancestor of popular science.[5] Johann Heinrich Zedler's sixty-eight-volume *Grosse vollständige Universallexikon aller Wissenschaften und Künste* (Large complete universal lexicon of all sciences and arts, 1732–54) was probably the first German work that could be called an encyclopedia, though in literary and intellectual quality it was certainly overshadowed by the work of Diderot and D'Alembert in France. The German lexicon came into its own only in the early nineteenth century with the work of F. A. Brockhaus and Joseph Meyer. The first edition of the *Brockhaus Lexikon* in 1808 was limited to two thousand copies, but by the fifth edition in 1820 it had achieved an unprecedented circulation of thirty-two thousand.[6] In 1837, the Brockhaus Publishing House came out with a *Bilder-Conversations-Lexicon für das deutsche Volk* (Illustrated encyclopedia for the German people) that aimed at a broader, less educated readership and can truly be called the first popular German encyclopedia.[7] Joseph Meyer's *Konversations-Lexicon* (1839–55), which sold seventy thousand copies, also typified the progressive democratic philosophy that had come down from the eighteenth century. In the foreword, Meyer spoke of the liberating power of knowledge: "Any encyclopedia accessible to the masses and tailored to their needs must by its very nature contribute to overthrowing the oppressive monopoly of knowledge that has so long burdened the people; by communicating all available human knowledge of positive value, it gives to thousands new means to prepare themselves for a better fate; and it thereby anchors the public welfare in a broader, more reasonable and lasting foundation."[8]

Despite Meyer's talk of the masses, the popular book that reached beyond the small, wealthy, and educated middle class was a rare exception before the late nineteenth century. Illiteracy suggests itself as one obvious reason for restricted book sales. To be sure, Prussia seems to have been the first large European country to achieve anything like mass literacy; but the statistics must be handled with care. As early as 1840, 90 percent of the Prussian army recruits were classified as literate. Carlo Cipolla, in his study of European literacy, estimates overall Prussian literacy at 80 percent by about 1850. According to the 1871 Prussian census, only 12 percent of those over ten years of age could neither read nor write.[9] Another study found that of those born between 1821 and 1825, 84 percent of the men and 60.5 percent of the women were literate; of those born forty years later (1861–65), 94.5 percent of the men and 96.3 percent of the women were literate.[10] Only in the east did literacy rates remain low until late in the century. The figures are similarly impressive for other German states and suggest that strict school attendance laws paid off in terms of rising literacy rates.

Unfortunately, literacy figures lend an air of false or deceptive precision to a very complex social phenomenon. What does literacy really mean? It may well mean no more than the ability to sign one's name or to recognize a few simple words. No one would deny that literacy rose dramatically in the course of the nineteenth century, but it would be ludicrous to assume that the 80 percent figure for 1850 meant that 80 percent of the population could read a serious newspaper or encyclopedia article. As will be seen in chapter 7, it was not until the 1880s that working people began to read in any number. Before this time there may have been a potential reading audience below the middle class, but it was small. For, even if he were literate, anyone who worked, say, twelve hours in a field or shop was unlikely to be in the mood for an evening of reading. In rural areas especially there were strong cultural prejudices against reading. It was said to be impractical, even dangerous. As late as 1900, among some peasants a reader was synonymous with a liar.[11] Those few poor people who did want to read usually could not afford to do so before the late nineteenth century. A two-volume edition of the works of the poet Novalis, to take but one example, cost three taler in 1802. The same amount would have bought twenty-eight kilograms of beef.[12] Libraries, too, were accessible only to the well-to-do. In the early nineteenth century it cost ten to twenty taler (as much as 15 percent of a worker's income) just to belong to one of the Berlin *Leseanstalten* (reading institutes). Circulation figures reflect this narrow reading public. Only a handful of titles sold more than a few hundred copies. Prominent among these were items that might not even be classed as books: almanacs, calendars, and various handbooks. Surely, Goethe was engaged in wishful thinking when he remarked to Johann Eckermann in 1816: "He who does not expect a million readers should not write a single line."[13]

The early nineteenth-century works of popular science were, then, "popular" only in a very limited sense of the word. In the tradition of the Enlightenment, they sought to break the scholar's monopoly on knowledge, but they made no concessions to the ignorant masses. Their real audience was the tiny educated elite. When the famous nature philosopher Lorenz Oken founded his journal *Isis* in 1817, his intent was to disseminate scientific knowledge. But a mere glance through the pages of *Isis* would have been enough to scare off all but the most determined of educated readers. Five years later, in 1822, Oken organized the first of the annual meetings of the Association of German Scientists and Physicians. His purpose was not only to promote the spiritual unity of the divided German peoples, but to make more people aware of the achievements of science. To attract a larger audience, Oken suggested "lively and impromptu" presentations rather than dull manuscript readings. But accounts of the proceedings remained as dry as dust for most of the nineteenth century. One member even read a Latin speech to the association in 1832.[14]

Books for the layman were no less formidable. Von Humboldt's famous encyclopedic description of the universe, *Kosmos* (1845), though perhaps the most widely read book of its time, contained mathematical formulas, statistical tables, footnotes, and a liberal sprinkling of untranslated Greek, Latin, Italian, French, and English quotations. And the third edition of his *Views of Nature* (1849) was, as he put it, explicitly addressed to the "so-called higher circles of social life."[15] The great chemist Justus von Liebig had the same notion of the meaning of popularization. His *Chemische Briefe* (*Familiar Letters on Chemistry,* 1844) originally appeared as a series in the *Augsburger Allgemeine Zeitung*; but, as he said in the foreword, his work was strictly for the "cultural world" and would scrupulously avoid any "concessions to the vulgar."[16] Even Ludwig Büchner, who blandly asserted in his *Kraft und Stoff* (*Force and Matter,* 1855) that "it is part of the very nature of philosophy to be intellectually the joint property *of all,*" revealed in his very next sentence that by "all" he meant "every educated man."[17]

But when Büchner wrote these lines, the age of truly widespread reading was not far off. The many later editions of Büchner's own book (twenty-one by 1900) would enjoy a mass audience he had not anticipated. It has been estimated that by the 1870s a majority of German adults did at least some reading. Perhaps three-fourths had contact with newspapers or magazines and as many as one-fourth did some serious reading. The circulations of Meyer's familiar *Konversations-Lexicon* tell a typical story: whereas the first edition (1839–55) was an astounding success with a sale of seventy thousand copies, the fourth edition (1885–92), even with more competition, sold two hundred thousand copies.[18] Newspaper sales also shot up during the same period. Both the *Berliner Lokal-Anzeiger* and the *Berliner Morgenpost* had passed the two hundred thousand mark by 1900.[19] Increases such as these were not due simply to the expanded ranks of the middle classes. By the end of the century, workers accounted for as much as one-fourth of the patrons of public libraries in many cities;[20] and circulations of socialist newspapers and magazines were soaring. Although the majority of the new readers on all social levels preferred fiction to nonfiction, popular science—as the mainstay of nonfiction—also benefited from the great reading revolution. Small home libraries for the middle class were by the 1890s rarely without a volume or two of popular science;[21] and the workingman was already using popular science as the main tool of his self-education.[22]

This general upsurge in reading was caused not only by the increase in literacy. Technical developments also played a role. Changes in papermaking, especially the introduction of wood-pulp paper in 1874, helped make the mass press possible. Between 1875 and 1898, the price of paper in Germany fell from 65 to 20 pfennigs per kilogram. Other improvements, such as the introduction of the rotation press in 1872, were also bringing down publication costs. Newspapers, magazines, and books, which had been prohibitively expensive to earlier generations, were now affordable even by those of modest means. In 1884 the *Tägliche Rundschau* in Berlin could legitimately bill itself as an "entertainment organ for the educated of *all* classes."[23] By this time, too, Philipp Reclam's paperback editions of the classics, begun in 1867 with the easing of copyright restrictions, were selling by the hitherto unheard-of hundreds of thousands.[24] And, finally, the widespread use of the petroleum lamp after about 1860 greatly facilitated nighttime reading.[25] Reading aloud in family gatherings became common evening entertainment, and with the prices of some "people's editions" as low as one to two marks, one no longer had to be wealthy to participate.

The rise of newspaper and magazine reading revolutionized popular science. By midcentury the press was paying a good deal of attention to scientific developments. The weekly *Leipziger Illustrierte*, founded in 1843, was a trend-setter providing easily readable coverage of people, art, and nature, over and above the traditional politics and diplomacy. As mentioned, Liebig's *Familiar Letters on Chemistry* were originally a series of articles in the *Augsburger Allgemeine Zeitung*. The famous materialism controversy of the 1850s began in the same paper. Such uses of the press as a forum would have a profoundly democratizing influence on popular science. Newspaper and magazine articles usually had an audience far larger than the traditional group of educated book buyers. Many of these new readers were not used to reading books and were totally unprepared for long and difficult discourses (such as those of von Humboldt). Thus, by its very nature, the newspaper or magazine popularization demanded a certain easy, light, quickly approachable style. It had to be short, to the point, and highly entertaining; otherwise it could scarcely hope to compete with the other stories and features that surrounded it. A book stood alone, aloof, demanding, "aristocratic," as it were. But a newspaper or magazine article was thrust into the mass marketplace where it had to compete and adapt or face the extinction of being unread.

Nowhere was this kind of popularization more dramatically evident than in the tremendously successful family magazine *Die Gartenlaube* (The arbor), founded in 1853. *Gartenlaube*'s circulation shot up to about four hundred thousand within twenty years, making it the most widely read magazine Germany had ever seen. With several persons reading each copy, the total number of readers in the 1870s may be conservatively estimated at two million. By 1890, *Gartenlaube* was truly ubiquitous; it was in every café, club, and waiting room and probably had five million readers, by no means all of them middle class.[26] *Gartenlaube's* creator, Ernst Keil, made no bones about giving his readers just what they wanted, while making no severe demands on their intellects. His greeting to his readers in the first edition set the homey and cozy tone that the name of the magazine suggested: "So we want to teach you and to entertain you as we teach. A breath of poetry will hover over the whole thing like the aroma of a blooming flower; and you should make yourself at home in our arbor where you'll find good German congeniality [*Gemütlichkeit*] that speaks to the heart."[27]

As this greeting implied, much of what would come in *Gartenlaube* was pure kitsch. The serialized novels and the accompanying illustrations were often terribly sentimental. But this was only half of the story. Keil took his self-assumed role as public educator very seriously. He was particularly concerned that most of his readers had had a poor or nonexistent science education, and in the tradition of a zealous philosophe he set out to remedy this deficiency. An important section of each issue was dedicated to scientific essays—"Letters from Nature," Keil called them. As he said in the program for the magazine, "These letters must have no pedantic overtones; rather, they must be written in a very easily understandable, elegant, and, where possible, aesthetic form, so that the average manual worker, and especially the women, can understand them."[28]

What Keil demanded and got was a high quality of feuilleton-like popular science that would fit comfortably alongside serialized novels, reports of exotic places and peoples, and other family fare. *Gartenlaube* was extremely successful in attracting respected names to write its science essays. Leafing through its pages one can find articles by such men as Carl Vogt, Alfred Brehm, Matthias Schleiden, Carus Sterne, and E. A. Rossmässler, usually discussing scientific questions that could easily captivate reader interest. As Rossmässler, one of the most popular contributors, stressed, people should learn to feel comfortable with science: "Nature is neither a prayer stool, nor a storehouse, nor a study room; it is, rather, our common homeland where being a stranger is both injurious and shameful."[29] Typical article titles were "What Today's Science Says about Lightning," "Animal Character: The Shepherd Dog," "Orphaned Birds in the Berlin Aquarium," "Fear of Comets, Then and Now," as well as a host of others on Darwinism and anthropology. The style of these articles was casual, chatty, and diverting, very much in the tradition of Fontenelle, though more "folksy," in keeping with the larger audience. Although the didactic element was never allowed to be obtrusive, Keil's writers managed to do a good deal of basic science teaching to millions of Germans. The *Allgemeine Deutsche Biographie* was not exaggerating when it said of Keil that his achievement in *Gartenlaube* was "epic-making for its influence in raising the general level of education [*Bildung*]."[30]

The movement of popular science into the mass entertainment market and the subsequent broadening of the readership are manifestations of the rise of mass culture in the second half of the nineteenth century. Such democratization of knowledge was, of course, occurring throughout the advanced societies of the West, relatively independent of any specific political developments. Nonetheless, it is evident that the rather stunted growth of German political liberalism in the nineteenth century did much to set a unique tone for German popular science. As far back as 1819, Metternich's so-called Carlsbad Decrees had laid the heavy hand of censorship on liberal or nationalist publications. The Decrees, though enforced with varying degrees of severity by the many states of the German Confederation, tended to channel much intellectual activity away from politics. As a result, culture began to acquire subtle, yet potent, political overtones that it otherwise might have lacked. In a sense, it could even be argued that the repressive atmosphere actually encouraged popular science because it stimulated a good deal of superficially "unpolitical" intellectual activity. Oken's *Isis* and the Association of German Scientists and Physicians are good examples. Both ran afoul of authorities for their liberal leanings.[31] It has even been suggested that a strong undercurrent of scientific analogies ran through the speeches of radical democrats in the Frankfurt Assembly in 1848. Carl Vogt, later a prominent Darwin popularizer, was particularly fond of invoking the catastrophe theory as a "natural" justification of revolution.[32]

Only after the defeat of the liberal movement in the revolutions of 1848, however, did the antiestablishment tone of popular science come clearly into focus. Whereas the forces of progress could be checked in the political arena, they could survive if they appeared in the guise of science. In the 1850s, popular science was practically synonymous with a radical, materialistic, antireligious Weltanschauung. Each of the great "triumvirate" of popular materialists in the 1850s—Ludwig Büchner, Carl Vogt, and Jakob Moleschott—believed in fighting reaction through ideas. Those on the barricades might be crushed, but science marched on with irresistible progress.[33] But, because the universities were bastions of the state, popularization did not mix well with an academic career. Büchner's *Force and Matter* met vehement charges of immorality and cost him his position in Tübingen,[34] and Vogt's revolutionary activity in 1848 made him persona non grata in Giessen.[35] Moleschott fared no better. His *Der Kreislauf des Lebens* (The cycle of life, 1852)— a work of materialist physiology that even reduced thought to phosphorous—gained him great notoriety. The rector of the University of Heidelberg accused him of corrupting the youth and threatened to withdraw his right to teach. Moleschott responded by resigning and taking a position in Switzerland.[36] These men were not alone. Ernst Keil had also been a forty-eighter, and his *Gartenlaube* was aimed directly at the progressive bourgeoisie whose aspirations had been shattered in 1848. *Gartenlaube* was actually banned in Prussia between 1863 and 1866. (War Minister Albrecht von Roon was said to have liked *Gartenlaube*'s conservative Catholic competitor *Daheim* [At home], founded in 1864; he ordered it placed in all the officers' clubs.[37]) Even when Keil, like many liberals, became an avid Bismarck supporter and Prussophile after 1866, *Gartenlaube* continued to trumpet progressive scientific viewpoints.

Perhaps no one embodied the fusion of popular science and democracy more than Keil's favorite science writer, E. A. Rossmässler. Rossmässler had been a zoology professor at the Tharandter Forest and Agricultural Academy before his election to the Frankfurt Assembly in 1848. As a radical democrat, he had moved with the rump of the parliament to Stuttgart, only to be hunted down and tried for high treason. Though he was eventually acquitted, Rossmässler's career was ruined. He turned to free-lance popular science not only as a means of support, but also as a relatively safe way of continuing the fight for democracy. In a testament written in the wake of the failure of the revolution, Rossmässler argued that the revolutionary momentum had been lost because the German people did not know the laws of nature; Germans were ignorant and priest-ridden, mere subjects of the church and state rather than real human beings (again, shades of the philosophes).[38] The answer, Rossmässler said, was mass education in materialistic science, which would break the shackles of superstition and attain the freedoms unrealized in 1848. There was no mistaking the political allusion of the erupting volcano pictured on the title page of *Die Natur*, a popular magazine Rossmässler co-founded in 1852. "The fire inside is not extinguished," readers were told, "its passion still breaks forth in catastrophic flaming streams from the pores of the earth."[39] Rossmässler's subsequent success as a lecturer and writer on scientific topics made him a popular hero among both workers and dispirited forty-eighters; but it also earned him the enmity of conservative authorities. He was hounded out of several cities and was in and out of jail. Like most materialists, Rossmässler was an early convert to Darwinism; with his death in 1866 popular Darwinism lost one of its greatest potential champions.[40]

It was no accident that materialists such as Rossmässler were attracted to Darwin, for the materialism of the 1850s did much to prepare the way for Darwinism, not only within the scientific community, but also among the educated public. It was not that materialism stressed evolution, for it did not. Büchner's first edition of *Force and Matter*, for example, discussed descent, as he proudly pointed out later; but he developed the idea only in later editions. What materialism did stress was the notion that life was a purely mechanical phenomenon, ultimately reducible to carbon and motion. Force was just an attribute of matter; there was no such thing as immaterial spirit, and hence no God. Nor was there any creation in the Christian sense. Matter had always existed because it was impossible for anything to arise out of nothing. In such a system, there was no room for destiny or purpose; everything was under the inexorable sway of causal laws. All this was little more than a vulgarized replay of eighteenth-century French materialism. Vogt's insistence that thought was to the brain as bile was to the liver and Ludwig Feuerbach's memorable "Man is what he eats" are flagrant examples of the arrogant and dismal naiveté of the new materialistic "philosophy." Indeed, by reducing man to a thing like all other things, the materialists actually outdid Darwin, who would only make an animal of man.

Still, materialism was not entirely pessimistic. True to its eighteenth-century heritage, it retained an enormous faith in the capacity of science to guide man to a better future. Once stripped of his illusions, man would no longer be dependent on God and traditional authority; he would reach a full maturity and, through science and technology, create a new life for himself. In the repressive atmosphere of the 1850s, this was a welcome message for many who had given up hope for change through direct political action. As Büchner remarked in 1855 while working on his *Force and Matter*: "This kind of thing [natural science] has strong appeal these days. The public is demoralized by the recent defeat of national and liberal aspirations and is turning its preference to the powerfully unfolding researches of natural science, in which it sees a new kind of opposition against the triumphant Reaction. Look at Vogt, Rossmässler, and Moleschott, all of them are finding good publishers."[41]

Feuerbach was probably right when in 1850 he pointed out that the guardians of order were terribly shortsighted not to censure science. Those "unpolitical" scientists were really subversives in disguise: "Of necessity the scientist is not only a democrat but even a socialist and communist (to be sure only in a reasonable and general sense of this word); for nature knows nothing of the presumptions and fictions by which man's law has limited and stunted the existence of his fellow men."[42] Feuerbach was more literal than Rossmässler in his belief that the failure of the revolution of 1848 was a failure of materialistic understanding. If only the masses had understood that they "are what they eat," said Feuerbach, then they would have filled themselves with nourishing "revolutionary" peas instead of stupefying oppressive potatoes![43] In retrospect, this is a preposterous analysis, but it does reveal how closely materialism could be identified with political progress. And when blended with Darwinism, a theory of change par excellence, materialism was to become all the more politically subversive.

Materialism was a revolt in a double sense. Not only were materialists eager to use science as a pseudopolitical weapon, they also wanted to overturn the old romantic *Naturphilosophie* (nature philosophy) that had dominated German universities throughout the first half of the nineteenth century. This was the tradition of Goethe, Schelling, and Oken, men who had an essentially idealistic, contemplative view of nature. They believed that nature was an external manifestation of the structure of the world spirit or God. By their stress on the unity of life and the progression of forms toward perfection (man), the *Naturphilosophen* seemed to hint at evolution; and indeed they were later misunderstood as direct forerunners of Darwin. In fact, the progress of forms they envisioned was not a historical sequence of physical forms, one descending from another; rather, the only sequence was outside of historical time in the mind of the creator. Because all life and nonlife were related, and man was the highest stage, man was a microcosm of the universe and his thought a mirror of external reality; hence the importance of contemplation rather than experimentation.[44]

Materialists viewed such lofty speculations with contempt. They wanted facts and results, not fuzzy metaphysics. But whatever the hostilities of the two approaches to nature, it is clear in retrospect that each, in its own way, had created a very favorable atmosphere for the reception of Darwinism. On the one hand, natural selection was a materialist's dream come true: it was mechanistic and materialistic; it challenged traditional religion; it dispensed with the teleology of *Naturphilosophie*; and, above all, it was empirical. What romantic scientist could rival Darwin's systematic assembly of thousands of facts? On the other hand, evolution (if not its process, natural selection) was congenial to romantic theories of the mystical chain of being, the essential oneness of all life. Had not the *Naturphilosophen* striven to break down man's isolation, to immerse him in nature as primus inter pares? And had not Darwin done just that in his theory of descent? When we consider all of this in conjunction with the strong historical bent of much German thought, it is easy to see why Darwinism found its true home in Germany.[45]

Ironically, Darwin's own work got off to an unpromising start in Germany. A few weeks after *The Origin* appeared in English, the paleontologist Heinrich Bronn undertook to translate it into German. Darwin knew of the project and encouraged it. "I am most anxious that the great and intellectual German people should know something about my book," he wrote to Bronn.[46] Unfortunately, the results of Bronn's labors were rather less than Darwin might have wished. The translation was literal and laborious; but what was worse, Bronn was an unsympathetic editor. He left out Darwin's remark that "much light will be thrown on the origin of man and his history," and he added an appendix of criticisms of the theory. His main objection was the central one that Darwin himself dealt with at length: If the species have blended into each other, why isn't nature today a chaos of forms?[47]

Darwin read German poorly, and it took him a while to plow through Bronn's appendix. There were, he conceded, "some good hits," but Bronn had misunderstood a great deal, Darwin thought. Darwin was grateful therefore when Viktor Carus, one of his admirers, suggested a new translation in 1866. This time he requested that the appendix be omitted, so that Germans could judge the book on its own merits.[48] With Darwin's approval, Carus then became Darwin's regular German translator, and in 1875 Carus issued a German edition of Darwin's collected works.[49]

Darwin hoped that Germany would be a center of evolutionary theory, and he was not disappointed. Darwinism made rapid and deep inroads in the German scientific community. From the beginning it was broadly identified with progressive views. The early converts tended to be young men outside the mainstream of established university science—either in small universities or without any academic position. Most were liberal in their political and religious views; many were freethinkers or materialists. In contrast, the early opponents of Darwin were older, in higher academic positions, and religiously more conservative. Strictly political views of the opponents were variable.[50] Although the opponents were quite vocal during the 1860s, Darwin already anticipated victory in the first few months after the publication of Bronn's translation. As he wrote to his colleague Wilhelm Preyer in March 1861, "The support which I receive from Germany is my chief ground for hoping that our views will ultimately prevail."[51]

By 1875, it had become clear that Darwinism had carried the day, at least within the scientific community. Darwinists were steadily growing in numbers and academic influence, and they controlled the influential scientific journals *Ausland* and *Kosmos*. The anti-Darwinian party was reduced to only a handful of well-known scientists, the most vocal being Adolf Bastian, Albert Wigand, and Rudolf Virchow. And Darwin himself was rapidly achieving a status of honor and reverence. In 1867, Darwin was made a knight of the Prussian order Pour le Mérite, and in 1878 he was elected a corresponding member of the Berlin Academy of Science. Even Virchow, who opposed Darwin's ideas, believed him worthy of this honor and seconded the nomination.[52] Of course, Darwin's victory in the German scientific community did not mean that there was a widespread, unqualified support of all that Darwin said. The details and interpretation of evolution and natural selection remained very much a matter of dispute. Nor, as we shall see, did Darwin's victory mean that all of his German disciples automatically shared his prestige.

Darwin's own works never achieved any mass popularity in Germany. Like most great books, *The Origin* was much discussed but little read. It was only indirectly, through the popular accounts, that the public discovered Darwinism. But these were not thirdhand accounts.

Actually the public got closer to the "real thing" because from the beginning professional scientists assumed the burden of popularization. Among the young scientists who read Bronn's translation in the early 1860s, there were many who saw science as an unstoppable, progressive force. These men were delighted by Darwinism because they saw in it a weapon in their battle for an a-teleological, rationalistic, and secular Weltanschauung. Darwinism was pregnant with cultural significance beyond the narrow confines of science; it was potentially subversive of established conservative values; and it was flexible enough to adapt to the most intricate cultural battles. Indeed, Darwinism was almost too good to be true; it was not something just for other professionals, it was something the whole world had to hear about.

Such thoughts were in the mind of the young Jena zoologist Ernst Haeckel when he addressed the annual conference of the Association of German Scientists and Physicians in 1863 at Stettin. This speech may be regarded as the public debut of German Darwinism. To Haeckel, *The Origin* had been a revelation, and he was filled with the zeal of a recent convert. He told his audience (made up of professionals and laymen alike) that Darwinism afforded an entirely new perspective on human knowledge. Darwin's message, he asserted, was "evolution and progress"—a liberating cry that resounded far beyond the confines of academia. Haeckel went on to present a judicious summary of *The Origin*, though he did indulge himself to the extent of inferring the descent of man from a primeval fish. But what is really striking about this speech is the none-too-subtle undercurrent of old-fashioned Enlightenment radicalism. Haeckel saw Darwinism as scientific proof that reactionary institutions (that is, the state, the church, and the schools) were out of step with the inexorable progress of nature: "Progress is a natural law that no human power, neither the weapons of tyrants nor the curses of priests, can ever succeed in suppressing. Only through progressive movement are life and development possible. Standing still is in itself regression, and regression carries with it death. The future belongs only to progress!"[53]

From its very early days, then, German Darwinism was closely identified with progressive attitudes. Some imitated Haeckel in forging an explicit alliance. The biologist Friedrich Ratzel prefaced his popular natural history (1869) with the remark that his aim was to make propaganda for "progressive tendencies."[54] Battle-scarred radicals such as Vogt, Moleschott, and Büchner were also quick to incorporate Darwinism into their opposition views. And the old Bible critic David Friedrich Strauss made Darwinism the centerpiece of his *Der alte und der neue Glaube* (*The Old Faith and the New*, 1872)—that generation's best-known plea for a new culture of liberal rationalism. Sometimes the alliance of Darwinism and progressivism was implicit or contextual. Thus the liberal *Gartenlaube* opened its pages to Darwinists, while its conservative competitor, *Daheim*, excluded them. But whether explicit or implicit, there was a certain inevitability about Darwinism's progressive image, for to accept Darwinism usually entailed challenging the church, and to challenge the church was to challenge the state itself. In time, everyone came to understand this line of reasoning, and the public fight about Darwinism became almost as much political as scientific. (See chapters 4 and 7.)

The great importance that scientists attached to Darwinism lent a certain urgency to the need to popularize. Few scientific theories, before or even to this day, reached the public so fast and remained for so long a subject of great interest. Coming as opportunely as it did, Darwinism could ride the crest of the great reading wave that swept through all social classes. In 1865, the geologist Charles Lyell wrote to Darwin that he had visited the crown princess of Prussia and found her already well acquainted with Darwinism.[55] Three years later, in 1868, the *Illustrierte Zeitung*, a weekly that paid close attention to science, asserted that "all the educated" (*Gebildete*) were familiar with Darwinism,[56] perhaps a slightly premature judgment. That year's edition of Georg Büchmann's *Geflügelte Worte* (Familiar quotations)—a popular self-help book of witty phrases for middle-class people to sprinkle in their conversation—still had no reference to Darwin. But the next edition (1871) listed "struggle for life" (*Kampf ums Dasein*) as a phrase on everyone's lips[57]—a good indication of when Darwinism, at least as a cliché, penetrated middle-class consciousness. And Darwinism did not stop with the middle class; by the 1890s, as will be seen in chapter 7, the workingman's philosophy could be summed up in one word: Darwinism. Based on a count of articles on Darwinism cataloged by the various editions of the *Bibliography of German Periodical Literature*, it appears that the peak of interest was in the middle and late 1870s. But this conclusion may be somewhat misleading; the great Darwin enthusiasm of the working class was still in the future, as were the sales records of Haeckel's *Die Welträtsel* (*Riddle of the Universe*, 1899) and the many works of Wilhelm Bölsche. At the end of 1899, the *Berliner Illustrierte Zeitung* asked its readers (most of them middle class) who they thought the greatest thinker of the century had been. Darwin came in third, after Helmuth von Moltke (!) and Kant (the latter basically an eighteenth-century figure). In the same survey, readers chose *The Origin* as the single most influential book written during the century.[58]

Haeckel set the pace of popularization. Indeed, some popularizers derived as much from Haeckel as from Darwin. The key to Haeckel's success was not so much his style, for he did not excel at feuilleton-type elegance and thus did little magazine writing, but rather, his ability to transform Darwinism into a philosophy of life—a Weltanschauung for the modern masses. Darwin himself had no such grandiose ambition. When Darwin remarked at the end of his *Origin*, "We can dimly foresee that there will be a considerable revolution in natural history,"[59] he was thinking mostly of new perspectives within the biological sciences. He showed little interest in setting forth the universal implications of his evolutionary theory. Haeckel, however, brushed aside any limitations. He saw Darwin's theory as the key to unlock all the mysteries of the universe. "Evolution," he wrote in 1868, "is now the magic word with which we will solve all of the riddles around us, or at least be on the way to solving them."[60] Haeckel called his universal, Darwin-inspired system "monism," a word that evokes a distinguished philosophical past. However, it would be a mistake to search for hidden depths in Haeckel's works; he was often superficial, inconsistent, and just plain muddleheaded. But this does not really matter because popular writers are likely to be judged only by the surface impression they give. To overanalyze Haeckel would be to misjudge both the man and his popular effect.

In Haeckel's defense, it should be pointed out that to a certain extent he merely partook of the vagueness already inherent in the term "monism." If defined broadly, monism may be traced back through Spinoza's "God Nature" (its first modern form) all the way to the "block universe" of Parmenides. Christian Wolff (1679–1754) was apparently the first to use the word *Monismus*; he applied it to both materialism and idealism because both saw reality as a manifestation of a single phenomenon, be it matter or spirit. This basic vagueness surrounding the word has been the source of great confusion; for if both idealists and materialists can be monists, then so can almost anyone who professes to see unity in the universe. Monism, then, becomes a term of easy praise or opprobrium to be hung indiscriminately on thinkers of the most radically diverse views.

During the first half of the nineteenth century in Germany, monism was usually associated with the *Identitätsphilosophie* (that mind and matter are merely two sides of a single phenomenon) and with the panpsychism and pantheism of romantic *Naturphilosophie*. After about 1850, however, monism began to change sides, as it were, gradually becoming identified with the militant anticlerical, materialist tradition that saw mind as merely a temporary by-product of matter. Haeckel's work is often viewed as the crowning glory of this last stage of monism. And, indeed, Haeckel's passion for Darwinism and popularization, as well as his vitriolic anticlericalism, are characteristic traits of materialistic monists. But Haeckel should not be pigeonholed as just another materialist. As will become clear, his type of monism was very susceptible to the subtle lure of romantic *Naturphilosophie*.

The chief popular statements of Haeckel's Darwinian monism are his *Die natürliche Schöpfungsgeschichte* (*The History of Creation*, 1868) and his *Riddle of the Universe*. Like many popular books, *The History of Creation* had its origin in the spoken rather than written word. Haeckel was troubled that his book of 1866 on morphology had not been a popular success. He therefore reworked the material into a more easily understandable form and presented it as a series of lectures to large audiences of laymen. Those very successful lectures formed the basis of *The History of Creation*, a two-volume celebration of the rise of life from a "nonmiraculous" perspective. In his introductory remarks, Haeckel placed himself squarely in the fighting tradition of the popular scientist as human liberator: "The highest triumph of the human mind, the true knowledge of the most general laws of nature, ought not to remain the private possession of a privileged class of learned men, but ought to become the common property of all mankind."[61] Erik Nordenskiöld, in his classic *History of Biology* (1936) called *The History of Creation* the "world's chief source of knowledge of Darwinism"[62]—probably an accurate assessment, at least for the period before 1900. By 1900 the book had gone through nine editions and was well established as the layman's starting point for a study of evolution.

When, at the end of the century, Haeckel felt compelled to summarize his life's work, he tried to appeal to an even larger audience. The resulting *Riddle of the Universe*, though more philosophic and speculative than his earlier work, was an unprecedented success. With some three hundred thousand sales by the outbreak of World War I, it was probably the single best-selling German nonfiction book up to that time. It has frequently been observed that in the thirty-one years between these two books, Haeckel's views underwent some subtle changes. His monism became somewhat less mechanistic and materialistic and began to take on vitalistic and religious overtones.[63] Indeed, his very late works—which were not widely read—were often eclipsed by a mystical fog. But because these changes were camouflaged in a confusing and inconsistent rhetoric, it is doubtful that the reading public was ever aware of them. Ignoring the late writings, one can certainly jump from *The History of Creation* to *The Riddle of the Universe* without a noticeable jolt in tone or content. Surely the public Haeckel is most accurately represented when his work is considered, with all its flaws, as a single, unified system.

Haeckel considered Darwin the great liberator from the crippling shackles of dualism. What he meant was that Darwin's natural selection had rendered superfluous any outside interference in the course of natural history. In the seventeenth century, Newton had shown that the inorganic universe ran by natural laws, that all was predictable cause and effect. Now, said Haeckel, Darwin had done the same for the organic world. No longer was it necessary to posit a guiding spirit behind all living matter, a spirit that had to intervene capriciously on every occasion to keep life on its course. Now everything was explained by natural selection, a purely mechanical process, self-starting and self-sustaining. Life was a simple matter of material cause and effect, everything ultimately dependent on the Law of Substance, which, to Haeckel, meant that the universe ran on the principles of the conservation of matter and energy. Although there were no blind-chance random events—the law of cause and effect kept things on a narrow and predictable path—neither was there any purpose to anything in the universe, living or nonliving. Darwin's monumental contribution, said Haeckel, had been the final destruction of teleology. Indeed, antiteleology was one of Haeckel's definitions of monism, for the fact that causal law could be extended from the inorganic to the organic world proved that there were no real boundaries between various kinds of matter. Life and nonlife were subsumed into the giant One.[64]

In bridging the gap between the organic and inorganic and dissolving the dualism of matter and spirit, Haeckel seemed to be embracing a crude materialism. As the materialists of the 1850s had done, he reduced all life to carbon. The way Haeckel interpreted Darwin, this carbon had produced living molecules by spontaneous generation. There was one source of life, which had yielded the first organic molecules at a specific moment in time. Darwin himself was unsure about spontaneous generation, and he had assumed four or five primal sources of life. According to Haeckel, once life had begun in its simplest forms, it was just a matter of time before natural selection brought forth complex organisms such as man.

In his *The History of Creation*, he confidently constructed a giant tree of life, a pedigree of man going all the way back through the apes to the primitive monera.[65] All this could be inferred from Darwin's *Origin*, of course, but Haeckel's dogmatism and certainty left Darwin aghast. As early as May 1867 (before the publication of *The History of Creation*), Darwin had sought to restrain Haeckel, warning him that his extreme views might make people angry and blind them to the facts. After reading *The History of Creation*, Darwin restated his reservations. He wrote to Haeckel: "Your boldness, however, sometimes makes me tremble, but as Huxley remarked, someone must be bold enough to make a beginning in drawing up tables of descent."[66] Actually Haeckel had stolen much of Darwin's thunder. *The Descent of Man* came as something of an anticlimax; Darwin admitted that he would not have published the book at all had he known about Haeckel's work before he was so far along in his own. It would have been an unfortunate loss, since most of *The Descent of Man* dealt with sexual selection, a topic that received little attention in Haeckel's works.

The whole of evolution, Haeckel said, was a purely chemical process, "*the attraction and repulsion of particles of matter, of molecules, and of atoms,*"[67] as heredity interacted with environment. Organic growth might even be compared to the formation of crystals. Man himself was currently the most intricate stage of life, but he, too, was just another form of carbon, not really distinct from other organic or even inorganic forms. Haeckel made much of his so-called biogenetic law (ontogeny recapitulates phylogeny), which he claimed proved the similarity between man and primitive animals. He frequently pictured the early stages of human embryos, alongside of those of lower animals, challenging readers to discern the uniqueness of man. Of course, there could be no free will in such a universe, gripped as it was by causal laws; all was strictly determined. Man's actions were simply the result of heredity and environment. Nor could man take comfort in the uniqueness of his soul, for soul was a "purely mechanical activity, the sum of the molecular phenomena of motion in the particles of the brain"[68]—an activity man shared with other animals. In fact, asserted Haeckel, the "lowest men" were much closer to apes than to "higher men." And as one moved "down" through the organic world, differences continued to be merely a matter of degree; everywhere varieties of carbon prevailed. For Haeckel, then, all life, even human life, was but an ephemeral stage in the universal evolution of matter.

It is no wonder that Haeckel was almost universally perceived as a materialist. His monism seemed to assert that everything was unified because everything was matter. But, in his *Riddle of the Universe*, where he summarized his ideas, Haeckel vehemently denied that he was a materialist because his system, unlike materialism, did not see matter as dead. Rather, Haeckel placed himself in what he thought was the tradition of Spinoza and Goethe. These thinkers, he believed, saw nature as a single universal substance that was both matter and spirit—a universe of animated matter.

Actually, Haeckel had unwittingly undercut his own materialism right from the beginning. With all his insistence that life was nothing but matter, he failed to explain how life could find its way into a part of the universe's matter except by a mysterious metaphysical or divine force—a possibility he rejected outright. Haeckel's mentor, Darwin, had failed him on this crucial point, preferring (at least publicly) to defer to the powers of God at the moment of organic creation.[69] Left without guidance in this philosophical quandary, Haeckel was forced into the explanation that all matter was alive and always had been. In effect, he abolished organic creation by making the life force an eternal manifestation of the universe.

This hylozoism or panpsychism was already evident in Haeckel's *The History of Creation*, where he remarked that all matter possessed sensation and will, albeit unconsciously.[70] Exactly what this meant is not too clear. Haeckel was fond of talking about plastidules, molecules with soul that were somehow the ultimate units of protoplasm. But gradually this distinction between inorganic molecules that were vaguely sentient and organic molecules that had complete soul or consciousness broke down altogether. More and more Haeckel began to speak of all matter as *"beseelt"* (possessed of soul). Atoms themselves were said to love and hate. In his *Riddle of the Universe*, he stated openly that plants are conscious and that atoms have soul.[71]

To be sure, Haeckel did not mean that matter had an immaterial aura about it; nor did he believe that soul could be present in the absence of matter. But there is no doubt that his animated matter represented a lapse into the very romantic *Naturphilosophie* that he had denounced as metaphysical and teleological. In spite of himself, Haeckel came close to succumbing to teleology. His plastidule souls, with their innate tendency to develop, were an obvious imposition of purpose onto nature. Moreover, Haeckel's entire view of nature was highly aesthetic and therefore anthropomorphic. He continually praised the beauty and charm of nature and painted many fine watercolors and oils of natural scenes. His view of nature resembled a giant work of art, almost yearning for the creator he kept begrudging it. It was almost as though Haeckel instinctively recoiled from the dismal implications of materialism and determinism and sought refuge in the comfortable folds of romanticism.

Although most popularizers were more subdued in their speculations than Haeckel, they had a tendency—a tendency that was perhaps peculiarly German—to mine Darwinism for its philosophical meaning. The usual procedure was to integrate Darwinism into a system of anti-teleological materialism. Of course, Vogt, Moleschott, and Büchner had such a system ready at hand. It took Vogt only three years to shift man from the category of just plain material to the evolved material presented in *Vorlesungen über den Menschen* (*Lectures on Man*, 1863). Likewise, Moleschott, though he wrote no books on Darwinism, did incorporate it into the later editions of his *Kreislauf des Lebens*. But most of all it was Büchner who forged the link between Darwinism and 1850s materialism. In his *Sechs Vorlesungen* (Six lectures, 1868) on Darwinism, Büchner praised Darwin for redirecting the study of nature into philosophical channels. At first, this looks like an odd compliment coming from such a fact-obsessed thinker as Büchner, but Büchner meant that Darwin had found a way to avoid both the empty metaphysics of the *Naturphilosophen* and the myopic detail collecting of the specialists. Darwin, Büchner said, had remarried philosophy and science, and in doing so he had made a contribution even greater than his theory of evolution, namely, the final destruction of teleology.[72]

Others, including many writers of encyclopedia articles, joined Büchner in writing the obituary of the designed universe. If one was not already a materialist before 1859, the end of design was a good first step on the road to materialism. With no need for design, there was no need for a spirit or mind to guide nature. By simple subtraction, all that remained was a universe composed exclusively of matter and the forces produced by that matter. In his popular lecture on Darwinism (1869), Wilhelm Preyer inferred that life was merely a complicated mechanism, made up of the same things as nonlife.[73] This was a common position, and it found one of its more refined expressions in Edward Aveling's *Die Darwin'sche Theorie* (The Darwinian theory, 1887). Aveling began a chapter entitled "Proof of the Correctness of the Darwinian Theory" by pointing to the perfect harmony between evolution and the laws of the conservation of matter and energy: "The creation of a species would be the equivalent of the creation of a certain quantum of matter and a certain quantum of movement out of nothing. Now, so long as the principle of the conservation of energy is recognized as correct, the special creation of an animal or a plant species is inconceivable."[74] Life, Aveling said, was matter in movement; the life force was similar to heat, light, electricity, or magnetism. It was not always clear for Aveling whether materialism was the premise of Darwinism or vice versa; and this ambiguity was widespread. By the 1870s, materialism and Darwinism had become so intertwined that most Germans had come to assume that support of one was tantamount to support of the other. It did not matter that Darwin himself had said nothing explicit about materialism because the public knew his work only through the filter of popularization.

The emphasis on materialism should not obscure the fact that the popularizers spent most of their time on a straightforward explication of Darwin's argument, and, in explaining the particulars, they were extremely responsible and accurate. Their job was made easy by the clarity and the logical structure of *The Origin*. The first four chapters laid out the entire argument in all its simplicity and grandeur. One had only to summarize, which is exactly what most popularizers did. Here is the way Büchner stated Darwin's case: "1) The struggle for existence. 2) The formation of sports, or the variation of individual organisms. 3) The transmission of these variations to the progeny. 4) The selection by nature of the favored among these variations by means of the struggle for existence. Combine these four components or natural influences, allow them to interact, and the result, the constant alteration of natural creatures, proceeds of itself."[75] Büchner then discussed each component, illustrating with a wealth of examples that his audience would easily recognize. Packaged in the dense prose of the *Brockhaus Lexikon*, the same idea had a different feel:

> The internal and external influences which affect the life of the animal in the natural state work in a similar manner as "artificial selection"; in the place of the weeding out by human hands, there appears the struggle for existence. The little deviations from the parental type that emerge in the progeny can be damaging, indifferent, or useful. In light of the discrepancy between the fecundity of animals and plants and the space available for them, those progeny afflicted with damaging deviations have a smaller

prospect of surviving the others and reproducing themselves, while those with useful deviations have a greater prospect. Frequently the survivors will transmit their useful deviations to their progeny and these variations will become fixed: Thus the origin of new forms, varieties, and species.[76]

The task of explaining Darwin's theory in German was complicated by the problem of translating the pivotal phrase "natural selection." Even in English it could easily be misleading. Some thought it implied conscious choice in animals (à la Lamarck), while others thought it necessarily entailed an outside selector, or God. In the later editions of *The Origin*, Darwin defended the phrase against what he considered overly literal interpretations, claiming that "every one knows what is meant and is implied by such metaphorical expressions."[77] However, not everyone did. In writing to Bronn in early 1860 about the translation, Darwin had admitted that the phrase was "not obvious." At that time, he had tapped his limited knowledge of German and suggested to Bronn the word *Adelung* (from *Adel*, meaning nobility), but he feared that it might be too metaphorical. Bronn, it seems, had originally suggested *Wahl der Lebensweise* (choice of life-style), but Darwin thought that too Lamarckian. In the end, Bronn settled on the expression *natürliche Zuchtung*. The later translation by Carus made it *natürliche Zuchtwahl*, and from there the phrase made its way into popular literature. All of this was more than semantic bickering because the German phrase *natürliche Zuchtwahl* meant "natural breeding choice (or selection)." As Ludwig Büchner pointed out, this was teleological and therefore very deceptive: "In the Darwinian sense, nature does not breed as does man, rather it merely selects—but without purpose or intent."[78] Philosophers might have understood the distinction, but the average layman, who was usually already inclined to think both teleologically and anthropocentrically, would likely take the "breeding" literally and thus fail to grasp Darwin's essential concept.

What really caught on as the Darwinian catch-phrase in Germany was *Kampf ums Dasein*—struggle for existence. But here again there were problems of connotation. Darwin had meant the phrase in both a metaphorical and a literal way: "Two canine animals, in a time of dearth, may truly be said to struggle with each other which shall get the food and live. But a plant on the edge of a desert is said to struggle for life against the drought, though more properly it should be said to be dependent on the moisture."[79] The word *Kampf* is harsher than the word struggle and was likely to provoke in the reader images of fierce physical battles. Some of the popularizers tended to use this harsh imagery as a heuristic device. "The world is a great battlefield. . . . Woe to the conquered!"[80] wrote Aveling, almost reveling in the good fight. But others were very careful to stress the metaphorical side. The struggle for existence, cautioned Moleschott in his *Kreislauf des Lebens*, "is more a competition than a war inflamed by the hatred of all for all. Just as the plant does not hate the animals whose decomposition provides it food, and just as the man bears no ill will to the ruminants who clothe and strengthen him, so the hairworm does not hate the humans whose muscles he gnaws. Nor does the fox hate the chickens whom he outwits."[81] This is nicely put, but subtleties and qualifications are ill-adapted for survival in the mass marketplace of ideas—to use Darwinian terms. When the phrase *Kampf ums Dasein* escaped from the confines of books into the common stock of clichés, it probably meant "Life is war" to most people.

On the whole, the popularizers were not cliché mongers. Their usual approach was businesslike and responsible. It was the opponents of Darwin who were more likely to distort or sensationalize. (See chapter 5.) The popularizers explained evolution from every angle. They did not pretend that Darwin had explained the origin of life, and they were also careful to point out that Darwin had not discovered the idea of evolution, but only its mechanism, natural selection. (There was, to be sure, some tendency to exaggerate the role of Darwin's German forerunners. Turning Goethe and the *Naturphilosophen* into proto-Darwinists was a misinterpretation, but it was probably not done out of nationalist pride; non-Germans made the same error.) The popularizers always described Darwin's personal background and his lines of reasoning leading up to his theory, as well as the various kinds of evidence supporting the theory. In *The Origin*, that evidence is scattered throughout many chapters of intricate argument, and it is embedded in often tortuous qualification. In popular works, which tended to condense material, the evidence is stripped to its bare essentials and rains down relentlessly upon the reader. The "facts" of geology, anatomy, embryology, morphology, physiology, pathology, psychology, and geography are all there; and they appear overwhelmingly, inescapably, and conclusively in support of Darwin's theory. Not that the popularizers ignored weaknesses and objections; they did not. Following Darwin's own example, they dealt fairly with what they considered serious objections, ridiculing only those they thought were based on ignorance or religious prejudice. Darwinism was, they conceded, no more than a hypothesis; but as the *Brockhaus Lexikon* put it, a "greatly justified hypothesis."[82]

The most spectacular part of Darwinism, the issue of man's own ancestry, was also handled judiciously. Of course, the idea of man as animal was old and familiar. Alfred Brehm, in his famous family animal guide begun in 1864, told his readers that science had established that man was an animal: "From the scientist's point of view man is bodily really nothing more and nothing less than a mammal." But, Brehm reassured, "In counting man among the animals, we scientists find nothing insulting to man."[83] When Darwin published his own observations in *The Descent of Man* (1871), there was already an ongoing discussion of man's apelike past. Haeckel, Vogt, and Büchner had all inferred man's ape nature from Darwin's theory, and they had had great fun pointing to the physical and psychological similarities between man and the apes. Try to find the qualitative difference between man and ape, they challenged. Before long, the epithet "ape theory" had joined *Kampf ums Dasein* as a popular cliché. "If you ask someone what Darwin has done for science," remarked Aveling at the beginning of his *Die Darwin'sche Theorie*, "you generally get the answer: 'Darwin? I know him. He says that man descends from the ape.' Incorrect and inappropriate as this judgment of Darwin is, it still corresponds to the views of the vast majority of even so-called educated people."[84] Such distortion was not really the fault of the popularizers. If anything, Darwin's opponents were to blame, for they claimed that Darwin tried to put apes in every family tree. Darwin, of course, had tried no such thing; and the popularizers followed him faithfully when they stressed that the issue was not descent from living ape species, but rather a common apelike ancestry for both man and present-day apes. Gorillas and chimpanzees were man's distant cousins, they pointed out, not his direct ancestors. Many popularizers paid scant attention to the issue. In this context, it is notable how much *The Origin* itself (which had only a sentence on man) was and remained the chief source for popular Darwinism generally. The later subtle changes in Darwin's thought, above all his downplaying of natural selection, found little echo in popular accounts.

In faithfully reporting on *The Origin*, the popularizers did not turn Darwin into an infallible source of ultimate truth. Rather, they frequently both criticized and modified some of the major concepts. Many were disappointed that Darwin had not offered a naturalistic explanation for the actual beginning of life. Evocation of the creator seemed somehow an evasion. Other objections had to do with basic definitions and the process of change. Vogt, for example, had his own definition of species, based on common traits rather than fertility of offspring. In his *Lectures on Man*, this definition led to the assertion that the various races of man were really separate species with no traceable common origin (polygenesis). A certain partiality to Lamarck could be detected in other popularizers, particularly Moleschott, who preferred Lamarck's spontaneous generation. Readers of the popular magazine *Westermanns Monatshefte* (Westermann's monthly) were introduced to one of the major modifications of Darwin's natural selection: Moritz Wagner's "migration law," which posited that development could take place only if the variations were geographically isolated from the rest of their species.[85] Challenging Haeckel's version of Darwinism was more common than questioning Darwin himself. Vogt, for instance, had no use for such "excesses" as the "biogenetic law,"[86] and Otto Zacharias, in his long obituary of Darwin in *Westermanns Monatshefte*, rebuked those who would go beyond Darwin's modest claims.[87] Above all it was Büchner who was respectfully critical of some of the details of Darwin's work. In some cases, his modifications were so subtle and implicit that it is doubtful that they were perceived by many people. But in two particular cases he was very explicit. First, he claimed that it was "a large and generally recognized error of his doctrine" that Darwin had not reduced all life to one spontaneously generated primeval form. "For if special acts of creation were necessary for eight or ten progenitors or original pairs, then why aren't special acts admissible for all creatures? And why bother at all about a naturalistic explanation for all the others?" The amazing advances of organic chemistry demonstrated to Büchner's satisfaction that life could originate in a primeval chemical reaction. Second, Büchner questioned whether natural selection was a sufficient explanation of change. He believed that Darwin had underestimated the power of external influences in changing an organism. Darwin stressed the effects of external conditions (climate, soil, nourishment, and the like), but only in connection with natural selection, whereas Büchner claimed that there was ample evidence that external conditions acted directly and quickly on organisms. People and animals are changed perceptibly just by moving them to another climate, he said.[88]

These deviations from Darwinism demonstrated the independence and vigor of the popular Darwinian genre, but style more than content separated one popular account from another. And style was the key to success. Such men as Friedrich Rolle or Wilhelm Preyer, who wrote in a watered-down professional style, were not likely to become household names. To be really successful required one of two styles. First, one could follow the straightforward, expository styles of Moleschott, Büchner, Haeckel, Aveling, and Arnold Dodel. These men pursued linear arguments; they challenged the intellect or occasionally provoked anger as a means of holding attention. Given these features, their writing was best suited for lectures and books; it did not adapt well to family magazines, where the pace was apt to be more relaxed and chatty and the reasoning less formally structured. Demanding as it often was, this expository style was nonetheless capable of capturing and holding a large number of educated readers. One of Büchner's obituaries in 1902 said that he had done more to popularize science than all the universities with all their professional scholars.[89] There was a good deal of truth in that assessment.

The second style, the gemütlich, feuilleton style, was well suited to both books and magazines. It would reach its ultimate refinement only in the works of Bölsche after 1900. (See chapter 3.) Its notable earlier masters included Vogt (also capable of the expository style), who was a longtime contributor of nature sketches to the *Frankfurter Zeitung*. Other masters were *Gartenlaube* regulars C. Bock and Carus Sterne, as well as Alfred Brehm, author of the household classic *Brehms Tierleben* (Brehm's animal life), a book still available today. The gemütlich style was gentle and relaxed and tended to be structured as a series of word pictures; it frequently taught by personal example or anecdote. In discussing rudimentary organs, for example, Sterne recalled for *Gartenlaube* readers a boy in his school who could wiggle his ears.[90] This is an example of what Otto Zacharias had in mind when he remarked in an article on popularization that the popularizer had to have the ability to "see the great in the small and the small in the great."[91] In a magazine, such a style was the perfect complement to the travel sketch or serialized novel.

Even when used in a book, the gemütlich style still tended to reflect the magazine format. *Brehms Tierleben* was a series of word and picture portraits of the various animals, and each portrait was like an individual family magazine article, with all the sentimentality that the genre implies. As a student of Haeckel, Brehm was an avid Darwinist, but as he described each animal in turn, he never made an issue of evolution. Instead, the anthropomorphic descriptions helped people to see the animal world as part of their own world. Thus the mouse, in Brehm's treatment, became a charming parlor guest—music-loving, cute, and childlike.[92] The gemütlich style also appeared in the massive natural histories such as Sterne's *Werden und Vergehen* (Evolving and vanishing, 1875), Oswald Köhler's *Weltschöpfung und Weltuntergang* (Creation and decline of the world, 1887), and Rudolf Bommeli's *Die Geschichte der Erde* (The history of the earth, 1890). These books were not directly focused on Darwinism. Rather, they showed the evolution of the entire cosmos within a grand, flowing panorama, triggering the imagination by a vivid succession of images. One saw one's reflection in the primitive plants, fish, birds, and horses of eons ago. On the whole, then, the gemütlich style was broader, more "modern" in its appeal, than the expository style, for it made fewer demands on the reader's intellect. Perhaps it would not be stretching the point to say that the gemütlich style, with its flow of word pictures, was an ancestor not only of today's nature picture book but also of the television nature program.

What is perhaps most striking about the genre of popular Darwinism is its extraordinary longevity. This may have been partly fortuitous—the reading audience was expanding rapidly at the time—or it may have been due to the "spicy," exciting idea of man as ape. But it went deeper: the Germans tended to conceive of Darwinism very broadly, as an epistemology that would bring new answers to any number of fundamental issues. Darwinism came to mean progress, not only in a political, but also in an almost cosmic, sense.[93] It was, as Haeckel said, a master key to the universe. Writer after writer retained the faith that that key would keep on unlocking political, philosophical, and religious treasure chests. But how long could it continue? Certainly it would have been reasonable to expect that Haeckel's last word on the subject, *The Riddle of the Universe* of 1899, would have been *the* last word. Yet popular Darwinism did not expire with the nineteenth century. It was destined to have one final burst of glory in the writings of Wilhelm Bölsche, a popularizer whose talent, energy, and success eclipsed all those who came before him. Before turning to popular Darwinism's effects on education, religion, and politics we need to complete our picture of the genre with a detailed look at Bölsche's work.

Chapter 3

Erotic Monism—The Climax

of Popular Darwinism

ONE morning in May of 1890, a young novelist and science writer was sitting in the Humboldt Garden in Berlin, lost in thought. Around him were the garden's carefully cultivated plants, each duly tagged with a long Latin name. Suddenly, the noon factory whistle sounded and a stream of workers poured into the garden. Jolted from his reverie by this intrusion, the young man was forced to confront the gap between two worlds: science and the masses. As he later recalled the moment: "I had lost from view the splendor of the green paradise around me. With my walking stick I had just scratched in the sand the Greek letters of the word 'cosmos.' Now the strange marks stared up helplessly from the ground. There was a huge journey in the contrast. And I felt we had made despairingly little progress in shortening it."[1]

The young man was Wilhelm Bölsche, and these rather commonplace thoughts on the inaccessibility of science would hardly merit repeating had they not stirred him to extraordinary deeds. In 1890, Bölsche was just another struggling writer in Berlin, the author of two charming but not very successful novels, a rather pedantic tract on naturalist literature, and a few magazine articles. Within a generation he had become probably the greatest science popularizer of all time; and as the author of dozens of best-selling books and hundreds of articles, his name was a household word to millions. When the popular journal *Kosmos* surveyed its readership after World War I, it found that Bölsche's name was virtually synonymous with popular science. He was more popular than both Haeckel (whose *Riddle of the Universe* was still going strong) and Alfred Brehm (whose *Tierleben* was a longtime classic).[2] A newspaper sketch of Bölsche on his sixtieth birthday in 1921 put the matter simply: "It would be superfluous here to refer to any particular book of his; every German who reads has read at least one of them."[3]

This fame has not lasted. Today Bölsche is almost totally forgotten, relegated to a footnote to discussions of his friend Ernst Haeckel. This is an unfortunate distortion, and it is time Bölsche's true importance is recognized. To be sure, Haeckel set the original tone of German popular Darwinism, and, unlike Bölsche, he made important scientific discoveries. But what is relevant here is popular success, and by that measure Bölsche is unmatched. The combined sales of Bölsche's books by 1914 may be very conservatively estimated at 1.5 million. This total is probably at least three times that of Haeckel's circulation and does not include the hundreds of articles Bölsche wrote for magazines and newspapers. Haeckel wrote almost no popular articles. Most of the paperbacks that Bölsche wrote for the *Kosmos Bändchen* (small books) series sold over one hundred thousand copies at a time when a nonfiction book that sold a quarter of that number was a tremendous bestseller. Bölsche was probably the single best-selling nonfiction author in the German language prior to 1933.[4] There is no doubt that he was a major cultural phenomenon, and, because his main interest was Darwinism, his story is central to understanding Darwin's fate in Germany.

As a child, Bölsche breathed the rich air of popular science. He was born in Cologne in 1861, the son of one of the editors of the *Kölnische Zeitung*. The elder Bölsche was also an amateur scientist, one of the founders of the Cologne Zoo, and a friend of some of the day's leading intellectuals. Von Humboldt, Vogt, and Moleschott were all guests in the Bölsche household.[5] Young Wilhelm hated school, but loved nature. He soon blossomed precociously into a self-taught amateur naturalist, amassing a large collection of flora and fauna, devouring *Brehms Tierleben*, and even meeting his friends on the sly in the back of a pub to discuss the revolutionary new ideas of Darwin and Haeckel.[6] His father's newspaper connections opened the door to his early publications, first of anonymous book reviews and then of full-scale signed articles. Karl Russ, a family friend and publisher of the popular science magazine *Die Gefiederte Welt* (The feathered world) printed many of Bölsche's early animal studies. An article from 1876, for example, finds the fifteen-year-old *Gymnasiat* describing a disastrous spring flood that engulfed the local zoo, drowning many prize animals. Already evident is the sensitive touch that would be the hallmark of his mature writings.[7]

Anyone meeting Bölsche in 1876 probably would have assumed that he would become a professor of biology. Instead, he became a dropout, leaving the *Gymnasium* without even receiving the *Abitur*. The ostensible reason for his failure was weak lungs, but the real reason was probably his hatred of traditional academic work. For several years he drifted, taking trips to Italy and France and casually attending university lectures. Eventually he decided he wanted to be a novelist, and so, like other young Germans with similar ambitions, he drifted to Berlin.[8]

In the mid-1880s, the imperial capital was filled with literary Young Turks in revolt against the established salon literature of the *Gründerzeit*. Bölsche soon found his niche among these so-called naturalists. A friend introduced him to Bruno Wille, the passionate socialist, Darwinist, panpsychic, and crusader for the new literature. And in the literary club *Durch* he mixed with other fiery young prophets of naturalism, absorbing a confusing brew of socialism, anarchism, Darwinism, and Bohemianism. Little of this was reflected in Bölsche's first two novels—*Paulus* (1885) and its humorous sequel *Der Zauber des Königs Arpus* (The magic of King Arpus, 1887). Both were conventional historical novels set in ancient Rome. *Paulus*, which deals with a young Roman aristocrat's confusion of Christian and sexual love, is of some interest in light of Bölsche's later "erotic monism." But neither book caused much of a stir.[9]

Bölsche had been paying close attention to the literary debates around him, and in 1887 he published his own theoretical statement of the meaning of naturalism. This little book, with the pretentious title *Die naturwissenschaftlichen Grundlagen der Poesie* (The scientific foundations of poetics), was little more than a rehash of Emile Zola's idea of the experimental novel. Science, said Bölsche, is the basis of all modern thought; therefore any serious adult literature is necessarily realistic simply because it must come to terms with scientific discoveries. Bölsche preferred the word "realism" to "naturalism" because the latter had dismal connotations. With the gap between science and literature closed, the novel would become an experiment exactly like a laboratory experiment, save that it is carried out entirely in the writer's mind. Just as there were laws governing the mixing of chemicals in a test tube, so, too, there were laws governing the mixing of characters in a novel. The novelist needed only to look to science for instruction. Science would teach him four lessons: (1) all behavior is strictly determined by combinations of hereditary and environmental influences; (2) science cannot prove its case against immortality, thus all tragedy is mitigated; (3) love is a natural and healthful expression of cosmic forces and must be treated openly; (4) Darwinism is the core of modern science. A Darwinian perspective should sharpen the writer's sense of the meaning of chance, small details, and the logic of development.[10]

This motley lot of scientific "lessons" for the writer reflects the very productive tensions within Bölsche's mind. He seems to be in the grip of a materialistic and deterministic positivism à la Büchner. Yet at the same time he resists the dismal implications of materialism, preferring somehow to save the soul from destruction at the hands of the materialists, thus his stress on the possibility of immortality and on the spirituality as well as the earthiness of love. (Bölsche later recalled that a reading of Friedrich Albert Lange's *History of Materialism* [1866] had cured him of a crude materialism.) How Darwinism fit into this pattern was not yet clear. Bölsche was convinced of its importance without being sure what part it would play in a larger Weltanschauung.[11]

What really troubled Bölsche was the apparent conflict between an aesthetic, poetic view of nature and the demands of science. Could one accept science and still find spiritual satisfaction? The problem was not simply that Bölsche could not make up his mind whether he wanted to be a novelist or a science journalist. His torment went deeper. As had been the case with the older Darwinians, a commitment to science and Darwinism tended to imply a social and political commitment. Like many young writers of the day, Bölsche was deeply affected by the poverty and ignorance he saw in Berlin. Bruno Wille had introduced him to socialist circles and enlisted him in the fight for workers' education and a free theater. Bölsche wanted to believe in the liberating power of knowledge, but he feared that people would gain enlightenment at the expense of spiritual comfort. (See chapter 7.)

This inner struggle was reflected in Bölsche's last, and only successful, novel, the semiautobiographical *Die Mittagsgöttin* (The noon goddess, 1891). It is the story of a young science writer and social activist who is driven by a sense of spiritual emptiness to abandon science and the urban struggle. He finds solace with a group of spiritualists in an idyllic castle in the *Spreewald*. As the foundations of his Darwinian scientific Weltanschauung are eroded, so, too, is his sense of social commitment. Just as it appears that the hero will give himself up to self-absorption, he learns that his spiritualist lover is actually a clever fake. Science is vindicated, and the hero returns to the city—into the arms of his working-class fiancée and back to the social struggle.

In real life, Bölsche's solution to his problem was not so clear-cut. Gradually he moved away from literature to popular science, but without abandoning a highly literary style. First, he tried science fiction. Sometime in the early 1890s, he began a novel called *Sternenfriede* (Peace of the stars) about a group of Martians who land near Berlin and explore the world, explaining it from their lofty scientific viewpoint. It was a clever idea, but Bölsche never finished the book.[12] Instead, he poured his efforts into a huge *Entwicklungsgeschichte der Natur* (Evolutionary history of nature, 1894–96)—a work of some sixteen hundred pages in which he attempted to describe all the achievements of modern science. But this was well-covered ground, and the book never transcended the works of Köhler, Sterne, or Bommeli. Then, in the spring of 1897, Bölsche found what he called the "longed-for synthesis." He was approached by Eugen Diederichs, who was looking for authors for his new publishing house. Diederichs wanted a new kind of book on love—neither a novel nor a philosophical tract. Sensing the chance to create an entirely new popular science book, Bölsche plunged hopefully into the writing.[13] As he explained to Diederichs while writing the first volume, "It's not going to be a popular science book on animal love-life in the conventional sense; rather, in style and in the entire conception of the problem, it will have that special formal charm of a work of belles lettres."[14] Bölsche called his new work *Das Liebesleben in der Natur: Eine Entwicklungsgeschichte der Liebe* (Love-Life in Nature: The Story of the Evolution of Love, 1898–1901). In three thick volumes it told the story of evolution from the perspective of sexual love. The book was a sensational success and established Bölsche as the new master of popular science.

In *Love-Life* and the dozens of books that followed it, Bölsche recast Haeckel's monism into a more palatable form. As will be recalled, Haeckel's monistic materialism had an undercurrent of romantic *Naturphilosophie* that his opposition to teleology and "metaphysics" forced him to deny. Bölsche, on the other hand, openly accepted a fusion of Darwinism and *Naturphilosophie* and thus worked out the full implications of Darwinian monism. Bölsche believed that the unity of nature felt by the romantics had been proved scientifically by Darwin. As Bölsche's friend, the panpsychic Bruno Wille, put it: "We both, friend Bölsche, are idealists in that we ascribe a psychical, spiritual character to all of nature. At the same time we profess Darwinism because in spite of its gaps it is a purely reasonable, clearly intelligible, and in a certain sense irrefutable theory. On our walks in the woods we have often sketched Darwin's theory into our panpsychic picture of nature."[15] Here we find correctly identified the two main ingredients of Bölsche's (and Haeckel's) monism: panpsychism and Darwinism. The two complement each other in Bölsche's works; but, as Wille suggests, it is Darwinism that is fit into a panpsychic framework, rather than the reverse.

The basis of romantic monism, as Bölsche saw it, was the belief that nature was a sensitive organic unity, of which man was a microcosm. In the early nineteenth century, science had not yet developed tools to examine this feeling, and, consequently, it found its outlet in a mystical awe of nature expressed in art. The artist felt, as Bölsche said, "the organic insertion of the little roundelay 'man' into the more complete dance of the infinite."[16] For the romantic poet Novalis (1772–1801), whom Bölsche greatly admired, the blue flower was the symbol of this mystical oneness in which the artist swam as in a timeless dream. Plants blended into the sky, the sky into the earth, the earth into man, and man into God. This romantic journey into the depths of the soul was for Bölsche protorealistic, because its goal was truth, not mere escapism into an unreal world. In Novalis, he said, art and science flowed together.

This view that nature has a soul of which man is a part had found its most elaborate exposition in the work of the philosopher and experimental psychologist Gustav Fechner (1801–87), whom Bölsche regarded as the spiritual son of Novalis. Aside from Darwin himself, Fechner was probably the greatest single influence on Bölsche. He referred to Fechner frequently and devoted a long laudatory essay to him.[17] In a book of 1848, *Nanna, oder das Seelenleben der Pflanzen* (Nanna, or the soul life of plants), Fechner had argued that the spiritual life of men is a part of a larger spiritual universe inaccessible to the science of physics. Granted, there was no direct proof for this contention, but the argument by analogy seemed compelling to Fechner—and to Bölsche. Briefly, it was as follows. Our knowledge that other people have souls (by soul, Fechner often seems to mean consciousness) is ultimately based on an analogy. We are directly aware only of our own soul, but we conclude that because other men are similar to us, they, too, have souls. Man, however, is not the only complex organized object in the universe. Because animals, plants, rocks, even the earth and stars, also show complex forms of organization, what prevents us from assuming that soul is a parallel phenomenon of all advanced systems? In Fechner's view, the entire universe consisted of these interlocking soul systems, God being the *All-Seele* (All-Soul). There could be no such thing as isolation; all was one because there was nothing outside of the All-Soul. Not even death destroyed the soul because its effects, like the light of long-dead stars, were intermeshed with countless other systems of souls that lived on. In a later book, *Die Tagesansicht gegenüber der Nachtansicht* (The daylight view as opposed to the night view, 1879), Fechner dubbed his view that the universe was alive the Daylight View or optimistic view. The contrary view of many materialists, that the universe consisted only of dead fragments of matter, he branded the pessimistic Night View. Ever sensitive to the speculative nature of his thought, Fechner appealed to the argument (later used by the Pragmatists) that if man feels more at home in an alive universe, then there is no reason to deny him his happiness.[18]

Darwinism, in Bölsche's view, had greatly strengthened Fechner's panpsychic monism by proving the smooth continuity of life from man on downward. All the barriers between life forms had become blurred and thus useless as a basis for sharp divisions between differing forms. If man blended into apes, and apes into still lower forms, then it was purely arbitrary to stop at any given point and proclaim: From here on down there can be no soul! Alfred Wallace, the co-discoverer of natural selection, had been quick to see this threat to man's uniqueness and continued to the end of his life to insist on a separate creation for man. But Bölsche, like most Darwinists, was undaunted by man's animal origins. Indeed, as a good Fechner student, he drew an even more radical inference from Darwinism. Why, he asked, abandon Darwinism at the bridge between the organic and the inorganic? Wasn't this distinction as arbitrary as that between man and animal?[19] Nonlife, he argued, had fundamental similarities to life: it tended to form into individual parts, such as crystals or stars; these parts tended further to divide like life; and, moreover, throughout the inorganic world we see forces of attraction at work, such as gravity and magnetism, that remind us of the sexual forces of life.[20] This closing of the gap between the organic and the inorganic did away with one of the basic dualities of nature and made possible a monism that integrated life into an infinitely spiraling development of the universe. Just as Haeckel had done, Bölsche sidestepped the question of organic creation by making life an eternal force. But whereas Haeckel's fierce antiteleology rendered this position a dead end, Bölsche was willing to ask: What is the purpose of the universe, and how is that purpose achieved? Bölsche focused, above all, on sex. Sexual love was the unifying principle of the universe, the engine of evolution. In Bölsche's hands, Darwinism was changed from a tale of bitter struggle to an erotic monism or paneroticism, a lyrical celebration of love. *Love-Life*, his most ambitious and endearing work, tells the story of sexual love from primitive life forms—flies, jellyfish, and tapeworms—to the rapturous human love, which ultimately transcends sexuality to find its final expression in art and religion. Here again, the anthropomorphism of German romanticism is injected as a foreign element into Darwinism. Each stage on the scale of being has already passed through every simpler stage and now longs to experience the ecstasy that accompanies climbing still higher on the ladder. Man's advancing culture is but an extension of this natural ladder and is thus drenched in sexuality. Every person has deeply buried within himself, in the hoary wisdom of the body, a primeval memory of the whole drama of eons of evolution. This is Bölsche's dramatic version of Haeckel's biogenetic law that ontogeny recapitulates phylogeny. The primeval memory that Bölsche seeks to activate in his *Love-Life* is no metaphor in his eyes, but rather a real and intensely personal "chapter of your history."

The story of love begins with the assumption of the primeval sympathy of all matter. Whereas his mentor, Fechner, had attributed soul only to systems, Bölsche, like Haeckel, believed that single units or cells might also possess soul. Once again, slippery analogies were advanced to support what amounted to a variation of the old pangenesis theory—the idea that each germ cell contains fragments from every body cell. If the single-celled sperm and egg contain all the ingredients that grow into a soul-possessing adult, then all the attributes of the adult, including the soul, must be present from the beginning in the single cells. And if sperm and egg cells have soul, why cannot all other cells, or even all other bits of matter?[21] As it had been for Fechner, soul for Bölsche was really consciousness. From the perspective of the empirical tradition within which Darwin worked, Bölsche's theory of the soul looks like sophistry: the anthropomorphism and the almost mystical confusion of the potential and the actual reveal a mind still steeped in *Naturphilosophie*.

Once we have conceded that individual cells are consciously aware, everything else falls into place. Love is present from the very beginning as the basic motivation for eternal renewal and development. "Beyond the shadow of a doubt," said Bölsche, "there were acts of love in the beginning, and for the purpose of these acts of love there were erotic feelings."[22] At first, simple division suffices, but eventually the primal feeling of *Gemeinschaft* (community) of all cells begins to assert itself. Division is complemented by fusion of two cells to form a new individual. Some cells learn to travel together as a group, "for company" and for the sake of efficiency through division of labor. Reproduction thus becomes specialized, ultimately in sexual organs, though the principle of divide and fuse remains. In these higher stages, the release of the sperm and its fusion with the egg correspond to the earlier breaking off of parts to unite with other parts. At first, sex and death are indistinguishable, for the destruction of one individual is simultaneous with the creation of a new one. Higher up the scale, sex and death begin to diverge somewhat, though they still maintain their intimate connection. In a memorable passage, Bölsche describes the life of the day fly, which emerges from its larva only long enough to mate and die—"killed by the lightning of love." Even in man, death remains an "unrecognized act of love" that throws him into the lap of nature, where he achieves immortality through the unbroken chain of life.[23]

Of course, there are important differences between bacillus love and human love. The former is exclusively "fusion love," as Bölsche called it, whereas the latter includes not only "fusion love," but also "distance love" and "lasting love." Fusion love is the oldest form of love, involving only the fusing cells themselves, and in the case of higher animals, the reproductive organs. Lasting love, which occurs only in advanced animals and man, is family love, the love of parent and child. Finally, the concept distance love evokes the rich context that surrounds the sexual act in humans. In Bölsche's words: "To distance love we ascribe all those things that build love and hold it together—whether by spirit alone, by spiritual instruments, or by sound waves, light waves, speech, writing, or aesthetic feelings."[24] This is most extraordinary, for, by this line of reasoning, everything that is associated with sexual activity assumes by a kind of osmosis its own erotic character. Eroticism becomes universalized, not only in the body, where all parts have a sexual function, but in the very air around the lovers that carries the sounds, sights, and smells from one to the other.

If it is to claim legitimate descent from Darwinism, erotic monism obviously must come to terms with the struggle for life and the resultant natural selection. Failure to do so would relegate erotic monism to a vulgarized neo-*Naturphilosophie*. At first glance, it might seem that Bölsche picked what suited him and ignored a great deal in Darwin's work. But this hardly makes him uniquely culpable, for Darwinism had both the advantage and disadvantage that it could be all things to all men. As a theory, it was anything but airtight and consistent, and its many ambiguities and infinite suggestiveness opened the floodgates for a plethora of often totally contradictory interpretations. Bölsche's reconciliation of Darwinism and erotic monism offers one of the classic examples of the almost infinite malleability of Darwinism. Bölsche claimed that Darwin's nature was not nearly as brutal and bloody as many (including Haeckel) had made it out to be, especially as one moved closer to man on the evolutionary ladder. Nature was filled with examples of love, cooperation, and symbiosis, all of which tended to mitigate the struggle for existence. In an essay called "Is Mutual Aid a Basic Principle of Organic Evolution?" Bölsche argued that struggle in nature was a secondary feature, a necessary by-product of the individuation that was a prerequisite of higher development. Struggle usually manifested itself not in a competition among the various forms of life, but rather between these forms of life and a common inorganic environment. Cooperation and love, which were the higher forms of a primal sympathy of all matter, would keep reappearing and would be positive variations in the struggle to survive in a hostile environment. Even at the primitive level, cells tended to cooperate rather than fight. As one ascended the evolutionary ladder, this cooperation became increasingly sophisticated until it found its natural extension in civilized man's ethics. Never did Bölsche deny the bitter realities of nature, but by relegating them to a transitional stage on the way to a finer harmony, he relieved Darwinism of some of its dismalness.[25]

This downplaying of the harsh survival-of-the-fittest philosophy finds some support in Darwin's own writings. In *The Descent of Man* and the later editions of *The Origin*, Darwin retreated noticeably from his earlier emphasis on "tooth and claw" struggle and put a much greater stress on sexual selection. The most beautiful, though not necessarily the best physically adapted to survive, are chosen as mates and leave progeny, while the drab tend to die out. Sexual selection seems to impute a human intellectual dimension to nature, because an animal in effect "decides" which is the most tastefully decorated mate. In Bölsche, sexual selection becomes "love-life" but the essential anthropomorphism was already present in Darwin. A further softening of the struggle for life is the Lamarckianism that crept into Darwin's later works. Natural selection is too deterministic to leave much room for man's rapid moral improvement through the benefits of culture. But the inheritance of acquired traits means that the positive effects of culture will not be lost with each generation. Bölsche followed the neo-Lamarckian controversy closely, and though he saw the evidence as inconclusive, he did lean somewhat toward accepting the inheritance of acquired traits."[26]

The anthropomorphism of sexual selection, which Bölsche eagerly seized upon, was part of a larger teleology that he read into Darwinism. Here again, Bölsche took advantage of a central philosophical ambiguity in Darwinism. Superficially, it appeared that Darwin had banished mind from nature. Many writers interpreted natural selection as a kind of mechanistic cosmic roulette game with chance variations pushing life forms aimlessly from one stage to another.[27] Such a reading of Darwin led straight into the dismal pessimism that Bölsche abhorred. As that prophet of materialism, Ludwig Büchner, put it: "What are the entire life and the yearnings of mankind in the face of a nature whose course is eternal, irresistible, and borne along by iron necessity and inexorable causal law? The short-lived play of a day fly hovering over the sea of eternity and infinity."[28] How different is the spirit of Bölsche, which celebrated the same day flies in their ecstatic moment of death and renewal. Even Haeckel would have recoiled from Büchner's views, preferring to see in causal law the eternal advancement of the universe.

The antiteleological interpretation, however, had serious difficulties that Haeckel did not see but Bölsche would exploit. If there were no overall plan in nature, how could one account for the development of extremely intricate organs that had every appearance of design and were totally devoid of survival value in their earlier developmental stages? Did not the very idea of adaptation imply that a species tended toward its own collective good? The eye was the classic example of an organ worthless in its early stages; the very thought of the eye, Darwin once admitted, made him "cold all over." A similar problem existed for the human brain, which, as Wallace pointed out, was fully developed before it was fully exploited by cultured man. Many passages in Darwin's own works seem to support the argument from design. At the end of *The Origin*, he remarked: "Hence we may look with some confidence to a secure future of great length. And as natural selection works solely by and for the good of each being, all corporeal and mental endowments will tend to progress towards perfection."[29] Elsewhere, as in his correspondence with the American, Asa Gray, Darwin seemed to contradict himself on the design problem; but, as he admitted in 1860, he was in an "utterly hopeless muddle."[30] Certainly Darwin was a better biologist than metaphysician.[31]

The root cause of the teleological confusion was that Darwin's theory addressed itself to the effects rather than to the causes of variations. This opened the way to those who would argue that not only was there a general plan for nature (as Darwin at least sometimes implied) but also that each variation was cunningly contrived to fit into the grand design. In this way, God could slip into Darwinism through the "back door." Just why He would choose to do His work so indirectly and awkwardly was still an embarrassing question; but the point is that as long as natural selection seemed to produce order out of chaos, it was defenseless against any sophisticated theologian or teleologist.

Bölsche's erotic monism is compatible with Darwinism only if the latter's teleological possibilities are fully exploited. Having taken over from *Naturphilosophie* the notion of a *beseelte Natur* (nature with soul), Bölsche was predisposed to see a spiritual idea at work behind the process of natural selection. He, too, used the argument from design, combining it with the romantic idea of man as a microcosm of the universe. "We seek a model for the world—we ourselves are the model," Novalis had said.[32] Volume 2 of *Love-Life* opened in the same spirit: "To speak of man does not mean to skim the flat surface of nature, but rather to plunge right into the secret depths."[33] Thus, implicitly, what was true of man could be universalized to nature as a whole. This is a slippery proposition indeed; but Bölsche applied it with a literalness that would have been foreign to most of the *Naturphilosophen*, who tended to remain within a vague realm of generalization.

If man really is a microcosm of the universe, then man's quest for purpose, sense, and harmony is of great significance, for it reveals a larger purpose in the universe: "Man acts with purpose, therefore nature at the stage of man acts with purpose," Bölsche asserted.[34] It may be objected that to say that man is an integral part of nature, or even a microcosm of nature, is not the same as to say that man is identical with nature. Man's sense of purpose may be an exception within a cruel and chaotic universe. Bölsche replied that man cannot be an exception or an isolated fragment because evolution proves that there are no sharp divisions in nature. Man's harmony must be predicated on a larger harmony stretching billions of years into the past and forever into the future. Since the chain of evolution is unbroken, the primeval forms of the universe must have contained the potential for everything that was to come. Nature cannot simply go through any stage (be it fish or man) without revealing its essence, its primeval ideal. And at the stage of man—the most fully developed stage to date—that essence justifies a teleological view.[35]

Bölsche claims to be appealing to Darwinism here, but actually he is again revealing his *naturphilosophische* prejudices. He has entered a realm quite alien to Darwin's empiricism. In fact, it could be argued that the idea that the past and future are inherent in every stage of the hierarchy of nature is based on a mystical conception of time, confuses the potential with the actual, and thus implicitly denies the need for evolution, which demands a sequential appearance of natural forms.[36] It is not surprising, therefore, that Bölsche also appealed to a non-evolutionary analogy to buttress his sagging argument. In a comparison of the natural world to the Cologne Cathedral, he argued that it would be absurd to describe its artistic spirituality in terms of separate fragments of stone. The glory of the spires at the top must be a fundamental principle of the whole structure, even of the rough foundation stones. Of course, like any argument by analogy, this one leaves much to be desired.

The major stumbling block in the way of the teleological interpretation was how to explain away the combination of accident and iron law that first produced and then selected the variations. How could an ideal purpose realize itself by such a process? Bölsche solved this problem deftly. He began by conceding that each of the countless individual variations is indeed an accident, in itself totally without any purpose. Only man can act directly with purpose, moving straight toward his goal. But nature, too, acts with purpose, though its method is less refined than man's. Bölsche used the analogy of two men hunting rabbits. The first man shoots directly at his rabbit and hits it. The second man is blind, so instead of aiming at the rabbit, he blasts away in all directions, covering all possible positions, until he eventually hits the rabbit. Both hunters achieve the same result using different means, but they both show sense and purpose. Nature, said Bölsche, is like the blind hunter who shows sense and purpose in the way he copes with his predicament. The tiny variations of nature (as well as the big ones resulting from mutations) are like the blind man's bullets shot at the rabbit, and any hit is analogous to a step upward on the ladder of increasing harmony of the universe.[37] In this way, Bölsche has nature realize an ideal goal by way of "mechanical laws," though once again it could be argued that human intentions are being imposed on nature. (We may assume that the blind hunter has purpose because he is a man, but what would Bölsche say about a flood that killed the rabbit by washing everything away?)

Ultimately, total harmony is the purpose of the universe, and natural selection (which for Bölsche begins before life itself) is the means by which nature approaches its goal. In the long run, there is a strict determinism, just as Haeckel had said. But Bölsche was more sanguine about the outcome of evolution. Harmony, he said, has the greatest survival potential and will always win in competition with chaos: "Nature has a primevally given law that the harmonious and good conquers the disharmonious and bad as soon as they enter into competition." The accidental variations can change only the timing of nature's plan, not its ultimate realization.[38] Thus for Bölsche there is a progress in nature that we can see in the steady improvement "from chaotic mist to the solar system, from a red-hot sphere to the inhabitable earth, from one-celled animals to man. And in man, from mammoth hunters to Plato, Copernicus, and Goethe."[39]

As he had done with sexual selection, Bölsche extended natural selection far beyond what Darwin ever intended. Both tended to become for Bölsche universal principles rather than limited theories to explain the process of organic evolution on earth, as they had been for Darwin. What for Darwin had been adaptation to the local environment became for Bölsche a quest for universal harmony, powered by a sexual attraction that gave a foretaste of what the universe would eventually be like. Sex was literally the ideal experience, yielding a brief glimpse of eternity. Because the laws of nature were universal, love was not unique to the earth; it would develop everywhere along the same lines (Bölsche believed that there was nonterrestrial love as close as Mars) as the universe progressed toward greater harmony.[40] Any event that moved the universe a step closer to its goal could be interpreted as a sexual act. Eros was the self-realization of the universe. Obviously, erotic monism is a philosophy of boundless optimism. Chaos and pain are downgraded to a transitional stage. They represent merely unfortunate variations that have not yet been excluded by natural selection. Even death takes on a larger meaning in this schema. As Bölsche remarked: "You don't fall into a bottomless gaping sea or an eternally sinking cloud of atomic dust. Wherever you are in the universe, you fall into the arms of nature. She directs you to a new place in the battle for order. She is with you every day. With her power of becoming, her logic. You fear for your spirit? But nature is in her innermost depths eternally spiritual."[41] No possible catastrophe could shake Bölsche's confidence in a better future. Should the earth collide with a comet, things would begin again after the dust settled. Should the sun begin to cool off, man could go somewhere else.[42] The future of life is boundless. Evolution teaches that eventually the earth will be inhabited by creatures as far advanced over man as man is over the amoeba.[43] To the pessimist who objects that, when all is said and done, we are still left with a meaningless circling of the heavens, Bölsche would reply that the heavens actually describe a spiral in space; and the spiral, he asserted ingenuously, is a progressive shape![44] But by this time, Bölsche has totally lost sight of Darwin. When he finished his *Love-Life* on the happy note, "The pessimist says: Everything is finished. I say with equal right: Everything is love,"[45] he is back at Fechner's Daylight View.

In short, although erotic monism began with Darwin, it quickly moved toward the aesthetic view of nature that had typified *Naturphilosophie*. Nature resembled a giant work of art whose beauty unfolded through evolution, linking the inorganic to the organic, the tiniest flowers to man's most glorious works of art. Bölsche called this aesthetic dimension of nature "the rhythmic-ornamental principle," and he elevated it to a universal law that existed parallel to the struggle for existence and moved nature toward ever greater aesthetic perfection. True "art forms of nature" would emerge in evolution wherever they did not interfere with useful adaptation.[46] Nature's artistry, evident even in the most primitive life forms, increased in complexity as one rose on the evolutionary ladder, but the great principle remained the same. Man's art was an outgrowth of the art of nature, the difference between a Raphael and deep-sea radiolarian one of degree rather than kind: "There is no doubt in my mind," he wrote, "that it is the same principle that creates the rhythmically beautiful armor of the radiolarian and the art of man."[47]

Only in his methods does man stand out from his plant and animal ancestors. The latter are only able to bring the innate beauty of their bodies into the world, but man, with his tools, can add to the world's beauty. Instead of growing, say, beautiful feathers, man feels the urge to pick up a pen or paint brush.[48] Here Bölsche pushes monism to its limits, as he stresses the connection between man's highest creation and his hoary past. The aesthetic bond of man and nature does not lower man in Bölsche's eyes, but rather raises nature to a spiritual realm. Like the beauty that man consciously creates, the beauty of nature is no accident; it is part of the larger teleology of nature, the push toward love and harmony in the universe. Animals, even plants, said Bölsche, again extending Fechner's nature with soul, can be artists, too. They may not be conscious in the same ways as the human artist, but, like the human artist, their beauty wells up from the depths of the soul.[49]

Because love is the engine of evolution, it is also the basic creative force behind nature's beauty and man's art. For Bölsche, the beautiful was sexual and the sexual beautiful. In stressing the intimate connection between sex and creative thought, Bölsche both looked back to the romantics, especially Novalis ("The organs of thought are the world's reproductive organs—the genitals of nature"[50]), and ahead to Freud's libido theory. Colorful decorations, haunting melodies, rhythmic dances—all these, said Bölsche, have their origins in the sexual foreplay of man's animal ancestors. The painting of a Raphael or the poetry of a Goethe are inspired by the same thrust toward universal harmony as are the love orgies of man's animal ancestors.

The human body was one of nature's most exquisite works, and, as with flowers, its most beautiful parts were the most erotic. Though warped by corsets, hidden by drab clothes, and surrounded by an aura of shame in modern society, the human body was actually pure, delightful, and inspiring. To Bölsche, every part of the body, even the anus, was worthy of admiration. He effusively praised the harmony and beauty of the male penis, mocking those who found it obscene.[51] But his greatest encomia were saved for the female derriere: "Let us not forget," he said in all earnestness, "that the backside of woman belongs among the most alluring art forms of the entire cosmos."[52] The female backside represented a grand ideal toward which the universe was evolving. Art and evolution went hand in hand for Bölsche because beauty was a positive variation. The invisible hand of Darwinian selection worked in the medium of nature just as the human hand might work with stone or paint or words—always selecting, refining, and integrating into a harmonious whole.[53] Thus the nude human body, which moved Bölsche so greatly, had been selected for not only because of its utility (nudity permitted clothes that gave great flexibility to man), but also because it appealed to man's innate sense of beauty. Yet there was a still deeper bond beween art and evolution. Not only did art grow out of nature, it also afforded a vision of the future. The ideal, as represented in art, was a foretaste of what evolution would later actually realize. Art was by its very nature progressive and healthy because, though it had its origins in a less perfect past, it looked forward to an improving future. By tying art to evolution, Bölsche believed that he had exposed the old dualism of ideal/real as the illusion of a static, mechanistic view of reality. Evolutionary monism revealed that the ideal (art) was actually the evolving real.[54] Poetry and science were but two sides of the same coin, two stages of man's perception of the order and unity of the universe. Both art and science, Bölsche stressed, envisioned the evolving harmony of the universe; the difference was that the more fluid, free-flowing images of art preceded the rigorous structural thought of science. Science derived its inspiration from man's primeval fantasies, reordering those fantasies in ways that could change reality, rather than merely represent it: "Art is the ideal model of the research goal—research in the highest sense, the ideal fulfillment of art."[55]

Again the categories of German romanticism lurk just below the surface of Bölsche's exposition. As the romantic Adam Müller (1779–1829) had said, the purpose of science was not "discovery" but rather "rediscovery."[56] Science, in Bölsche's eyes, was really a process of déjà vu. This conclusion followed logically from one of the major premises of monism, which Bölsche had taken from Novalis, namely, that man was a metaphor of the universe and thus had, at least metaphorically, "seen it all before." Bölsche never tired of finding examples of fantasy and myth that predicted later scientific discoveries. Dragon and monster stories were exaggerated memories of real reptiles that science later rediscovered.[57] Indeed, folk fantasy had foreshadowed the theory of evolution in that it had intuitively grasped the unity of life forms: "In the fairy tale (the ancestral form of all human philosophy and science) animals are disguised people, who need only to crawl out of the shell. In the frog is hidden a prince who waits for his hour to come. The sorceress changes people back into swine whenever it gives her pleasure. Soldiers evolve out of dragon's teeth."[58]

Bölsche's interest in tapping the folk fantasy reflected his general belief that popular science had to be more than a neutral conduit between professionals and laymen. The function of popular science was to help people overcome their alienation from nature by means of a judicious blend of knowledge and emotion. Professional scientists, Bölsche believed, bore much of the blame for this alienation from nature, because they had abdicated their responsibility to explain and enrich their empirical discoveries by placing them in an understandable philosophical context. Bölsche took issue with those scientists who claimed that Weltanschauung was better left to theologians or philosophers. Why shouldn't famous researchers lend their prestige to optimistic speculation? he asked rhetorically. Only science had the authority to combat the spiritual malaise that had been the unfortunate by-product of its great achievements. The ranks of these "guilty scientists" who neglected their duty to philosophize were legion; but, for Bölsche, the great biologist Emil Du Bois-Reymond stood out as the prime offender. His famous *Über die Grenzen des Naturerkennens* (On the limits of natural knowledge, 1872), in which he insisted that science was forever doomed to say "*ignoramus et ignorabimus*" about the ultimate questions of matter and consciousness, became the classic statement of the self-imposed limitations of science.[59] It was hardly surprising that the general public had gotten the impression that scientists trafficked in dismal formulas, which were progressively reducing human beings to hapless cogs in a giant machine. Cut loose from their old spiritual moorings, the people cried out for a new Weltanschauung: "Everyone needs Weltanschauung; and the way is paved by a universal, truly democratic hunger for science, a feeling unknown to earlier times. Today, and even more in the years to come, we seek from research more than just steps toward technical perfection or cures for physical disease. Rather, the full passion of our religious and worldly needs is focused on science."[60]

Yet, instead of providing Weltanschauung, as Bölsche wanted, most scientists were retreating ever further into their own world of specialized language. Paradoxically, just at the time when democracy seemed to be pervading many areas of life, science was moving in the opposite direction, becoming more elitist and isolated. The ranks of professional scientists had become in effect a new priesthood. Unlike the old priests, however, these new ones failed to talk to the outside world, but instead often seemed to revel in the arcaneness of their work and the unintelligibility of their writings. In addition, laboratory work was contributing to the atomization and fragmentation of the world. The general public saw only the effects of science, which were either marvelously incomprehensible, or disturbing, or both. Science appeared to be undercutting all the old value systems, while shirking its role to propagate new ones. In order to analyze and control, it took the world apart, but then disdained to put it back together again for the bewildered onlookers. No wonder, then, that the hopes inspired by science were mingled with fear and awe. Science had become an authority at once unchallengeable and unapproachable. (Of course, all of what Bölsche says here has become stale and clichéd in our day; but at the turn of the century, when so many hopes were pinned on scientific advancements, these issues were fresh and urgent.)

Bölsche expected the popularizer to bridge this gap between the isolated professional and the confused public. He would do what the professionals scorned—reassemble dissected nature and return it to the public as an intelligible whole. Here Darwin showed the way because his theory of evolution was a simple demonstration that man was part of a unified nature. As Bölsche saw it, however, a mere recounting of the facts would not do, for that would only magnify the confusion. Aesthetic feelings, personal experience, and value judgments had to be mixed into the popularization, so that the reader could rediscover his affinity with nature. This restoration of the aesthetic unity of nature was an essential task of popular science, and it demanded a suitable aesthetic literary style. The popularizer was called upon to imitate in his own works the artistry of nature. In an essay on Carus Sterne, Bölsche summarized: "[The task of popularization] is to put back together what has been destroyed in the idea of science; to give a complete picture again, a picture suffused with the spirit that has been gained by a look deep into nature. It is a mistake to try to accomplish this restoration with the instruments of research. The only tools are the aesthetic and creative imagery of art. Therefore popular expositions of even the most abstruse and difficult scientific discoveries demand a certain plastic and dramatic style."[61]

This sounds much like a description of the approaches used all the way back to Fontenelle; yet Bölsche carried the aesthetic style further than anyone had before. He called for a complete breakdown of the distinction between fictional and nonfictional styles in popular science. In his work the novel blended into the science book just as he thought art blended into science. Bölsche's ideas were like "Zola in reverse." Instead of a scientific novel, he proposed a novelistic science. Hence, the role of popular science was not primarily to disseminate facts, but to promote fantasy and nature worship, so that the individual would feel a part of an ever-improving nature. As Bölsche freely admitted, the important thing was not so much what the popular work said (as long as it was accurate and up-to-date), but how it got its message across.[62] The subjective was allowed to overshadow the objective on the grounds that the subjective would make the more lasting impression. Bölsche once said in defense of Ernst Haeckel's supposed subjectivity, "After a hundred years the books that an era regarded as objective are totally obsolete; what still interests people are the subjective books."[63] This remark applies even more to his own work. Neither formulas, diagrams, nor intricate explanations could take the place of elegantly fashioned word pictures. Albert Einstein once said in reference to popular science that clarity was everything and "elegance should be left to tailors and shoemakers."[64] Bölsche believed, in contrast, that ideas should not be merely baldly stated, as in a "watered-down" lab report; they should arise naturally from a richly textured visual context. Thus an essay might record a daydream on a train trip, ponderings by an idyllic brook, or a stroll through a field of flowers. The genre ideally suited to this kind of presentation was the so-called scientific *Plauderei*—of which Bölsche was the undisputed master. The *Plauderei*, a form of light, impressionistic newspaper essay, seeks, by a few carefully chosen words, to evoke a particular mood. A good *Plauderei* is chatty, personal, and entertaining, its style elegant and aesthetic. Like a fine conversation (the verb *plaudern* means to chat), the *Plauderei* moves easily from one point to the next without cumbersome transitions. It hits the peaks of experience, offering a provocative kaleidoscope of life. Whereas it may have almost anything as its subject matter, the *Plauderei* always focuses on a captivating, highly concrete situation, be it a coffeehouse encounter or a saunter across a heath. If it makes a general point, it does so not by systematic argumentation, but by evoking intuitive associations. Setting just the right scene is of paramount importance in the *Plauderei*, because it never deals directly with abstractions; any ideas it conveys are affixed to a vivid visual impression.[65] Almost all of Bölsche's books carry the unmistakable stamp of the *Plauderei*. In many cases, he merely assembled *Plaudereien* that had first appeared in newspapers or magazines. Elsewhere, the *Plauderei* form was used in an indirect or disguised form. In *Love-Life*, for example, the narrative flows through three thick volumes, but its structure is kaleidoscopic—a series of memorable scenes into which the facts of evolution are woven. Bölsche's use of this technique seems natural, since he began his career as a popularizer not by writing but by talking to groups of workingmen. In transferring his informal lecture style to the printed page, he somehow managed to retain the sense of personal immediacy, as though he were in the room speaking to the reader, teaching him without appearing to do so. Bölsche never loses sight of his didactic intentions, but never does he plunge directly into his instruction. First, he takes great care to set the proper mood—the "introductory mood color," as he called it—an atmosphere of feeling into which the reader is transported. Thus in his *Die Abstammung des Menschen* (*Descent of Man,* 1904) we read first about a beautiful meadow and the universal brotherhood of man and only then is it appropriate to raise that "tremendous question"—the evolution of man.[66] But by far the finest example of this mood setting is the extraordinary opening paragraph of *Love-Life,* which is worth citing in its entirety:

> I should like to carry you off to a lovely spot; and there I should like to tell you a story . . . East of San Remo, in the paradise of the Riviera, towers Capo Verde, a brown rock jutting out against the open sea. Strata of stone, that once were soft ocean bottom

millions of years ago, crop out of the soft green contour of the coast like a phantastic citadel. The blue Mediterranean exposed them, wearing them away, not with rough fist, but through an infinite length of time touching them over and over again as in a dream with delicate white foam hands. Now the eroded, bared heads of strata lie there like pieces of the skeleton of a long extinct giant animal, whose grave had suddenly opened on the border of the sea. Between them, they form niches of soapy green, where the shallow water moves lazily and where, on the flat bottom, mysterious violet-red shadows of waving sea weeds loom up and fade away. At the outermost rim of the cliff the foamy coronet of the free onrushing waves flashes incessantly like dazzling white wings that close and spread fanlike in the sunlight. Beyond, far as the eye can see, all is blue; deep and bewitching blue. . . .[67]

A bit further on, he says, "Here let us speak of love," and the reader is off on a sensuous journey of love and adventure, as Bölsche guides him up the evolutionary ladder from the day fly to man. To be sure, not every stage is covered, only those that lend themselves to dramatic visual presentation. The book moves in a series of pictures, as in effect one *Plauderei* follows the next—all tied together by the grand theme of indomitable love. When the talk is of the day fly, the scene is a "wild summer evening on the river"; we learn of the herring on a "silver island of love"; and of bees while resting our head "in red heather." A piquant sexuality arises naturally out of these seductive, almost lurid scenes, where everything is idyllic, esoteric, or bizarre.

Here indeed is the grandiose climax of the tradition running all the way back to Fontenelle. Bölsche squeezes the very last drops out of all the old techniques. But in doing so, he comes dangerously close to losing control of his own style, thus creating an unintentional caricature of folksy popular science. Yet somehow he remains in control; somehow his extravagance is not ridiculous, but spectacularly successful. The secret of this success would appear to be the elegant harmony between Bölsche's style and his monistic Weltanschauung. How he says things seems to be a natural outgrowth of what he says. Thus the somewhat unsystematic series of *Plauderei*-like scenes is not disorganization or subjectivity run wild, but a reflection of his image of nature herself, where everything is interrelated and represents more than itself. Because nature is conceived monistically, Bölsche can move in at any point and jump all around without any discontinuity. Nature is like a giant gallery of beautifully colored erotic paintings. Once the general theme is understood, one may tour the "gallery" in any number of ways. Nothing in this titillating panorama can be irrelevant or out of order. Everything sheds light on everything else.[68] Descriptions of jellyfish love may provoke speculation on immortality; snails may evoke a rapturous discourse on the grandeur of the cosmos; and the behavior of the stickleback fish may raise philosophical questions about marriage.

Scattered throughout the text of *Love-Life* in no particular order are drawings by the book illustrator Müller-Schönefeld, reinforcing this sense of primeval unity, independent of systematic development. Insects alight on exotic flowers, whose long, curled stems seem to be everywhere at once; lizards intertwine their hoary tails; birds perch in trees, their feet and feathers scarcely discernible from the twigs and leaves; primeval amphibians slip quietly from lily pad covered ponds. Even a more "realistic" drawing, comparing the embryonic development of the cat and man (taken from Ernst Haeckel), may not stand by itself; it is framed by a plant whose roots seem to begin as sunbeams. Bölsche's long, meandering sentences with their stacks of adjectives seem almost to wind in and out of the drawings, which hook one word picture to the next. Everything is rank, pulsating, voluptuous, and entangled.

Equally remarkable is the way Bölsche's highly personalized style—the reader is always addressed as "*Du*"—expresses his anthropomorphic view of sexual love. The pulse of personified sensuality begins in the sea with its "tender, white, foamy hands" and flows up through the animal world to man. Along this upward journey, there is nothing that the reader cannot immediately identify with, because as the end product of evolution, he has passed through these earlier stages and carries a memory of them deep within him. This is Bölsche's very shrewd application of Haeckel's biogenetic law. What better way to grip the reader than to convince him that even eons back, "love-life in nature" is a part of his own personal experience? What reader could possibly find his own sex life uninteresting to read about? Remember, Bölsche repeats over and over; tap the primeval memory of your body that will link you to the primitive wild love orgies of bygone eons. You are the herring on the "island of love": "Millions of years ago: And man is a fish, a primeval fish of forgotten eons with only the potential of someday becoming a man."[69]

Such far-reaching speculation and poetic imagery would have perplexed the cautious, unphilosophical Darwin. Evolution, driven by love, was for Bölsche more than an explanation of the development of life forms; rather, it became an all-encompassing Weltanschauung, a monism that viewed everything as interrelated and moving toward greater harmony. This process of grandiose extrapolation from Darwinism had been begun by Haeckel, not by Bölsche. It was Haeckel who unwittingly recast Darwinism into the old romantic mold. Terms like the plastidule and the Law of Substance sounded materialistic and antimetaphysical, but they only veiled the romantic anthropomorphism that was always close to the surface of Haeckel's thought. Only when Bölsche restated Haeckel's monism in an overtly teleological form did the romantic base become fully obvious. Bölsche gave Haeckel's monistic evolutionism the love and harmony that the system implied but had been begrudged by its creator. And especially when presented in Bölsche's folksy style, monism stood revealed for what even Haeckel admitted it was: a new scientific folk religion.

What accounts for Bölsche's success? The easy answer is to be found in the lurid, sensual quality of much of his writing. He made sex "scientific" and respectable. In his hands, delicate subjects were made to seem beautiful and uplifting rather than dirty or offensive to religion. His work may be viewed, then, as both a cause and a symptom of the cracks that were appearing in the puritanism of nineteenth-century European culture. But it was not enough to say the right things at the right time—that did not ensure a huge audience. Bölsche stretched the publishing potentials of his day by drawing in both the audience for literature and the audience for popular science. But, more important, he mastered the art of newspaper and magazine writing. Unlike Haeckel, he knew how to say interesting and provocative things without offending or estranging large groups of readers. His cozy gemütlichkeit could endear him to the bourgeoisie, while his vision of the liberating power of nature attracted the working class. He managed to offer something to everyone. In today's jargon, we might say that he was the first popularizer to exploit the potentials of the mass media. Yet, remarkably, he did so without reducing everything to the lowest common denominator. He seemed to have the best of two ages: the mass appeal of the new and the aesthetic and intellectual refinement of the old. That delicate balance was the secret of his success.

Chapter 4

Darwinism and the Schools

THE zealousness of the popular Darwinists—"ape fanatics," as they were soon dubbed—was bound to produce a backlash. Predictably, the question of teaching Darwinism in the schools became the main focus of public debate. To conservatives and devout Christians, both Catholic and Protestant, Darwinism was a materialistic, anti-Christian threat to public morality. These groups believed that the popularizers were already dangerous enough just publishing and lecturing; they were horrified by the possibility that Darwinian ideas might infiltrate the schools and corrupt the nation's youth. But the controversy was slow in coming. The early 1870s, when the full implications of Darwinism were becoming increasingly clear, happened to be a period of anticlericalism in most of Germany. This so-called Kulturkampf, or battle for modern culture, had been begun by Bismarck as a strictly political battle against the Catholic church; but it created an atmosphere in which it would have been difficult for the state to take the church's side on any cultural issue. Thus, even though there were probably a few Darwinists in the schools by the early 1870s, their presence provoked no official response.

There would have been little to protest in any case. Science education in most German secondary schools—where the issue of evolution would most likely arise—was poor. According to the 1856 curriculum plan for the Prussian Gymnasium, science could be dropped entirely if no suitable teacher were available. In Bavaria, science was not even required in the Gymnasium. What passed for biology was usually called *Naturbeschreibung* (nature description), largely a rote memorization of plant and animal parts. On the whole, the main purpose of biology was to promote an almost religious respect and awe for God's creations. Great stress was also placed on the potential usefulness or danger to man of various plants and animals. A typical, highly stylized classroom exchange might go like this: Teacher: "How are the snakes classified?" Pupil: "As dangerous, suspicious, and harmless." Teacher: "Correct!"[1] Such an atmosphere left little room for any innovation, not to speak of unsettling theories like Darwinism.

With the waning of the Kulturkampf in the late 1870s, the issue of whether Darwin would find a place in the classroom came out into the open. The first round of the controversy came in September 1877 with a dramatic confrontation between Haeckel and his former professor

Rudolf Virchow. In a speech before the Fiftieth Congress of the Association of German Scientists and Physicians in Munich, Haeckel asserted with his usual brashness that Darwinism was incontrovertibly true. He brushed aside as sheer ignorance calls for experimental proof. Science was now in a position, he claimed, to answer the "question of all questions": What is man's place in nature? This was an extravagant claim indeed; but by this time, Haeckel's colleagues were used to his style of argument. What his audience was probably not prepared for was Haeckel's conclusion that Darwinian evolution ought to become the centerpiece of the school curriculum. Haeckel had more than biology in mind. Rather, he would have every subject enlivened by the evolutionary approach. He envisioned a thoroughgoing school reform whose aim was to show students the unity of nature and of all human knowledge. The Christian religion—a fundamental part of the traditional curriculum—would be exposed by evolution as an ephemeral dogma. Its place would be taken by the new pure nature religion whose commandments of love were based on social instincts going back to the animal world.[2]

Whatever one's position on Darwinism might have been, there was no doubt that Haeckel's speech was provocative and irresponsible. Apparently, the audience was not pleased by the performance; they even refrained from the usual polite applause. But if Haeckel had wanted to start a fight, he had chosen his forum well. Four days later, Haeckel's old mentor, the renowned pathologist and liberal politician Rudolf Virchow, rose to deliver a stirring rebuttal. Virchow called his address "The Freedom of Science in the Modern State," a vague title, though one certainly in keeping with his reputation as a liberal. What followed was actually a plea for the restraint of intellectual freedom, lest the great gains of the past be squandered. Vehemently attacking his former student, Virchow argued that since Darwinism was a mere hypothesis (as yet unproven), its inclusion in the school curriculum could well damage the reputation of science. The schools, he said, should deal only with certain knowledge. Schoolchildren did not yet have the maturity of judgment necessary to distinguish between hypothesis and knowledge. They would absorb all as gospel, only to discover later that science had moved on to new hypotheses. The inevitable result would be to breed a public cynicism and disillusionment that would ultimately pose a threat to intellectual freedom.[3]

With such strict standards as Virchow suggested, it might well be asked what could be taught in school. Virchow himself conceded the tenuousness of most scientific "knowledge." Still, given Haeckel's reckless confidence, there was food for thought in Virchow's warning; at least, most of his audience thought so. Haeckel's hyperbole made him very vulnerable, and Virchow got in some good rhetorical hits. He ridiculed Haeckel's much-touted ape-man skulls, dismissing them as diseased modern skulls (Virchow was, after all, a pathologist; and besides, this was a legitimate point in the 1870s). And he exposed the empty verbiage of terms like the "plastidule soul." Thus spoke the sober scientist who demanded cautious empiricism from his colleagues.

Yet in the midst of this assessment, Virchow let drop these startling lines, which revealed the true basis of his caution: "Now imagine for a moment how the theory of evolution looks today in the mind of a socialist. [Laughter.] Yes, gentlemen, that may appear funny to some, but it's very serious; and I hope that the theory of evolution will not bring to us all the horrors which similar theories have actually wrought in a neighboring country. After all, if pursued logically, this theory has an unusually ominous side; and I hope it hasn't escaped you that socialism is in close sympathy with it. We must be clear about this."[4] The laughter could not have been more appropriate. Blithely equating socialism and Darwinism was problematic enough; but to blame Darwinism for the Paris Commune (the target of the oblique reference to neighboring horrors) was the height of absurdity, and as a political man himself, Virchow must have known it. Most likely, he had been provoked by Haeckel into a rhetorical overkill.

Haeckel hit back in his polemical *Freedom in Science and Teaching* (June 1878), which accused Virchow of incompetence on the subject of evolution. Virchow's success in Berlin had gone to his head, Haeckel charged. He had in effect sold out to the reactionary establishment by becoming a dualist, that is, by doubting Haeckel's brand of monism. The choice was clear, Haeckel said: one must believe in either Darwinian evolution or miracles. There was no middle ground. Darwinism might not be subject to experimental proof, but it was still the only theory to account for all the known facts. The most Haeckel would concede was that man's descent from apes was only a "relative" certainty, whereas the general theory of evolution was an "absolute" certainty. As to Virchow's equation of Darwinism with socialism, Haeckel expressed shock and surprise: "What in the world does the doctrine of descent have to do with socialism?" he asked. To Haeckel, Darwinism was if anything aristocratic in its implications. But he warned (in a passage that has frequently been overlooked) that scientists should not meddle in politics—the results would be "dangerous."[5]

Reaction to the Haeckel-Virchow confrontation was predictably mixed. Virchow seemed to be saying that the constitutional guarantee of the freedom of science and teaching did not apply to the secondary schools. This idea alarmed liberals, and they moved in for the kill. *Kosmos* and *Ausland*, the two leading Darwin-oriented scientific journals, attacked Virchow for obscurantism, as did the progressive *Frankfurter Zeitung*, which observed: "It should not have escaped a man like Virchow that the modern outlook and the practical effects of science have already gone too far to be locked up in the specialist's closet."[6]

The Darwinists, meanwhile, poured scorn on the idea that hypotheses should not be presented in the schools. To omit all but proved facts would leave only lower mathematics in the curriculum, Vogt remarked. He suggested that the German universities be dissolved and remanned every thirty years as a way of getting rid of men like Virchow.[7] Büchner agreed that if Virchow's proposal was taken seriously, it would be difficult to teach anything in the schools—especially religion. It should be permissible to teach theories, Büchner said, as long as those theories were presented objectively. Evolution must not be allowed to become a new dogma.[8] Moleschott, too, was basically on Haeckel's side, but he tried to take a balanced position. Teachers needed to know, he said, "what you can say to children and what is better withheld from them for the time being. The highest principle must always be that the truth is not concealed from them, especially by forcing myths on them as knowledge. Even children will benefit when they are shown how imperfect our knowledge really is."[9]

Conservatives and clerics disagreed. They were delighted with Virchow; and the fact that such views could come from a famous liberal, the coiner of the term Kulturkampf, was all the more gratifying. *Germania*, the leading Center party paper, praised Virchow for his successful "club blows against the ape fanatics"; and the *Neue Evangelische Kirchenzeitung* of the court chaplain Adolf Stöcker saw in Virchow's remarks a "conservative impulse in the best sense of the word."[10] For Haeckel's enemies, the issue was not really the problem of teaching theory to pupils—that was just a convenient ploy. The real issue was Darwinism itself. Repeatedly, the argument was advanced that Darwinism destroyed Christian morality and was therefore a threat to the nation's youth.[11]

The school controversy came at a good time for Haeckel's enemies. Just prior to the publication of Haeckel's 1878 pamphlet, two attacks on the kaiser—falsely attributed to the socialists—furnished the excuse to outlaw much socialist activity. Much as he railed against the stupidity and unnaturalness of socialism, Haeckel could not dispel a widespread sympathy for Virchow's simplistic equation, Darwinism = Socialism = Subversion. The late 1870s were not a good time to make fine distinctions in the public arena; the air was filled with inflammatory rhetoric and recriminations (of which Haeckel contributed his share). Even the staid *Preussische Jahrbücher* was not immune to the hysteria. Its editor, the famous historian Heinrich von Treitschke, used its pages to charge that all shared the blame for the socialist outrages, particularly the "fashionable philosophers"[12]—a not too oblique reference to popular Darwinists. The *Kreuzzeitung* was more blunt. It simply blamed the attacks on the kaiser on the "ape theory."[13]

It was no accident, then, that the beginning of a showdown on the question of Darwinism in the schools came in the late 1870s. Although the journal *Kosmos*, which kept close tabs on the fortunes of Darwinism, noted several little-known incidents of teachers being disciplined for teaching Darwinism,[14] only the so-called Müller-Lippstadt affair attracted widespread attention. Hermann Müller was a biology teacher in the *Realschule* in the Westphalian city of Lippstadt. A noted botanist in his own right (Darwin knew and admired his work on flower fertilization), Müller was also well known as a progressive and dynamic teacher. Since the early 1870s his lesson plans had included discussions of evolution based on Darwin and Haeckel.

In 1876, Müller's activities came to the attention of the ultramontane newspaper, the *Westfälischer Merkur*, which ran an article accusing Müller of subverting religion by teaching evolution. Someone apparently sent the article to the Prussian cultural minister, Adalbert von Falk. Even though he had presided over the Kulturkampf, Falk was in no position to condone any actual antireligious activity in the schools. Religion was, after all, one of the main pillars of the social order. He therefore routinely ordered the provincial school board in Münster to look into the Müller case. When questioned on the matter, Müller replied that he taught the evolution of lower animals only and that he in no way intended to offend religious sensibilities. The reply apparently satisfied Falk, for he made no attempt to follow up on the matter.[15]

But Müller's opponents were not satisfied, and in early 1877 they renewed their campaign against him. This time their ire was aroused by Müller's reading to his advanced students from Ernst Krause's *Werden und Vergehen*. Krause (who went by the pen name Carus Sterne) was editor of the journal *Kosmos* and a "notorious" Darwinist. The particularly offensive passage from the book was: "A modern chemist who wanted to translate the history of creation into his preferred special language could not begin as Faust did: In the beginning was the word, or sensation, or force. He cannot possibly put so high a value on force. Rather, he would at once see the light and exclaim: In the beginning was carbon with its extraordinary inner forces! Only where enough carbon was present in suitable form could organic life, as we know it, begin."[16]

The passage seems innocuous enough now, but at the time many found it outrageous. The critics moved in for the kill. It was alleged that in religion class one student had countered the teacher's reading from the Gospel of St. John, which begins, "In the beginning was the Word," with catcalls of "Carbon! Carbon!" Versions of the story varied; some charged that Müller had also read passages that contended that Christianity was degenerating into fetishism. Others maintained that he had read from Haeckel's works. But the conservative newspapers took no trouble to confirm the details. They denounced Müller as a corrupter of the youth and demanded his ouster. Several newspapers, including *Der Reichsbote* in Berlin, printed an inflammatory statement sent to them by a Westphalian evangelical pastor named Krepeler. "Take care for your children," the statement warned; for there was a state of "spiritual emergency" at the Lippstadt *Realschule*, where Dr. Müller preached venomous hatred of Christianity. Alarmed by Krepeler's report, a group of Catholic clerics called for an investigation by the provincial school authorities, who in turn demanded a full explanation from both Müller and the school director.

With the support of the school director, Müller fought back. He denied reading any anti-Christian passages to his class and blamed "fanatical clerics" for stirring up all the trouble. He conceded that as a scientist he did work within the framework of evolutionary theory; but in no case, he insisted, did he present it dogmatically, and never had he read to the class from Haeckel's works. The school board agreed that the charges had been exaggerated, but suggested that *Werden und Vergehen* was inappropriate for the classroom. They urged Müller to be more tactful in the future. In the meantime, Müller had sued all the newspapers that had printed Krepeler's charges against him. Eventually he won judgments against all of them. The courts found no evidence that Müller was an enemy of Christianity.

It is difficult to say whether Müller's classes really were an indirect threat to religion. Müller claimed he was always very careful to separate theories and personal opinions from firmly established scientific facts. One of his former students recalled that the classes were always exciting and that no one was misled or encouraged to question religion.[17] But another Müller student disagreed. E. Dennert, who later became an outspoken opponent of Darwinism (but not of evolution as such), claimed that Müller's good intentions did not prevent him from corrupting his students. Darwinism, Dennert said, was inevitably associated in the students' minds with materialism and atheism; there was no way that Müller could teach about evolution without provoking some youngsters to doubt what they heard in religion class.[18]

Doubts like these were surely on the mind of Johann Stauder, an official of the Cultural Ministry, who visited the Lippstadt *Realschule* in May 1877 for a routine inspection. Stauder had great praise for Müller's knowledge and teaching skills, but he agreed with Müller's critics that the botanist's zeal was undermining the foundations of the students' Christianity. As Stauder said in his report to Cultural Minister Falk: "I pointed out to him [Müller] that he must avoid anything that might threaten the educational task of a Christian school, particularly things dealing with very difficult problems that his own science was still uncertain about. Above all, he had to be more careful in his public statements, and avoid any polemical clashes with clerics in the newspapers."[19] Müller promised to take the warning to heart, and Stauder believed him. So, too, apparently, did Cultural Minister Falk; he signed Stauder's report, and the affair seemed closed. Whether or not Müller mended his ways completely is not clear. He was certainly more careful in the future. Shortly before his death in 1883, he was granted the title Professor in recognition of his distinguished services.

Müller had apparently won at least a compromise in his confrontation with the Cultural Ministry in 1876 and 1877. But the affair would not go away. As usual, the wheels of justice in the courts ground slowly, and Müller's case against the *Reichsbote* did not come to trial until January 1879. The *Reichsbote* was a Berlin paper, and its own reports of the proceedings against it caught the eye of conservatives in the capital city. It was not long before the newly reopened Müller affair became a political football. The Kulturkampf under Falk had proven a failure, and the cultural minister's days were numbered. His political opponents in the Prussian Landtag could hardly resist the chance to embarrass him further. The Müller affair served their ends well.

It was no surprise, then, when the Old Conservative, Wilhelm von Hammerstein, managed to slip the Müller affair into a Lower House debate on the Cultural Ministry budget. His remarks were predictable. Basing his charges on the *Reichsbote* accounts, von Hammerstein painted a grim picture for his fellow representatives: "I must say that when Haeckel-Darwinism is allowed as a subject in our schools; that when it is permitted to inoculate young pupils with materialism in our public institutions of learning; then the school authorities are not doing their duty. (Very true! from the center.) And they will bear the responsibility when there grows up within our fatherland a generation whose confessions are atheism and nihilism and whose political philosophy is communism. (Very good! from the right and center.)"[20]

Speaking for the Cultural Ministry, Stauder (who had done the inspection of the Lippstadt *Realschule*), sought to play down the importance of the Müller affair and to vindicate the cultural minister. He explained that Müller had been "censured" for his behavior and that thereafter the damaging reports from Lippstadt had ceased. In a statement that was later widely misunderstood, he told the House: "I told the teacher [Müller] in the strongest possible language that with all due respect to scholarly convictions, the Herr Minister [Falk] absolutely demanded that theories and unproven hypotheses, such as are frequently found in the writings of Haeckel, Darwin, and Carus Sterne, do not at all belong before pupils of our secondary schools."[21]

These reassurances hardly satisfied Falk's enemies. Another Old Conservative, Representative von Meyer, continued the intemperate attack. Accompanied by "Bravos" from the right and center and hisses from the left half of the chamber, he charged Falk with neglect of duty. That Müller could get away with presenting such disgusting views to thirteen-year-old children was outrageous.[22] Like the others, von Meyer had not bothered to acquaint himself with the facts; the pupils in question were at least seventeen.

It did not help matters when Falk himself appeared, seemingly unprepared, and denied that Müller had ever read the offending passage ("In the beginning was carbon . . . ")—a statement Falk had to retract when presented with the evidence. Three other representatives, including Virchow and the leader of the Catholic Center party, Ludwig Windthorst, spoke up in favor of the government's handling of the Müller affair. Virchow repeated his earlier warnings about teaching hypotheses; but he added (to cheers from the left) that if evolution were ever proved conclusively, the church would have to yield, as it always had had to yield before science. Windthorst announced his dismay over Müller's actions, but thought that the Cultural Ministry had acted forcefully enough to prevent a moral disaster.[23] Neither man appeared to be closely acquainted with the case.

In itself, the Müller-Lippstadt affair was petty. Falk seems not to have taken the episode too seriously. And though Müller's enemies were genuinely upset, their behavior was self-serving and hysterical. The affair nevertheless had a far-reaching denouement, which marks it as at least a psychological watershed in the controversy over evolution. It was widely believed that Falk had officially prohibited the teaching of Darwinism in the Prussian secondary schools. In fact, this was not, strictly speaking, true. Stauder was actually exaggerating when he told the House that Müller had been given a censure (*Rüge*) from the Cultural Ministry. Müller had merely been warned verbally. Apparently, it was Stauder's remark in the Lower House—that the cultural minister would not tolerate in the schools unproven hypotheses like those of Haeckel, Darwin, and Sterne—that led to the belief in the official ban. But it should be remembered that this remark was a recollection of what Stauder had said to Müller two years before, and it was made as Stauder defended himself and his boss against charges of negligence. Although it would be stretching a point to call such a remark an official prohibition, there was no question that Darwinism was in disfavor at the very highest levels of authority. In September 1879, Falk's successor, Robert von Puttkamer, sent a notice to the provincial school board in Münster asking it to watch Müller. There was to be no more anti-Christian activity, lest the Lippstadt *Realschule* be further damaged.[24]

The new Prussian curriculum plans emerged in 1882 in the anti-Darwinian atmosphere following the Müller affair. By the 1880s, the secondary school system was diverse and complex, but the general pattern of the curricula was clear: no biology was to be taught at the upper levels.[25] The ostensible reason for the cuts in biology teaching in Prussia was that the school week was becoming too crowded and cuts had to be made somewhere. Philipp Depdolla, in his excellent article on the Müller affair, largely accepts this explanation, but he points out that buried in the instructions accompanying the new curriculum plan was an oblique reference to the Müller-Lippstadt affair. The Cultural Ministry said that the teaching of biology in the secondary schools had opened the door to unproven hypotheses that were appropriate only on a university level.[26] Whatever the exact motivations behind the curriculum changes, it was universally assumed that the Müller affair had been the real cause. It could hardly have been accidental that other German states generally followed the Prussian example. As they revised their curricula in the years to come, Württemberg, Bavaria, Saxony, Baden, and Hesse all gave short shrift to biology.[27] Some biology was still allowed on the lower levels, but it was usually very out-of-date.

The comments and explanations issued with the Prussian curriculum plans of 1882 did acknowledge that biology had made great strides in the last decade. Yet they made no mention of the greatest advance of all—evolutionary theory. As before, students were supposed to learn about the Linnaean system, the local flora and fauna (including their danger or benefit to man), and the health of their own bodies.[28] Subsequent curriculum plans were no different.[29] A quick look at the comments prescribing the function of religion class shows why school authorities were suspicious of new scientific theories. The 1892 Prussian curriculum plan was typical. It asserted: "Special weight is to be put on the doctrine of the church; for the church is the divinely sanctioned guardian and interpreter of God's laws. Obedience to the church is the foundation of true moral life and also a special protection against the perverse tendencies of the time."[30] In other words, religion was a bulwark against materialism, atheism, and socialism. Since Darwin and his disciples were associated with all three, they were persona non grata in the schools.

Nor did Darwinism have much chance in biology textbooks, for they continued in their antiquated ways. The material found in schoolbooks is usually a good barometer of what constitutes "safe," established opinion. And on this score, Darwin was bound to be excluded. Evolution did not mix well with the avowed purpose of science teaching— namely, the promotion of religion and political stability. Next to the revelations of Christ himself, wrote K. A. Schönke in the introduction to his natural history (1866), there is no better means than the study of nature to awaken religious feeling. For Schönke and many others, a true understanding of biology was an antidote to materialism and a prop for civic virtue.[31] Johannes Leunis, who wrote a teacher's handbook widely used in the 1870s, agreed. He saw science as a safeguard against egotism and political fanaticism, because science taught the young to resign themselves to the eternal, immutable laws of nature.[32] These men were using a kind of code when they talked of fanaticism, materialism, or the laws of nature. Yet their intent was clear. They really meant that science as a cultural weapon should not be abandoned to the enemies of the established religious and political order. Rather, if handled cautiously and kept immune from unsettling theories (like Darwinism), science could be exploited to promote respect and awe for the present order.

No real adjustments were required, then, in the wake of the Müller affair because there had always been a tacit conspiracy of silence surrounding Darwinism. After the Müller affair, the silence merely continued, with but a few breaks, until World War I. Indeed, it is almost impossible to find references to Darwin or to evolution in the German school biology books of the late nineteenth century. The 1877 edition of Johannes Leunis's teacher's handbook included a long list of the most important scientists of the century. Neither Darwin nor Haeckel appeared; Lamarck's name was present, but not as an evolutionist.[33] Carl Baenitz's botany book of the same year mentioned Darwin in passing, but not in connection with evolution. Rather, Darwin was cited as an authority on the digestive process of an insect-eating plant.[34] (Perhaps Darwin might have been pleased at this minor form of recognition; even after becoming world famous, he still modestly cultivated esoteric specialties.)

In an age when Darwinism dominated biology, it was not easy to evade the question of evolution in a biology text. Many authors merely described one organism after another, without ever discussing the relationships among them. Others tread cautiously around the subject, hinting at relationships, without mentioning actual common descent. Many, following the example of Samuel Schelling, whose natural history had gone through twenty editions by 1893, spoke of the great antiquity of life and suggested that it had arisen in stages.[35] But the crucial point was whether those stages had appeared suddenly in perfect form or evolved from one another. And here most textbook authors were silent.

Even so avowed a Darwinist as Oscar Schmidt, who tried his hand at school-book writing, retreated from evolution. Schmidt wrote the zoology volume (1878) of a series of school science books that were approved for use in several German states. The author of the first volume—a general introduction to science—was Thomas Huxley, who made no reference to evolution. Apparently agreeing with Virchow that Darwinism had no place before schoolchildren, Schmidt very neatly sidestepped the question. First, he acknowledged that there was a progression toward completeness in nature; for example, frogs were fish before becoming frogs; birds were related to reptiles; and mammals were higher than all other animals. But just when it looked as though all of this might lead somewhere, there came a masterful piece of evasion. Why do certain animals resemble others? Schmidt asked. His answer: We are close to knowing why and have made "great strides" in recent years, but zoology cannot yet speak with the certainty of physics. Moreover, only the expert can understand: "It is the goal of zoology to understand the conditions under which living creatures grow and multiply, as well as the true causes for animals being separated into groups and then varying within those groups. But because all is so complicated and requires so much specialized knowledge, we can only hint at this goal here."[36] Schmidt followed with an extremely vague discussion of adaptation to the environment, but he still drew no conclusions.

What scared so many textbook writers was the question of man's place in nature. Most authors did discuss man, but they were very careful to put him into a category by himself. Otto Schmeil, who wrote a study guide for teachers, refused as late as 1903 to classify man as an animal at all.[37] Carl Baenitz and others were willing to concede that man was an animal in body, but in body only. Man's spirit lifted him far above the animal world.[38] K. A. Schönke spoke for these writers when he said that man, as the crown of creation, the image of God, and the bearer of an immortal spirit, stood so far above the animals that he required treatment as a special creature.[39]

Even those who acknowledged that man was an animal would not go beyond classifying him as a mammal. No one accepted that man was a kind of ape. Schelling's books would not even allow man in the same biological order as the primates.[40] As late as 1909, he was still insisting on a "huge chasm" between man and ape.[41] Leunis, too, would make no concessions on the ape question. Even his teacher's handbook (of 1883), which included a very brief discussion of evolution (though without acknowledging its importance), made no mention of man being a part of the process.[42]

Occasional books flirted dangerously with the question of man as ape. H. Wettstein's teacher's guide for biology (1902) contained illustrations comparing men and gorillas. As the text put it, men were *similar* to apes, *but not related* to them—a distinction that could well break down in the classroom in view of Wettstein's suggested study questions. Thus, students were asked, "In what way can the apes be considered bodily and mental caricatures [*Zerrbilder*] of man?" And, "Compare the hand and foot of man with the corresponding organs of the gorilla."[43] One wonders just how far the student was supposed to take these comparisons. Schmidt, too, came very close to talking about a descent of man. He called the last section of his book "Animals and Man" and pointed out that zoology helps you know yourself because man is subject to the same laws as other animals. He cited Herder's remark that "the animals are man's older brothers." Schmidt then added gratuitously: "The maturity of age and many years of scientific experience are needed in order to appreciate the full meaning of this statement."[44] Once again, one wonders what direction a classroom discussion might have taken. A group of adolescents has its own dynamic, independent of textbooks, lesson plans, and teacher discretion. There was no way that the schools could be completely sealed off from an idea as socially pervasive as Darwinism.

Yet there were many who wanted to do just that. The years following the Müller-Lippstadt affair saw a continuing struggle over the question of Darwinism in the schools. For the most part, this battle was fought out among educators themselves. But as always in such conflicts, the particular interests reflected more general ideological considerations. Those opposing Darwinism in the schools were generally the conservative and the religious, both Protestant and Catholic. These people saw their effort to keep the classroom free from Darwinism as part of a larger campaign to protect the public from dangerous ideas in any form. They were, in effect, opposed to scientific popularization as such. For them, science, especially Darwinism, carried overtones of godless materialism and political radicalism, and their fears were exaggerated by the occasional excesses of popular science. They found ideas like Darwinism hard enough to control within the academies and among elites. Once outside these narrow confines, such ideas could wreak moral havoc on the nation. On the other hand, those who supported Darwinism, or at least saw no threat in it, tended, in the broadest sense, to be either liberal or radical. They were people whose religious ties were weaker and who favored a democratic secular society, advanced by science and education.

Although there is nothing very surprising about this ideological lineup, it is nonetheless striking to see the opposing forces in action. In February 1883, shortly after Darwin's death, there was an extraordinary debate on Darwinism in the Lower House of the Prussian Landtag—the same body that had dealt with the Müller affair. In a way, this second, much longer, debate could be considered a continuation of the Müller debate, for the immediate issue was analogous. The rector of the University of Berlin, the renowned biologist Emil Du Bois-Reymond, had given a public speech before the Berlin Academy of Science. The occasion was the birthday of Frederick the Great, and the speech dealt with British perceptions of the king. What caused the trouble was that Du Bois-Reymond chose to append a short eulogy in memory of the recently deceased Darwin. What he said was pretty standard fare: Darwin is the Copernicus of the nineteenth century, the man who put man into the animal world, and so forth. But this was too much for conservatives in the Landtag.

Court Chaplain Adolf Stöcker began the attack. In the midst of a debate on the Cultural Ministry budget, he paused to accuse Du Bois-Reymond of spreading moral corruption. Darwinism, Stöcker said, was barely tolerable inside the university, but Du Bois-Reymond had had the outrageous audacity to praise Darwin publicly, in the presence of impressionable young people and hapless laymen. The public had no way of knowing, Stöcker insisted, that the rector's remarks were a subjective personal opinion; for Germans stood in awe of professors and believed indiscriminately everything they said. All would naturally assume that what the rector said was established scientific truth, little realizing that Darwin's much praised work was actually a confused mass of hypotheses. Here Stöcker invoked the authority of Rudolf Virchow, who had expressed doubts about the various "missing links."[45]

It was pointed out to Stöcker that Frederick the Great, whose birthday had been the occasion for the rector's speech, had himself been a rationalist and a skeptic. Stöcker replied, perhaps aptly, that the freethinkers of the eighteenth century had had enough sense to keep their thoughts to themselves, whereas their contemporary counterparts dared to popularize their views. Indeed, for Stöcker, this was exactly the issue: the quarantining of dangerous ideas. He had no shortage of horror stories "proving" the moral degeneracy which Darwinism spread in public life: "Gentlemen," Stöcker warned the Landtag, "it happened that last New Year's Eve a medical student abused his mother in the worst possible manner; he's been sentenced to prison for the deed; and it is said in certain circles that Darwinism was connected with such an impiety. (Yes indeed! from the right and center; laughter from the left.)"[46] As if this were not enough, Stöcker later read a statement from a Rhineland judge, decrying the dramatic rise in "bestial crimes" within his jurisdiction. What could be expected, Stöcker asked, when the Darwinists have told people that they are in fact wild beasts, condemned to a godless struggle for existence. The chaplain demanded that the offending professors be brought under control. He wanted to see the professoriat as the "apex of the spirit," not the "apex of the animal world."[47]

It was a fine rhetorical performance with the expected reactions—cheers from the right and center, groans and ridicule from the left. But the absurdity of Stöcker's charges was exceeded only by his ignorance of Darwinism. He even claimed to support Darwinism as long as it was confined within one species! Thus, for man, it proved scientifically that all were descended from one pair—Adam and Eve. He also trotted out some confused skull measurements that purported to show the enormous gap between man and ape.[48]

Stöcker should have been more cautious, for in his audience sat Rudolf Virchow, a man who knew a great deal about skulls. Ever since his famous Munich speech in 1877, Virchow had been a source of comfort to anti-Darwinists. His opposition to Darwinism in the schools and his cautious skepticism about archaeological finds were well known. But Virchow was probably tiring of rightist appeals to his lofty authority, for, as a liberal, he had little in common with most anti-

Darwinists. So it was not surprising that he rose to defend Du Bois-Reymond and that he directed a barrage of scathing ridicule at Stöcker and his supporters.

The Landtag was not an inquisition, Virchow began. The rector's remarks had been a polite formality, which politicians were totally incompetent to judge in any case. Darwinism, he continued, had nothing to do with religion. Like all science, it was mechanistic rather than materialistic, which meant only that it sought causal laws as explanations. Furthermore, Stöcker's Bible was no more than a tangle of ancient legends, many of which would actually embarrass the chaplain. Virchow pointed out that speculations about man's animal origin were old; and he referred to Herder, implying snidely that Stöcker had not heard of him. As for those troublesome skulls, the chaplain received a condescending invitation to drop by for a friendly science lesson. He might learn then that the difference between man and ape was not as great as he had thought. Never did Virchow actually endorse Darwinism or its unbridled popularization; he merely insisted that scientific questions would be answered on their own terms, without regard to religious opinions.[49]

All this was too much for Ludwig Windthorst. The Center party leader agreed wholeheartedly with Stöcker that Darwinism was a dangerous threat to religion. He rejected Virchow's separation of science and religion as a figment of the pathologist's liberal imagination. Such a separation was possible, Windthorst asserted, only if Christianity was reduced to Virchow's vapid do-goodism. But if the essence of Christianity was the redemption of man's eternal soul through the sufferings of Christ, then a doctrine that made of man a mere mechanical animal was profoundly subversive. Christ was not an ape who died for other apes. Windthorst scoffed at Virchow's contention that religion had to yield before the authority of science. Just the opposite was true, he maintained; therefore it was essential that the much-touted freedom of science and teaching be extended to the church. For only the church could judge scientific statements about man.[50]

The Landtag debate of 1883 was a classic liberal-conservative confrontation. The frequent interruptions from the floor (the left friendly to Darwin, the center and right, hostile) are significant signposts of attitudes toward Darwinism. Most politicians knew little about the technical details of Darwinian theory, but they did have a keen sense of the theory's social implications. Liberals saw in Darwinism a test case of the freedom of thought, especially freedom from church meddling in scholarship and teaching. And to the extent that they wanted to weaken the church's influence on public life, liberals were glad to use Darwinism to embarrass Christianity. Christian apologists such as Stöcker and Windthorst were therefore particularly sensitive about allowing public access to Darwinism. These men and their colleagues shared a belief in a conservative, authoritarian, Christian society—a society that the "ape theory" could only corrupt. If their estimate of the moral impact of Darwinism was exaggerated, this was only a reflection of their conscientiousness as custodians of the nation's moral life.

The issues raised in the Landtag debate presaged a generation of debate about whether Darwinism should be introduced into the secondary schools. But there was really little new left to say. Typical of the zealous promoters of Darwinism in the schools was Arnold Dodel, a botany professor in Zurich. His fighting polemic *Moses or Darwin?* (1889) lambasted the school system for ruining children with a "medieval scholasticism." Teaching the myths of the Bible was a sin against the natural development of a child's intelligence, he maintained, and would inevitably result in a generation of cynics. The solution, for Dodel, was to expel Moses from the schools and install Darwin in his privileged place. Only then would children feel the "true bliss" and confidence of being in tune with nature.[51] Meanwhile, opponents of Darwinism in the schools, such as Otto Schmeil, made much use of Virchow's old argument that Darwinism was a "mere" hypothesis;[52] while the writers for the Catholic journals, for example, stressed the threat to religion, insisting that science should be used to promote Christian values in the young.[53]

By the turn of the century, many devout Christians were adopting a less fearful attitude toward Darwinism, or at least toward some form of evolution. E. Dennert and J. Reinke (both biologists and devout Christians) began to concede the need for some evolutionary education. But as opponents of Darwinian evolution, they demanded that all sides (including the biblical) be presented objectively. Reinke, a professor in Kiel, went so far as to call Darwinian monism "barbaric." He urged that students be taught Darwinism so that they could understand how erroneous it was.[54] Dennert, author of *Am Sterbelager des Darwinismus* (*At the Deathbed of Darwinism*, 1902), also wanted teachers to expose the weaknesses of Darwinian evolution. In its place he advocated teaching the "true" evolution—a divinely directed harmonious process.[55] Both Dennert and Reinke were confident that Darwinism would be devastated by critical exposure in the classroom. They and many others were also becoming increasingly aware that the exclusion of Darwinism from the schools merely made the subject all the more alluring and thus drove students into the arms of the hated popularizers. It was better, perhaps, to confront Darwin than to ignore him, better to admit Darwinism to the schools than to allow the likes of Haeckel and Bölsche to go unchallenged.[56]

It is useful to view the fight to get a place for Darwinism in the classroom as part of the larger school reform movement. In the 1890s, many hostile critics denounced the German schools as obsolete and soul-destroying. They called for a modernization of the curriculum, taking into account the practical and emotional needs of the students. One of the most eloquent of these critics was Bölsche himself, who saw the introduction of evolution as part of a general opening up of the schools to the joys of living. He viewed the current schools as sterile prisons, poisoning their students' minds with an overdose of memorized classics, all the while oblivious to the wonderful world of nature outside. Weighted down with meaningless homework, the student saw the world "through clouded windows and eyeglasses, like a distant forbidden paradise."[57] To Bölsche, the failure of the schools was most alarming in the science curriculum. School science destroyed the child's natural joy and affinity for nature by burdening him with a tedious "medieval scholasticism." As Bölsche put it: "This kind of instruction plants in the young sensitive mind the unhappy notion that nature is something foreign and exotic; something usually locked up in the school closet, smelling of formaldehyde, pinned down with needles and wires, and cut off by a soul-destroying technical jargon and labels with Latin names."[58] No curriculum, Bölsche protested, could begin to be adequate unless it included Darwinism. He was sharply critical of those who wanted to exclude Darwinism on the grounds that it was unproved or subversive. What would be left of the curriculum, he asked, if everything hypothetical or incomplete were excluded? And could any really vital moral or religious belief be destroyed merely by bringing science up-to-date?[59] Bölsche thought the study of Darwinism would renew the students' contact with their own bodies and the beauty of nature.

But, as Bölsche realized, evolutionary education meant sexual education, and here there was bound to be resistance. Indeed, probably one of the reasons why the schools avoided Darwinism was that it would raise embarrassing sexual questions. The biology texts of the time completely omitted the reproductive system. In fact, when compelled to illustrate the lower body to show some other system, they concealed the genital area with the proverbial fig leaf. Frank Wedekind's famous play, *Spring's Awakening* (1891), in which young adolescents are destroyed by their sexual ignorance, poignantly dramatized the sexual repression of the schools. In the play, a boy is expelled from school because he has written a factual essay on sexual reproduction. He later kills himself. A young girl in the school, unaware of the facts of life, becomes pregnant and dies from the abortion potion administered by the family doctor. The play was banned in most German states.

Bölsche believed that a science curriculum that included sex and evolution would break through the unhealthy sexual repression of the day. He called his plan "reality instruction." It involved dispensing with the classics except for those students genuinely interested in them. With the school schedule opened up, the student would then go out into nature and begin to break down the barriers between himself and the world around him. He would study his body, his food, the earth, plants, and animals; and the great process of evolution would unify it all for him into a harmonious and satisfying whole. Understanding evolution would help end the damaging alienation from nature.[60] Bölsche was not the only one to link the study of evolution to joy and liberation. In 1900, a play by Max Dreyer, *Der Probekandidat* (The assistant master), was seen on stages throughout Germany. Based loosely on the Müller-Lippstadt affair, the play deals with a young biology teacher, Fritz Heitmann, disciplined for teaching Darwinism to his advanced students. The school authorities see him as a threat to state and society and call upon him to repent. At first, Heitmann agrees, but when the faculty and students are called together for the occasion, he changes his mind and launches into a stirring defense of his actions. He is, of course, immediately fired; but the students cheer him as a hero, for his classes had been the most exciting at the school. By all accounts, the play was a great success with audiences everywhere.

But despite pleas for reform coming from several directions, very little was accomplished. At the famous school conference convened by the kaiser in 1890, there was a great deal of talk about a modern curriculum, but surprisingly little was said about science. The conference did pass a resolution, proposed by Virchow and others, saying that "instruction held in the outdoors in natural history as well as in local geography and history is to be promoted by every means."[61] That sounded vaguely promising, but the conference's curriculum proposals still showed no biology in the last years of the secondary schools.[62] In the early years of the century, the journal *Natur und Schule* was filled with articles calling for the reinstatement of biology, including evolution. And from 1901 on, the prestigious Association of German Scientists and Physicians was also on record in favor of better biology instruction, although not all members were enthusiastic about evolution. At the association's seventy-fifth meeting in 1903, Professor Karl Kraepelin of Hamburg reviewed the situation for the members. He claimed that the association's proposals to upgrade biology had been generally well received, but he complained that most state governments were doing nothing, probably hoping that the problem would go away if they delayed. Part of the difficulty, Kraepelin said, was that there were few good teachers because opportunities to teach biology were so scarce.[63]

In fact, it was so difficult to regain lost momentum that almost nothing happened before the war. Kraepelin himself was in the forefront of introducing Darwinism into the schoolbooks. His teacher's guide of 1907 recommended an objective discussion of evolution in the last year of secondary school,[64] and his biology text of 1912 was one of the first to deal openly with the subject.[65] But these remained exceptions. Evolution did not come into its own as an integral part of the curriculum plan until after the war.[66]

The exclusion of Darwinism from the schools during the period of its greatest influence was of pivotal importance in determining the character and impact of popular Darwinism. By ignoring Darwinism in the classroom, the schools in effect officially confirmed the outsider status of the popularizers. But that exclusion created a giant vacuum which the popularizers rushed in to fill. As the dispensers of a forbidden fruit, they gained an exaggerated influence that they otherwise would have lacked. And, inevitably, their outsider status tended to heighten the tension between them and established society. With no foothold in the schools, Darwinism could not easily become part of the mainstream of conventional wisdom. Nonetheless, it was unstoppable as a powerful cultural undercurrent. Such men as Haeckel and Bölsche were keenly aware that a cloud of suspicion hung over their work. However much they might protest, they were probably also aware that their dubious reputation helped make them the potent forces they were.

Chapter 5

The Holiness of Science

"A MONG the most noticeable characteristics of the outgoing nine-teenth century is the increasing vehemence of the confrontation between science and Christianity," remarked Ernst Haeckel in 1899.[1] The conflict was inevitable and natural, Haeckel thought, for science, especially Darwinism, was continually reducing the number of mystical occurrences. Backed ever farther into a corner by the triumphant forces of rational thought, the Christians were beginning to strike back with an irrational fury. This conflict was one of Haeckel's favorite themes. In his Stettin speech of 1863 he had depicted the battle over evolution as one between Bible-bearing conservatives and progressive scientists.[2] Haeckel was not alone in these views. Perhaps the most sober assessment of the resolutely scientific, anti-Christian position came from the old Bible critic David Friedrich Strauss. The first chapter of his *The Old Faith and the New* was entitled "Are We Still Christians?" Strauss's answer was simple: "In short, if we would speak as honest, upright men, we must answer that we are no longer Christians."[3] By "we" Strauss meant all those who had accepted modern science, above all Darwinism, as the sole legitimate path to truth.

To be sure, the attack of science on Christianity was as old as modern science. It had reached both substantive and rhetorical peaks with the philosophes of the eighteenth century and had resurfaced with the materialists of the 1850s. "Only ignorance is barbarity" had been the materialist Moleschott's rallying call.[4] The wide acceptance of Darwinism in the 1860s and 1870s gave a new and powerful impetus to the anti-Christian forces. More than any previous scientific theory, organic evolution, implicitly banishing God and "demoting" man back into the animal world, appeared to cut to the heart of Christian theology. German Protestantism, although less fundamentalist than its Anglo-Saxon counterpart, proved particularly vulnerable to the Darwinian "threat." But Catholicism, too, was an easy target for the skillful polemicists of science. With Pius IX's *Syllabus of the Principle Errors of Our Time* (1864) the Catholic church had explicitly rejected modern science and culture; while the proclamation of papal infallibility in 1870 rebuffed those who believed that the only path to truth was experimentation.

Not everyone, however, agreed with Haeckel that Darwin had dealt a fatal blow to Christianity. In fact, many—in the worlds of both science and theology—believed the exact opposite. Darwinism and Christianity could be reconciled, assuming a nonliteral interpretation of Genesis and a teleological interpretation of Darwinism. The bounty of nature remained a tribute to God's grandeur, and natural selection merely became God's way of working out His plan on earth—"design on the installment plan," John Dewey scoffed.[5] Doubtless such a reconciliation of Darwinism and Christianity required a considerable retreat from traditional dogma into a theological no-man's-land of ill-defined allegory and philosophy. God could easily become little more than Samuel Taylor Coleridge's "something-nothing-everything which does all of which we know,"[6] with Adam politely retained as a kind of poetic first man. If sin and redemption were not quite respectable scientifically, Christ could be demoted to the status of an exemplary man whose legacy was to "do good." If religious revelation made the rational conscience uneasy, science could become the ultimate path to truth. To be sure, it was not only Darwinism that forced many people into such a position ("pseudo-Christianity," Haeckel called it), but history as well. Strauss and the Tübingen school of biblical criticism had chipped away at the historical foundation of Christianity, dismissing most of it as a tangle of myths. Adolf von Harnack, one of Germany's foremost theologians, may well have been right when he remarked in 1907 that the quiet work of historical criticism had done more damage to religion than all the shrill and spectacular onslaughts of science.[7]

Those who debated the merits of Christianity in the wake of Darwinian evolution found little guidance from the master. Fearing that he might prejudice a fair reception of his entire argument, Darwin was very careful not to offend religious sensibilities. "I see no good reason why the views given in this volume should shock the religious feelings of any one," he wrote in the conclusion of *The Origin.* Darwin then quoted a letter he had received from a divine to the effect that "he [the divine] has gradually learnt to see that it is just as noble a conception of the deity to believe that He created a few original forms capable of self-development into other and needful forms, as to believe that He required a fresh act of creation to supply the voids caused by the action of His laws."[8] And in the very last paragraph of the book, Darwin found it expedient to invoke a creator who had breathed life into those few primeval forms to which the theory of evolution had reduced the organic world.[9] There was nothing incongruous, then, when Darwin was buried in Westminster Abbey, eulogized by the religious as well as the nonreligious. All his life Darwin had been a sheltered figure, with few personal enemies. Such figures as Thomas Huxley and Haeckel, who had reputations for vehement godlessness, tended to be the targets of the harshest criticism of evolutionary theory, leaving their master personally unscathed and his reputation for piety intact.

However cautious his public position may have been, Darwin certainly had private doubts about religion. His skepticism dated from the years shortly after the *Beagle* voyage and grew as he got older. By the time of *The Origin*, Darwin was no longer a believing Christian, although, as the statements from *The Origin* suggest, he may still have been a theist. How long his beliefs lasted (in any form) is difficult to tell.[10] When two of the prominent German popularizers, Edward Aveling and Ludwig Büchner, visited Darwin in September 1881, he told them that he had been an agnostic for over forty years. Aveling remarked that Darwin's views were no different from his or Büchner's and that Darwin was merely a polite atheist.[11] This assessment was probably fair. Darwin's rooting of all human feelings in the animal past certainly called into question all forms of religion, not to speak of the unique truth of Christianity. For Darwin, nature, not God, was the source of morality. Man had inherited socially useful altruistic instincts that corresponded to what the religious called God-given morality. This position was implicit, especially in *The Descent of Man*, although Darwin never made a public issue of his belief that naturalistic ethics had replaced divinely inspired ethics.

Darwin's caution on the religious question was not widely imitated. Even encyclopedia articles, with their pretense of objectivity, found it difficult to avoid religious issues. The *Brockhaus* article on Darwinism rejected out of hand any objections that stemmed from religious principles.[12] Friedrich Rolle, one of the first Germans to write a book on Darwinism (1863), was equally adamant. The scientist, he said, was concerned only with natural explanations; religion was totally irrelevant.[13] Generally, it was simply considered bad form even to consider "childish" religious arguments in a scientific discourse. As Brehm said in the introduction to his *Tierleben*, he would deal only in facts: "It's far from my mind to see a wonder of creation in the similarity between the animal and his habitat, because I regard the animal simply as a product of his habitat. And as to the How of this correlation I don't want to wrack my brains beyond the graspable naturalistic explanation of science."[14] But not everyone was as gentle and restrained as Brehm. Many popularizers who took a purely scientific approach concealed an aggressive hostility to religion that could burst forth at any time. Carl Vogt, one of the first to infer the descent of man from Darwinism, contained himself quite well throughout his *Lectures on Man*; but on the last page he could not resist directing a few barbs at the moralists: "Let them rage! *They* require the fear of punishment, the hope of reward in a dreamt-of beyond, to keep in the right path—for us suffices the consciousness of being men amongst men, and an acknowledgment of their equal rights. We have no other hope than that of receiving the acknowledgments of our fellow men; no other fear than that of seeing our human dignity violated—a dignity we value the more, since it has been conquered by the greatest labor by us and our ancestors, down to the ape."[15]

Those writers who attracted the most attention posited a harsh dichotomy: one must choose either Darwinism or Christian revelation. *Moses or Darwin?* was the way Dodel put it—provocative language indeed, but the kind that the opposition could understand, for many Christians shared with these popularizers the firm belief that Darwinism and Christianity were irreconcilable.[16] In their war against the churches these popularizers had three main objectives: (1) to discredit teleology and thus deny the Christian God; (2) to discredit the Bible; and (3) to construct a non-Christian ethic based upon man's natural heritage.

Such arguments were, of course, not the sole province of the Darwin popularizers. They were very common in the late nineteenth century. But when others, such as Strauss or Max Nordau—perhaps the two most widely read social critics of the time—made the same case, they always appealed to Darwin's authority. Strauss, who had already dismissed the Bible as myth in his *Life of Jesus* (1835), believed that Darwinism had finally cleared the way for a rational religion by proving that man's dignity came from his own efforts, not from God. How much more dignified it was for man to have risen from animals than to have fallen from a state of perfection! For Strauss, such a view led straight to the worship of modern scientific culture. But he brushed aside the need for a formal church, "as if meditation were only possible in a church, edification only to be found in a sermon!"[17] The "New Faith" was an individual declaration of independence from the past. It needed no institutional expression. Nordau, who also believed in the liberating power of Darwinism, argued in his popular *Conventional Lies of Our Civilization* (1883) that religion belonged to the childhood of mankind. Darwinian struggle would refine the human race to the point where cultural pursuits alone (poetry, concerts, science, and the like) would elevate man's spirit. Eventually, rationality would bring a deeper nature-based morality that proclaimed: "Do everything which promotes the welfare of humanity; leave everything undone which inflicts injury or pain upon humanity." And then there would emerge a "civilization of truth, love of one's neighbor, and cheerfulness."[18]

Among the popularizers, Haeckel was not the only one to turn Darwinism against religion. Friedrich Ratzel made it clear at the beginning of his *Sein und Werden der organischen Welt* (The existence and development of the organic world, 1869) that God and the Bible had been pushed aside. The discovery that man was part of a mechanical nature was shocking at first because it destroyed all the old comforts. But Ratzel reminded his readers that they were on the threshold of a new freedom based on a real appreciation of man's true potential.[19] Wilhelm Preyer was another early popularizer who insisted that Darwin had given back more than he had taken away when he had destroyed teleology. In a public lecture in 1869, Preyer told his audience that the discovery of progress and improvement in nature was truly morally uplifting. No longer would man blindly worship a false harmony of nature.[20] Later popularizers hammered away at the same themes. It became common to develop the case for Darwinism by first showing the limitations of the biblical account of creation. Both Oswald Köhler and Rudolf Bommeli used this technique as a way of showing off the superiority of scientific explanations. Because science dispensed with God, they said, the door was opened for the achievement of infinite human potential.[21] All of these men believed that the power of science gave man new dignity and maturity by freeing him from dependence on a false God.

Few were more resolutely atheist than Ludwig Büchner. In his lectures and in the later editions of his perennially best-selling *Force and Matter*, Büchner tried to convince people that they had been "brainwashed" into believing in God. Darwin himself, he argued, had missed the obvious atheistic implications of his theory. Natural selection was the working of inexorable natural law, not God showing off his skill with limited materials, as Darwin had hinted. Büchner would not even admit Haeckel's pantheistic God-Nature. Evolution *"has, and must have, happened without the interference of a supernatural power,"* for what sort of God could ever have been content with such an awkward process? What sort of God could have tolerated the persistence of useless rudimentary organs? Büchner quoted Schleiden's provocative statement on rudimentary organs: "For God, who was able to create the whole universe in six days, would surely have been able, in an equal space of time, to get rid of an organ which had become useless."[22]

According to Büchner, the biblical notion that man was the centerpiece of creation was a childish fantasy, and anyone who believed it was "bereft of his senses." Man was merely a natural product of the animal world, and there were no qualitative differences between him and other animals. His spirit was simply the physical activity of his large brain, his morals nothing more than the elaborate ramifications of animal instincts. No human activity was so sophisticated that it was without precedent among our animal ancestors. Animals, said Büchner (probably enjoying the shock value), had morality and law, including all the institutions needed to support them: soldiers, slaves, palaces, jails, and halls of justice![23] The sooner man faced up to his animal nature, the better equipped he would be to exploit the useful social instincts that his heritage had bequeathed him. As man evolved further from the animals, these instincts would become ever more refined. Already we can see, said Büchner, that inherited cultural improvements have made man more moral by making him less dependent on the physical side of the *Kampf ums Dasein*. Eventually, sin, the vestigial egotism of older, harsher times, would disappear. Science and culture would lift man into a realm of supreme happiness and harmony.

With Strauss and Nordau, Büchner shows his Enlightenment heritage by tying his vision of a new evolving age to a damning critique of Christianity. Born in faith rather than reason, Christianity had suppressed knowledge, culture, and morality throughout its long, dark reign. How fortunate, thought Büchner, that the end was at hand: "As regards Christianity, or the *Paulinism* which is falsely called Christianity, it stands, by its dogmatic portion or contents in such striking and irreconcilable, nay absolutely absurd contradiction with all the acquisitions and principles of modern science that its future tragical fate can only be a matter of time."[24] What separated Büchner's anti-Christianity from that of his eighteenth-century predecessors was a belief that Darwinism had proved progress, as well as the independence of morality from religion.

Nor was Arnold Dodel one to make any compromises. The very fact that Darwin had been buried in Westminster Abbey upset this popularizer. Surely the location had been against the master's wishes, he lamented. Dodel believed that man created God, rather than the reverse. He wrote off the Old Testament as a "fairy-tale of oriental beauty," a mass of contradictions when viewed scientifically. What are we to make of the nonsense of the fifth day of creation, he asked: "Paleontology teaches us that the animal world coexisted with the vegetable world, and that the birds in the air were preceded by land animals, whereas Moses wishes us to believe that the latter did not enter into existence before the sixth day." The New Testament fared no better under Dodel's savage attack. It revealed an unparalleled contempt for nature and its beauties and the beginnings of an arrogant ignorance that would stifle humanity for centuries until science came to the rescue.[25]

Like Strauss, Dodel wanted a "New Faith" of science, a monistic "gospel of naturalistic reasoning." Dodel's new God was scientific truth. As science progressed, man would come to worship truth instead of the Christian God. This new religion could be based totally on evolution because evolution proved that all life was related and marching toward perfection. To be just was to be in tune with (or ahead of) evolving nature; to be sinful was to be out of tune (or behind). For two thousand years, Christianity had promised hope and had not delivered, said Dodel. But now we know that evolution will root out the bad and bring happiness and peace to all. Dodel's book ended with lofty paeans of praise for science.[26]

Dodel's monism was very much like Haeckel's except that Haeckel identified God with nature as well as with truth. Like most of the prophets of science, Haeckel began with a fairly unoriginal attack on Christianity. He relied mostly on a scurrilous brew of Voltairian mockery, 1850s materialism, and anthropological critiques of the Bible. Thus he denied the virgin birth, the divinity of Christ, miracles, and the legitimacy of the church tradition. Everything of value in the teachings of Jesus had been betrayed by the ignorant degenerates of the church. To Haeckel, all church doctrine was rubbish because it was dualistic, pitting an immortal human soul against a dead material world. In a passage of consummate polemical skill in his *Riddle of the Universe*, he challenged Christians to catch the escaping soul of a dying believer. Was the soul an invisible gas? If so, it could be solidified into "soul snow," Haeckel scoffed.[27]

However much he hated the church, Haeckel was not opposed to what he considered the true essence of Christianity—the golden rule. Buy why, he asked, let the Christians appropriate what was really a natural ethic, an inheritance of positive social instincts from the animal world? Once man understands the basis of his ethics he will begin to worship nature, which is the manifestation of the imminent divine force. Darwinism led logically to pantheism, Haeckel asserted, although he conceded that atheism was a negative way of expressing what he meant.[28] This new monistic nature religion was designed to restore to man the world the Christians had denied him. In compensation for the loss of the Christian God, and immortality, man would acquire a lofty appreciation of the true, the good, and the beautiful. Instead of being oppressed by an irrational theology, he would use his reason to understand his place in the temple of nature. Science and nature would exalt man:

> The goddess of truth dwells in the temple of nature, in the green woods, or on the blue sea, on the snowy summits of the hills—not in the gloom of the cloister, nor in the narrow prisons of our jail-like schools, nor in the clouds of incense of the Christian churches. The paths which lead to the noble divinity of truth and knowledge are the loving study of nature and its laws, the observation of the infinitely great star-world with the aid of the telescope and the infinitely tiny cell-world with the aid of the microscope—not senseless ceremonies and unthinking prayers, not alms and Peter's pence.[29]

Such attacks on Christianity are well known and are the source of common historical generalizations about the late nineteenth century. Nonetheless, there were equally effective popularizers who took their cue from Darwin's public position and sought to play down the conflict between science and religion. Otto Zacharias wrote in *Westermanns Monatshefte* shortly after Darwin's death that anyone who thinks Darwinism is impious has not read a line of the master's works.[30] Most of these men did not take the Bible literally, and many agreed with Haeckel and Dodel on the need for a new rational religion. But in contrast to the harsh polemicists, who wanted to destroy Christianity, these conciliatory popularizers wanted to transcend it. For them, science did not undercut old truths, it merely expressed those truths in a new language.

Often this conciliation was more a matter of style and tone than of substance, but in popular literature these factors may be as important as any substantive argument. Thus Carus Sterne in his *Werden und Vergehen* could agree with Haeckel that Darwin had destroyed teleology, that man's morality stemmed from the animal world, and that science was the new religion. But as Sterne argued correctly at the time of the Müller affair, *Werden und Vergehen* was not at all anti-Christian. He opposed only a very literal biblical interpretation because it was unscientific and would drive the educated out of the church. In Sterne's view, religion evolved just as all other things. First came primitive personal gods; then the great monotheistic religions like Christianity; and, finally, transcending them all, came evolutionary science. Each was true on its own terms and complemented the others. The scientists might be the new priests, but the old priests had nothing to fear as long as they did not try to interfere in science. Evolution was a noble process, and there was no reason why its glory could not redound to traditional gods.[31]

Conciliatory arguments like these were very common in the popular literature. Friedrich Dahl, in a book provocatively entitled *Die Nothwendigkeit der Religion, eine letzte Consequenz der Darwinischen Lehre* (The necessity of religion, a final consequence of Darwinian theory, 1886), maintained that the Bible spoke a language of its own that was not refutable by scientific analysis. An article in Friedrich Naumann's *Göttinger Arbeiterbibliothek* (Göttingen library for workers, 1896) made a similar case, stating that the Bible is a moral book, not a science book. God did create the world, but not as it is today.[32] And in the early 1870s, Bock was telling his many *Gartenlaube* readers that Darwinism made God all the more impressive as the craftsman of universal progress.[33] Such arguments usually entailed a teleological view of natural selection or a dose of Lamarckianism. A fascinating article in the family magazine *Nord und Süd* (North and south) in 1886 raised in a new light the old point that progress in nature was impossible without some will or direction to select the variations. The author was unconvinced by the classic argument about rudimentary organs. We see analogous vestiges on countless human contrivances, he pointed out, yet we never question that they were designed. Why should we question design in nature?[34]

Bölsche brought this tradition of reconciliation to a poetic consummation, revealing at once its potential and its limitations. His attempts to hook a monistic nature worship onto traditional Christianity (a concept implicit in Sterne's book, which Bölsche admired and edited) were truly ingenious. Yet, on balance, it must be asked whether Bölsche's efforts to "improve" Christianity with a kind of second Reformation did not entail the destruction of the very core of Christian theology—the fall and salvation of man. Bölsche's reconciliation of Darwinism and the Bible reflected his general belief that the scientific spirit was at root the same as the religious. Religion and science sprang from the same depths of the soul, just as did art and science. Ideally, their relationship was complementary, not antagonistic. Any religion that regarded science as an enemy had lost its original impulse and become rigidly insensitive to man's yearnings. That impulse, Bölsche thought, was the quest to be a part of a harmonious, loving universe, a quest that fitted easily into a scientific view of the world. Did not the scientist, too, seek the ultimate harmonies, which he then expressed in laws? Indeed, what prevented one from calling these scientific laws "holy"? This was what Bölsche had in mind at the beginning of his most widely read book, *The Descent of Man*, where he remarked: "And from the depths of the human soul, whence also the lessons of the gospels have come, still another voice whispers into my inner ear, a voice first heard in the wisdom of the ancient Indians. And it says that the bond of community and brotherhood is not limited to men, but that it encompasses all things on this earth, all things that grow up and evolve to their peak under the sun's rays and in the silent grasp of holy universal laws."³⁵ "Holy universal laws!" Some might have choked on the phrase, but to Bölsche science was actually the only remaining foundation for religion. The modern man was compelled to recast all of his spiritual needs in a scientific mold. Here we see Bölsche moving very close to a simple nature worship that is totally divorced from any theology. Like Haeckel, he believed that merely staring at the stars was a greater religious experience than any organized church could offer.³⁶

The notion of "holy universal laws" is one more expression of Bölsche's optimistic monism; for there would be little point in worshiping science if it merely uncovered a dismal and alien universe. Those inexorable laws of Büchner and Haeckel had made the universe sound threatening and any religious optimism rather forced. But the "friendly universe" that Bölsche took over from Fechner was very amenable to the fusion of science and religion. As an intellectual construct, the "Daylight View," the animated universe suffused with the All-Soul, was in a gray area between science, religion, and philosophy. Like much of German romantic thought, it could be interpreted both pantheistically and monotheistically. Identifying God with nature could mean that there are as many Gods as there are plants and animals (or even atoms), or it could mean that there is one God who manifests himself everywhere. Unlike Haeckel, Bölsche never called himself a pantheist, but he did see an intimate connection between monism and monotheism. There was a single force pushing the world toward harmony, order, and happiness. Thus God was just a convenient label for the beauty and harmony of nature, and the strivings toward God were no more than the aesthetic appreciation of nature's artistry.[37] This sounds like a gentle version of Haeckel's ideas, but, unlike Haeckel, Bölsche firmly believed that nature worship need involve no repudiation of Christianity. The problem was not with the Bible itself, but rather with the organized church, which had perverted the original pure spirit of Christian love and pitted itself against the forces of scientific enlightenment. Whereas the true essence of Christianity was supple, poetic, and evolving, institutionalized Christianity had fossilized the teachings of the church into a static, anachronistic creed. Literalism, for Bölsche, was the enemy of religion. No informed modern could read the Bible in the same way he read a scientific work. In this light, the Bible was indeed ridiculous and outmoded. But such a comparison was not only unworthy of science, it was also a violation of everything that Bölsche thought Christianity should stand for. Science, particularly evolution, needed to confront the basic ethical impulse of Christianity: "[Evolutionary theory] must come to grips in a positive sense with the ethical foundations of Christianity as a cultural force. Not with legends and miracles and an erroneous interpretation of old symbols, but with the idea of human love, of mutual aid and sacrifice."[38]

Bölsche's hero and mentor, Novalis, had asked, "Who has declared the Bible complete? Should the Bible not still be in the process of growth?" Novalis had even planned to write a "scientific Bible" that would embody an experimental religion.[39] Bölsche had no such ambitious plan; but he was constantly concerned to show that, if read allegorically, the Bible was thoroughly consistent with science—indeed, he said, the Bible actually predicted later scientific discoveries. In this sense, he viewed the Bible as he did other myth and folklore: as a vital, yet primitive expression of the human spirit, later systematized by science on a different level of expression.

To Bölsche, the story of evolution was symbolically foreshadowed in the Book of Genesis. Everything appeared there in just the order that science now insisted on, except that the poetic vision was not bound by the scientist's time frame: "What appears to the scientist as a slow development over millions of years can be compressed by the poetic vision into a few seconds of creation."[40] Thus, the Book of Genesis saw the universe developing from an ill-defined mist to man, smoothly following the will of God, and without the catastrophes so dear to many pre-Darwinian theorists. Light was seen correctly as the prerequisite for everything; and from the sea sprang the first teeming life. A graphic scene in *Love-Life* depicts a love orgy of millions of herring clouding the sea with semen, recalling the divine orgasm that once begat all life: "Thus the naive mind once pictured the creation: That at a lofty consecrated hour the power of God poured out the infinite semen of all life into the dead waste of the ocean."[41]

Likewise, the story of Adam and Eve could be correlated to the sexual evolution detailed throughout *Love-Life*: "Our Adam is the primeval bacillus, a kind of one-celled primitive being that forms the basic pattern of all subsequent living beings including men. Did not this primeval bacillus (like the Adam of legend) actually first reproduce without two sexes? And didn't it then split into Adam and Eve, that is into a male and female bacillus?"[42] And just as Adam and Eve were driven from the Garden of Eden, so primitive man was driven from his paradise by the ice age—a crisis that he overcame with tools and evolving culture.[43]

Not only did the Old Testament correspond symbolically to natural developments, its relation to the New Testament also paralleled nature. The transcending of the Old Testament by the Christian Gospels represented a new stage in the universal drive toward love and harmony. The Old Testament universe was raw and severe, its order prescribed by a stern lawgiver. What Bölsche liked to call the "Must Principle" prevailed, that "tooth and claw" nature of the Social Darwinists. But the teachings of Jesus were a watershed because they introduced the commandment of love, thus symbolizing the elevation of man above his struggling animal ancestors, the next step toward the perfection of the universe: "There [in the Old Testament] it said simply 'Thou shalt not.' Now [in the New Testament] the positive commandment drowns out the negative. And with this step mankind rises out of the animal world."[44]

Bölsche saw the emergence of Christian love as an inevitable and necessary prerequisite for all the higher stages of human culture. Once man's brain had given him a little relief from the constant struggle for existence that tormented his ancestors, his very cleverness was likely to get him into trouble unless he had a sense of the basic unity of humanity. This intraspecies love was a natural protective principle built into the teleology of man's development, and it found a magnificent expression in the teachings of Christ. As man continued to evolve, this protective principle (or Christian love) would be increasingly vigilant against his self-destruction.

The major difficulty with Christian love, as Bölsche saw it, was that it tried to leap beyond nature and escape into an artificial spiritual realm. Fortunately, because man was so deeply rooted in his natural past, this quest could be only partially successful. Love would inevitably remain linked to sex. Raphael's painting of the Madonna and child, which for Bölsche was the ultimate symbol of Christian love, dramatized the tensions within the Christian concept of love. The Madonna was at once a sensual primeval being (a *Weib-an-sich*) and an ethereal being from a higher world, uncorrupted by an earthly past. Yet no matter how much tradition sanctified her spiritual side as a symbol of a higher love of humanity, her animal past would always break through; for even the most sublime love must rest on the bedrock of hoary primeval experience: "The whole colossal wild foundation of sexual love—from the animals on up, from the fish, from the day fly—all that is necessary for the growth of that great human creation, brotherly love."[45]

Thus, when Bölsche spoke of Christian love, he often meant little more than his usual idealization of sexual love. The human body itself, linked as it was to the great rhythms of nature, was a sacred object. And sexual union was a holy act affording a glimpse of the final blissful harmony of the universe; it was time travel to paradise: "The infinite joy of sexual love, the complete forgetting of the world, of pain, and of death, all these melt into the desire for a harmony of the whole world, for an order in the universe leading upward, beyond man and his love, to the divine light."[46]

All this talk of the sexual foundations of Christian love did not mean that for Bölsche a good Christian was one who had a great many orgasms. What he was really aiming for was a naturalistic view of Christian ethics. It is clear, however, that such a view effectively scrubs the theology off of Christianity and reduces it to mere civilized behavior. In his essay on Fechner, Bölsche approvingly noted that Fechner believed he was a Christian even though he rejected original sin, damnation, and redemption through Christ. All that really counted, then, was to follow the ethical example of Christ, that "very good man," as Bölsche called him. Whether in or out of the church, all cultured people, Bölsche said, agreed that one ought to love, share, and worship.[47]

But why, then, pay any attention to the Bible? After all, according to Bölsche, science had shown that the Bible was myth rather than historical truth; its God could no longer be taken seriously by any informed modern; and its attitude toward sex was hopelessly out of tune with nature. Moreover, the everyday wonders of nature far surpassed the so-called miracles of Christ. Even the resurrection paled in comparison to the simple wondrous fact that man is born at all.[48]

Bölsche saved the Bible from extinction by his usual broad application of the idea of evolution. If the Bible was to remain meaningful, it had to grow as mankind grew. As Novalis had said, the Bible was not a single and complete unit, fixed for eternity. Just as the New Testament had been appended to the Old, adding new material without rejecting the old, so now evolutionary science would add still another testament. This "Third Testament" would not violate the spirit of the first two—it would correct and transcend them. Thus, despair about the fate of religion and man's spirit was inappropriate; for, as the old beliefs became untenable if taken at their literal face value, the new evolutionary science breathed new life and hope into them. Old beliefs crumbled, but, as Bölsche assured his *Love-Life* readers: "Remain strong. From nature comes to you the idea of evolution. Stars come to life and life rises ever higher. It rises from form to form, up to spirit itself, which not only *lives* evolution, but also understands it. And here is the great consolation. Here arises the optimism."[49] Two thousand years ago Christianity had created a new optimism at a crucial juncture in history; now it was the turn of evolutionary science to perform the same function under similarly trying circumstances.

For Bölsche, the major way that evolution transcended Christianity was through new insights into the problems of evil and sin. Christianity taught that man's unique ability to acquire knowledge had introduced evil and sin into the world. Adam's fall condemned mankind to an endless cycle of suffering that Christ had only partially mitigated. The Christians had no adequate explanation of why a good and omnipotent God could have allowed evil to enter the world. But evolution was able to break through the dismal determinism of Christianity and provide a convincing explanation of evil. Evil, according to Bölsche, was a transient by-product of the breakdown of the primeval unity of the universe. The increasing fragmentation of life into countless cells and organisms was necessary for the development of intelligence. But this individualization brought with it the Darwinian struggle for life, or, in theological terms, evil. Fortunately, however, the struggle for life carried within it the seeds of its own overcoming; for evil was merely a catalyst in the increasing harmony and goodness of the universe. As Bölsche continually stressed, the struggle for life was the way the universe refined and improved itself. The further life developed, the less need there would be for evil, and it would eventually disappear of its own accord. Already there were discernible signs of the lessening of evil—the co-operation seen in nature and, above all, the rise of human culture and religion, which sought to hasten the natural decline of evil.[50]

This metaphysical optimism, tenuous though it was, put human sin in an altogether different perspective. Original sin lost its meaning; man was no longer trapped by his past. In the Bible, knowledge had been the cause of his downfall. Now knowledge (of evolution) returned to liberate him—to show him the necessary but transient role of evil. The iron grip of sin was broken at last. Bölsche thought that Goethe had been the first to grasp the optimistic consequences of evolution. *Faust* was the first and classic expression of evolutionary optimism; for in redeeming Faust and Gretchen, Goethe rejected evil as static and inexorable and reduced it to a stage on the way to a finer harmony.[51] This new freedom and independence would put man on the road to his lost paradise. The story of the Garden of Eden would be symbolically completed. A new chapter would be added to the Bible, glorifying man's transcendence of shame through knowledge.

As usual, Bölsche stressed the sensual consequences. Darwinian evolution reduced "sexual sin" to its proper perspective. The crudeness of sexuality stemmed from deep in the animal world, but there was now no reason to be trapped by the past. Once again man would walk naked in the sun, only this time his innocence would be based not on naiveté, but on the knowledge of how far he had developed toward ultimate love and harmony. As Bölsche put it in the second volume of *Love-Life*, the biblical story of man could now be told—"From the hour when Adam and Eve drew the loincloth over those organs that seemed most animal-like to them—to the hour when in silent blessed knowledge of the silvery heavens they throw away the loincloth with a smile and say 'I was an animal, but I am no more, what am I ashamed of?' "[52] In this golden hour of the future, knowledge would be a blessing rather than a curse, and soul and sensuality would fuse into a pure harmony.

In view of Bölsche's constant reiteration of the themes of love, harmony, unity, and bliss and his highly vague, symbolic conception of Christianity, it is hardly surprising that he drew much inspiration from the Christian mystical tradition. In 1904, Bölsche edited and introduced a new edition of the work of the seventeenth-century Silesian mystic, Johann Scheffler (better known as Angelus Silesius). Scheffler was of Protestant background, but converted to Catholicism during the 1660s while he was writing his *Cherubic Wanderer*. The 262 poetic aphorisms in this work reveal the ambivalence in Scheffler's mind. In his long introductory essay, discussing the modern significance of mysticism, Bölsche implied that Scheffler had captured the pure essence of Christian love in his mystical monism. Scheffler's mysticism, he claimed, might almost represent religion. It was indeed elegantly suited to complement the modern scientific Weltanschauung, for both the old and the new arrived at similar optimistic conclusions, although they began from radically different perspectives.

According to Bölsche, it was only cheap mysticism that tried to "compete" with science, contradicting natural laws or turning them on and off as was convenient. True mysticism did not wait for science to fail so that it might then step in with a supernatural explanation; rather, it was a quest for sense within the accepted, observable laws of nature, a desire to gain perspective on the universe by getting beyond space and time. This mystical inward journey could not be construed as a substitute for science, because it did not concern itself with the scientists' categories of time, space, and causal laws.[53]

The mystical yearning for meaning had two sides, both of which were complemented by science. One was the desire to escape from the banal, dismal world into a higher world of harmony and bliss. We have seen how, in Bölsche's view, evolution explained the discrepancy between good and bad and lent credence to the belief that mystical harmony would actually be the future reality, and that, in fact, it could already be envisioned in art and sex. The other side of mysticism was the tendency to see the universal within the particular, to range back and forth in eternity, to "find the universe in a drop of water," as it were.[54] But was this not also the goal of science, to be able to infer everything from the smallest objects or events? Had not science itself proved that time and space were relative, merely forms of perception? Actually, the mystic's view of the future could be of great value to science and society. Having contemplated the ultimate harmony and love of the universe, having ranged back and forth in the great chain of being, the mystic could return to the mundane and live his life as though the future of love and bliss were already here. Especially if evolutionary science lent its prestige to his vision, his life would be an inspiration and example to all. If people saw the future, they might like it and want to hasten its arrival.[55]

Sun worship was another form of mysticism that had meaning for modern man. Science, Bölsche said, now lent support to the ancient mystical ideal of man as sun child. The evolution of life was like an eternal flame created by father sun. All culture began with an evolutionary response to sunlight—the eye, which permitted man to formulate goals and strive toward further enlightenment.[56] Those who fled the city (where they saw artificial light as the enemy of culture) and strove toward the sun were in many cases crackpot faddists, Bölsche realized; nonetheless, evolution supported many of their basic claims about the sun. A frequent image in Bölsche's own works was a natural scene flooded by rich golden sunlight, usually signifying the triumph of love, harmony, and beauty. And sun worship could be tied not only to science, but also to Christianity. In one of his few ventures into poetry, "The New Commandments—A Dream" (1901), Bölsche lies in a meadow and dreams that the sun speaks to him, commanding a universal love that "improves" on Christian love. Thus: "'Love your enemy!' What once dying on the enemy's cross/Your Savior cried out to you/I give you now in a better form/'There is no enemy!'"[57]

Throughout Bölsche's discussion of mysticism there is hardly any mention of the church. Scheffler's mysticism and sun worship are considered to represent religion generally, uncluttered by institutions. Bölsche believed that the Christian spirit would thrive better without a formal Christian church to mire it in dogma. Such was the theme of a favorable introduction he wrote for a book advocating the abolition of the established church, Rudolf Penzig's *Ohne Kirche* (Without the church, 1907). Penzig was one of many freethinkers who were calling for a mass exodus from the church in the first decade of the century. The movement had the support of a wide variety of people ranging from Marxists, to ethical culturists, to *völkisch* cultists. Bölsche was attracted by the belief that Christianity as simple human love did not need the support of an organized church but would thrive better as an individual matter. The church held back scientific progress because it wanted to hand out "completed knowledge." As an institution, it was incapable of evolution and thus quickly out of tune with nature, whose essence was evolution. The fact that great religious art remained alive, while the old theology appeared ever more ridiculous, dramatized the discrepancy between the true, evolving religious spirit and church theology. Art envisioned the future and thus moved with the times, whereas theology stagnated, corrupting those who took it seriously. Bölsche therefore proposed that jurisdiction over the spiritual life of the people be taken away from the church and transferred into the hands of the individual. Mature and educated people from all walks of life could then rehumanize the great moments of life by attending such events as births, marriages, and deaths. Guided by evolutionary science, the people could see new meaning and hope in the ups and downs of their everyday lives. Bölsche probably saw himself in the role of one of these secular pastors; yet, despite his rhetoric, he did not leave the church until 1911.[58]

All this sounds like still another call to break the age-old tyranny of the priests; and, indeed, Bölsche, like Haeckel, saw parallels between the Reformation and the present. In the sixteenth century, the study of the Bible could free the individual from the priests; now, science could further this liberation through knowledge, so that not only were the priests superfluous, they had actually been left behind by their more informed flocks. Self-assertion and self-improvement were the cries of the day, said Bölsche. What is significant here is how this "second Reformation" is linked to Bölsche's notion of the role of popularization. In a way, professional scientists formed a kind of priesthood themselves. The triumph of the scientific Weltanschauung depended as much on breaking their monopoly as it did on crushing the authority of the church. Once well informed by the popularizer, he thought, each man would become in effect his own priest. Armed with the triumphant methods of science, the average man of the second Reformation could then interpret the whole world for himself, just as in the first Reformation the ability to read the Bible had given him the more limited power to interpret Christianity for himself.

In short, religion for Bölsche was totally divorced from any traditional theology. All religions had value to the extent that they stressed a yearning for a better world where human love would reign. Since monistic science "proved" the truth of any such vision of the future, there could be no fundamental conflict between science and religion as long as religion did not degenerate into dogma. Not every religion was equal, however, for religion had to evolve as did everything else in nature. As with life itself, the higher forms were variations on the themes of lower forms, transcending but never invalidating them. The most appropriate religion for modern man was therefore the scientific Weltanschauung, because it was the one most closely in tune with the present stage of evolution. Other religions retained their validity to the degree that they did not contradict evolutionary science. In practice, this meant a stress on ethics and love as the center of any religion, because they were usually vaguely formulated concepts, easily reconcilable with Bölsche's vision of future love. The dominant theme of nature herself was love; struggle was a secondary feature, designed to increase love in the long run. As long as Bölsche believed in the goodness of nature, there could be no pessimism in his positivism and determinism; he could still logically stress ethical love. For, to love and yearn for unity with the universe was merely to be swept along by natural evolution. Those who understood this had grasped the modern Weltanschauung and had seen how, like a new Reformation, it added to the past without totally breaking with it.

Yet, almost inevitably, such a view entailed at least some deification of both science and nature. To put it in a somewhat exaggerated form, for Bölsche, Darwin worked in the temple of nature, picking up where Jesus left off. In fact, in spite of himself, Bölsche came very close to turning Darwin into a priest. As Dolf Sternberger has pointed out, there is an undercurrent of idolatry in Bölsche's short popular biography of Darwin (1901). Darwin is seen as the white-haired patriarch of infinite love and wisdom, the "silent sufferer of Down."[59] What is more, even Bölsche himself could take on the role of the high priest of the modern Weltanschauung. One enthusiastic reviewer of a Bölsche lecture in the *Singakademie* in Berlin (1910) summarized his impressions of Bölsche this way: "The poetic materialist in the velvet jacket speaks for two hours. Now and then a sip from a glass of water. And it's quiet. 'As in a church,' says the feuilletonist. But there really is a church here among the chestnut trees. A church of the thirst for knowledge, of yearning. And Bölsche is its priest."[60]

Many of those who, with Bölsche, favored some form of free thought or wanted religion without a church ended up forming their own organizations to challenge the established churches. In the period from the 1880s to World War I, dozens of free-thought organizations of all stripes sprang up all over Germany. Among the best known were Ludwig Büchner's German Freethinkers' League (1881), a more militant offshoot of the older Free Religious Congregation movement (the two rejoined in 1891); the German Society for Ethical Culture (1892); the Goethe League (1900); the Giordano Bruno League (1900); and finally, the German Monist League (1906). In 1909, all of these organizations and many other lesser known ones coalesced into the so-called Weimar Cartel, which claimed to represent some sixty thousand members. The basic goals of the free-thought, churchless movement were summed up in the demands of the cartel for "intellectual freedom, separation of church and education, and a complete secularization of the state."[61]

Yet none of these organizations ever turned into the mass movements that their founders had hoped for; certainly there never really was any second Reformation. Two reasons suggest themselves for this failure; in both cases Bölsche's loose association with the free-thought movement illustrates its basic weaknesses. In the first place, the groups involved in the free-thought movement represented widely divergent interests. A good example is the Ethical Culture Society. Its founder, Wilhelm Förster, was an advocate of Kantian ethics; but there were about as many different views of ethics as there were members of the society. Bölsche attended the society's organizational meeting in Berlin in 1892 and summed up the chaos: "On the basis of the first evening, one could with some justification define ethics as that which everyone disagrees about when a few hundred modern people are brought together."[62]

Bölsche's own idea was, predictably, that the society should glorify the ethical impulse of scientific advancement. Others had different views. The socialists, represented by Julius Türk, protested that ethics meant nothing unless the issue of capitalist exploitation was addressed; the socialists could have nothing to do with the society unless it became part of the political struggle of the working class. Still another viewpoint was advanced by Moritz von Egidy, a former army colonel who had stunned Imperial Germany by renouncing his military career to crusade for a mystic Christian humanism. Egidy expressed sympathy for the society but demurred from joining because he wanted a less rationalistic ethics. It was typical of Bölsche's view of Christianity that he remarked of Egidy that there was little difference between Egidy's Christianity and a simple humanity.[63] In the end, the Ethical Culture Society revealed its essentially liberal stripe by proclaiming a vague ethics "independent of all differences of social class, religion, and politics."[64] As Hermann Lübbe has pointed out, the ethical culture movement was basically an attempt to enlarge the sphere of private individual freedom against the encroachments of the state.[65] And the same could be said of most of the other free-thought organizations of the time. Because their essence was the limitation of politics and the humane toleration of diversity, they could never really get off the ground as mass movements. As Bölsche said of his own hesitant membership in the Ethical Culture Society, "I became a member of the Society partly 'because,' partly 'in spite of.'"[66] With members like that, any organization was condemned to remain on the sidelines.

All of this suggests the second weakness of the movement to find an alternative to the established church. How could those who were suspicious of organized religion organize an alternative to organized religion? If churches had rigidified Christianity, then wouldn't they also rigidify a monistic rational religion? The Monist League even had its own catechism. Haeckel envisioned a monist takeover of Christian churches, which, stripped of their outmoded ornaments, would be refurnished with scientific and natural symbols. In place of the altar would be Urania, the Greek muse of astronomy, and along the walls would be tropical flowers and trees, as well as aquariums of fish and coral.[67] Bölsche was never very explicit about his fears, but his disinclination to be passionately involved in any organization seems to indicate that Friedrich Schleiermacher's dictum, "The more church, the less religion," was always in the back of his mind. Though a willing joiner, Bölsche always remained somewhat aloof, shirking positions of power and influence that might easily have been his. He seemed particularly aloof in regard to the Monist League, Haeckel's pet project. Haeckel was on *"du"* terms with Bölsche in late 1905 when the league was being organized, and it is clear that he hoped Bölsche would be an active and powerful member.[68] Although Bölsche appeared at the league's founding conference, it is characteristic of him that he did not contribute to the league's journal. Weltanschauung, he apparently thought, could be better cultivated by means of mild-mannered lectures and books than by organizational agitation.

Thus the free-thought movement never amounted to much as a political force. It tended to exhaust itself in harmless symbolic gestures, such as the election of Haeckel as antipope. The movement was too diffuse to succeed on a large scale. With the battle for Darwinism largely won, the only rallying point was scientific rationality. To many this was a noble goal; but it was not one that could be translated into a widely accepted set of political tenets. Bölsche, potentially the movement's most able publicist, was loath to enter political battles and remained on the sidelines; Haeckel was an old man with many enemies and commanded little respect in the established scientific community. Few major scientists, aside from Wilhelm Ostwald (president of the Monist League), lent their voices to the free-thought movement. And what support there was among the educated was badly fragmented, from socialists on the left to *völkisch* racists on the right. Those humanistic liberals who made up the bulk of the rank-and-file freethinkers were not disposed ideologically to use political power to further rational culture—even if they had been able to agree on what a rational culture was. This is not to suggest that individual freethinkers were without influence, but only that that influence did not derive from organizational positions.

Nonetheless, Christian apologists were alarmed by the free-thought movement. Attacks on Haeckel were frequent and vicious in the conservative Christian-oriented press. He was still the "atheist ape-professor," destroying public morality. In May of 1907, J. Reinke, the Hamburg biologist, delivered a scathing denunciation of the monists to the Prussian House of Lords. He told his aristocratic audience that monism was to the spirit of the state what social democracy was to the economy. Unless stopped, the monists would plunge the nation into "barbarity."

Reinke suggested more school biology, so students could learn the errors of Darwinian monism.[69] Haeckel responded by reissuing his 1877 Munich speech—a sign that little had changed in the Darwinian debate. Antimonists also founded a kind of counter-Monist League, the Kepler League, which was supposed to demonstrate the virtues of a Christian-oriented science and keep the Haeckel men on the run.[70] Even the modernist theologian Adolf von Harnack was upset by monism. He told the Evangelical Church Congress that Ostwald's monism was a philosophy of "beetle legs" and "electrical substances." Ostwald left the church in protest.[71]

Religious anti-Darwinists generally found few readers. The Catholic *Natur und Offenbarung* (Nature and revelation), founded in 1855 to promote "true science," railed against Haeckel's Darwinism as "pure atheism and absolute materialism" and attacked evolutionists as "cultural heroes and friends of progress who drag everything Catholic into the dirt."[72] But few were listening, for this journal, like many other similar ones, had only about a thousand readers.[73] Christian anti-Darwinian books fared little better; none were widely read or went through many editions. The respected *Allgemeine Zeitung* of Munich did run occasional articles criticizing Darwinism from a Christian perspective. But usually it was Haeckel's excesses rather than Darwinism itself that came under attack. The *Allgemeine Zeitung* review of Haeckel's *Anthropogenie* (1875) was significantly entitled "Ultra-Darwinism and Dilettantism." The reviewer lamented the arrogant, condescending, "science knows best" attitude of most Darwin popularizers. Under their sway, the public had been gripped by a mass hysteria of popular, dilettantish materialism. This was far beyond what Darwin intended, but there was no way to stop men like Haeckel. Mocking Haeckel, the reviewer asked, "And what is neo-Darwinism itself? An involuntary cell-soul secretion."[74]

Christian apologists were partly to blame for their own frustration and pessimism. Almost without exception, the devout defenders of Christianity simply surrendered to the enemy the techniques of popular science that could have helped them fight Darwinism. No popular writer of the stature of Büchner, Haeckel, or Bölsche rallied to the Christian side. The few widely read authors who did oppose Darwin— most notably Nietzsche, Julius Langbehn, and Houston Stewart Chamberlain—did so ambiguously and certainly not for Christian reasons. Without a Christian genre of popular science, Christians missed the opportunity to give the Darwinians some of their own medicine.

That it was indeed possible to fight Darwinism with popular science is shown by an unusual article that appeared in *Daheim* in 1865. *Daheim*, it will be recalled, was a Catholic family magazine founded to compete with the liberal *Gartenlaube*. Its peak circulation was about sixty thousand. The magazine's avowed purpose was to promote religion and to "cultivate the decency and morals of the German household."[75] The article in question took the form of a conversation during a visit to a zoo by a scientist, a poet, a philosopher, and an old man. Provoked by the poet's wonder at the richness of nature, the scientist launches into an explanation of Darwinism. But no sooner has the scientist finished than his companions press their objections upon him. Evolution might just as well work backward from higher to lower forms, say the poet and philosopher. They are unimpressed by the analogy of man's animal breeding experience, for that is man mixing in nature with design. The old man finds fault with a fossil record that reveals no transitional species. He points out that there is no reason to infer development from variety; we do not assume that the various chemical elements derive from one another. And, finally, the philosopher is unmoved by the developmental stages of embryos, for analogies prove nothing, he maintains. The scientist is forced to retreat, leaving the others to compose an impromptu post-mortem on Darwinism. They agree that it is one more symptom of science trying to deny God. Perhaps, says the philosopher (taking his cue from the old *Naturphilosophie*), there is development in the mind of God, but the Darwinists have vulgarized this process into a material historical occurrence, which it is not. The old man comments that errors often contain a kernel of truth and may actually advance science. Eventually, Darwinism will be just another historical curiosity.[76]

The story is presented in a good, gemütlich, family-magazine style. Yet it includes powerful and sophisticated arguments—some of which troubled Darwin himself. That articles of this sort remained rare exceptions is symptomatic of the fact that Christian apologists did not adapt quickly to the potentials of a mass reading market. Christians seemed to harbor a deep suspicion of scientific popularization. In 1855, the founder of *Natur und Offenbarung*, Friedrich Michelis, had written an open letter to Matthias Schleiden, complimenting the great botanist on his antimaterialistic position. And yet Michelis had gone on to criticize Schleiden for following in Humboldt's footsteps and trying to popularize science.[77] It was almost as though popular science—even "correct" popular science—was a danger to faith. With the advent of Darwinism, this fear seems to have become more widespread among Christians and prevented them from being very resourceful in their own defense. Of course, it can be argued that their failure to do battle publicly with the Darwinians made some tactical sense. Any defense of the status quo, especially against an exciting and upsetting challenge, is at a distinct polemical disadvantage in the battle for public opinion. Doing public battle with the Darwinians would probably have meant fighting on enemy territory, on the enemy's terms. That enemy was formidable, and outright victory for the Christians would have been very unlikely. Whatever the reasons, the Christians' failure to come out fighting against the popularizers was an odd complement to their success in keeping Darwinism out of the schools, for in both cases they made the job of the Darwinians all the easier by allowing them alone to define the issues for the public. Once again, what is not done may be as important in the dynamics of popularization as what actually is done.

The arguments of the Christian anti-Darwinists are worth confronting, however, for though they were not popular with the public, their works were read by the Darwinists. Much of what the popularizers said was a response to or anticipation of the Christian objections to Darwinism. Without an understanding of those objections, the picture of popular Darwinism is incomplete and out of perspective. It is all too easy to forget, now that Darwin's works have ossified into classics, that late-nineteenth-century Christians could draw upon a well-stocked arsenal of potent arguments in their fight against Darwinism. We are concerned here not so much with the many technical arguments against Darwinism as with those arguments that used Christianity as a base of authority to criticize Darwinism.

As seen in the case of the Landtag debate of 1883 (see chapter 4), Protestants and Catholics had essentially the same objections to Darwinism. Both deemed it a morally odious hypothesis that demeaned man and corrupted public life. The differences were more of tone than substance. Conservative Protestants were often inclined, like Adolf Stöcker, to posit a stark contrast between the Bible and Darwinism. As a pamphlet put out by the German Tent Mission Publishers put it in 1909, only "dilettantes, the half educated, and the undiscerning masses" could believe Darwinism. All compromise was hypocrisy: "If Darwinism were correct then we'd have to throw out the Bible and Christianity."[78] Catholics were equally appalled by the moral dangers of Darwinism; but, especially after 1900, they were more likely than Protestants to stake out a middle ground of subtle opposition.[79] Haeckel's nemesis, the Jesuit ant specialist, Father Erich Wasmann, was typical. He conceded Darwinism as a theory of physical descent only; God was still the creator of the first living cell; and man's soul had been a special, separate creation.[80] Such dualism infuriated Haeckel even more than an uncompromising, outright rejection of Darwinism.

The Christian critics of Darwinism were usually willing to accept evolution if it was confined to animals and plants. That science had dared to eliminate God was what appalled them. Perhaps no one expressed this horror more eloquently than Albert Wigand, a professor of botany in Marburg and author of the polemical pamphlet *Der Darwinismus: Ein Zeichen der Zeit* (Darwinism as a sign of the times, 1878). Wigand attempted to dismiss Darwinism as an incoherent and contradictory hypothesis; but as his title hints, his main concern was to show that Darwinism was both a symptom and a cause of the pervasive atheism and arrogance of the age. Even if some kind of evolution occurred, he asserted, a creator was still necessary to begin and guide the process. An age that seized the opportunity to eliminate God and design was morally sick.[81]

Wigand placed the blame for this degeneracy at the door of unscrupulous popularizers, above all Vogt and Haeckel. They and other materialists had misled the lay public into believing that the universe was a meaningless machine; they had glibly made the "ape-theory" the centerpiece of Darwinism, convincing people that man was not a divine creation, but just another animal. Wigand painted an alarming picture of the consequences of the ape hysteria. Morality would collapse as the feeling of duty to God was supplanted by egotism. There could be no naturalistic ethics, for a Darwinian society was a war of all against all, with the stronger, not the more moral, prevailing. If persuaded that he was a beast, man would begin to act like one. Wigand, like many other opponents of Darwinism, blamed Darwinism for the plumber Max Hödel's assassination attempt on the emperor. Wasn't Hödel a nihilist and socialist? Wigand asked. And weren't nihilism and socialism direct results of the Darwinian destruction of social morality?[82]

Wigand was not alone in his charge that science was trying to defy God. The late 1870s witnessed the climax of the Christian counterattack against the Darwin popularizers (see chapter 4). The charge was always that Darwinism was a mere hypothesis foisted upon an unsuspecting public. Even those who would yield on the question of physical descent insisted that man's spirit lifted him out of the animal world. All agreed that there could be no moral standards without God and no ethics based on man as he was rather than as he should be. Some forecast the imminent demise of German society, as attested by the purported rise in bestial crimes, the growth of socialism, and the assassination attempts. Others saw the decline as slow and subtle, a historical regression to less civilized times (Bölsche in reverse). In a way, the Christians had an odd argument: they seemed to be at once denying the reality of natural selection and admitting that it would take place as soon as people believed in it.[83]

Ironically, what hope the Christian anti-Darwinists harbored derived as much from science as from faith. Properly interpreted, science would advance faith, not destroy it, they said. As Joseph Kuhl argued in 1879, science can at most affect transient dogma; it can never go to the heart of Christianity.[84] In defense of their faith, Christians always appealed to "true science" which they claimed would expose the intellectual poverty of Darwinism. As early as 1878, Wigand had already announced the decline of Darwinism in the scientific community.[85] Materialists like Haeckel and Vogt were supposedly anachronisms who would soon be discredited by their colleagues. There was some truth in this, of course. Popular materialism was an obsolete hangover from the 1850s; but

Darwinism, with its subtle pervasiveness and adaptability, was certainly no anachronism. Anti-Darwinian Christians often uncritically accepted their opponents' identification of Darwinism with materialism. Christian apologists never abandoned their hope that the established scientific community would come to their rescue. Every modification or correction of Darwin's ideas was greeted as the beginning of the end of Darwinism. In 1902, E. Dennert claimed in his *At the Deathbed of Darwinism* that biologists were abandoning Darwinism in droves. Dennert was a Christian evolutionist who believed in a God-directed evolution limited to the nonhuman organic world. He attacked Darwinism for undercutting the concepts of sin and redemption through Christ. According to Dennert, the dying dogma of Darwinism was based on six false premises: (1) there is no need for a creator; (2) pure chance produces variations; (3) there is no purpose or finality in the world; (4) the engine of evolution is egotism; (5) in the struggle for existence the strongest, fleetest, and most cunning prevail; and (6) man is merely a highly developed animal. Dennert then proceeded to show that many Darwinists questioned some of these premises.[86]

But the limitations of Dennert's (and other Christians') characterizations of Darwinism are revealing. Darwin himself would not have embraced all six points. He invoked a creator, was evasive about teleology, saw struggle more metaphorically, and placed increasingly less emphasis on natural selection. Bölsche would have disagreed with or qualified the first five points; and even Haeckel would have wanted to soften "pure chance" by tying it to causal law. Given Dennert's idea of Darwinism, it is no wonder that he could find biologists who had doubts. Like many Christians, Dennert chose to define Darwinism as harsh, dismal, and atheistic, and then to oppose it to a reassuring Christian faith. In the process he ignored the fact that the Darwinists did not comprise a monolithic anti-Christian conspiracy, but rather were an extremely varied lot.

Dennert was wrong; Darwinism did not die, abandoned by science. Nor was there any chance of Christianity dealing the fatal blow. In the end, Darwinism and Christianity simply reached a stalemate, with both sides talking past each other. Over the years, the antagonists in the popular debate had relied on the same old arguments, ones that had already been old hat in 1870. Subtle new ideas like mutations and Mendelian law were important to scholars, but made little popular impression. Proponents of neither side realized that they were often stereotyping their opponents and fighting bogus enemies. How many useless battles were fought on the fallacious assumption that all Darwinians were atheistic materialists and all Christians ignorant literalists! Under such circumstances, total victory was impossible for either side, for both were so broadly defended, so flexible, indeed so confused, that they could make countless small concessions without great risk. Moreover, both yearned to share some of the enemy's prestige. Christians appealed to *their* version of science and Darwinians to *their* version of Christianity. Perhaps the old faith and the new were not as antagonistic as Strauss had thought.

Chapter 6

Social Darwinism and

the Popularizers

DARWINISM'S enormous popularity in the latter part of the nineteenth century was due in part to its apparent profound social and political implications. More than a biological theory for the specialists, Darwinism seemed, if only indirectly, to speak to the fundamental questions that lie at the heart of all social theory: What is man's nature, and what is the natural order of human society? The desire to be on the side of nature—long a preoccupation of social theorists—tempted advocates of almost every cause to rummage among the rich ambiguities of evolutionary theory in the hope of uncovering scientific evidence in support of their views. Many capitalists, liberals, democrats, conservatives, nationalists, racists, and socialists convinced themselves that Darwinism could settle age-old controversies in their favor. And, in truth, almost anything could be inferred from Darwinism, provided that one was at once highly selective and oblivious to contradictory evidence. Apologists for capitalism, for instance, could glorify the struggle for life, while those pressing for radical egalitarianism could point to the common origin of all men or the natural necessity of change. That Darwin himself saw no broader social implications for his theories and was contemptuous of those who did, did nothing to still these often simplistic debates. In fact, Darwin's failure to throw his immense prestige onto any one side probably contributed to the confusion and controversy. But, no matter how much he might share Darwin's reluctance, no serious thinker or popularizer could hope to keep Darwinism confined to the realm of biology. Every Darwinist became ipso facto a social theorist.

To oversimplify somewhat, there were two basic answers to the question, what does Darwinism mean for human society? The first stressed struggle and saw in Darwinism, with its natural selection of the fittest, proof of the naturalness (and hence justice) of the competitive, hierarchical, bourgeois society. In this view, the economic struggle had selected the fittest, who were now rich and powerful, and left the less fit behind. If the sufferings of the less fit masses were regrettable in the short term, they were nonetheless natural and necessary, and any attempt to alleviate them through social welfare would only contribute to the degeneration of the race. Carried to its logical extreme, and it often was, this interpretation of Darwinism could lead to eugenics or racial hygiene—attempts to "help" nature improve the race by speeding up natural selection in a desired direction. The second answer was given by socialists and radicals, who were never at ease with biological analogies to society, but still were able to find some comfort in Darwin's implicit challenge to a static society. Accordingly, they saw change as the main message of Darwinism and stressed that existing elites were by no means the fittest in any Darwinian sense. Only when everyone had an equal start, as in nature, would men be able to reach their true potential. The term "Social Darwinism" has generally been associated with the first of these two positions and will be used that way here, but it may with almost equal justification be applied to the second. No one in the late nineteenth century called himself a Social Darwinist. The term is a creation of later historians, and its restricted application reflects more their interests and limitations than the merit of anyone's special claim to Darwinism.[1]

Nowhere is the task of disentangling the various strands of Social Darwinism more formidable than in Germany. For the historian, German Social Darwinism seems trapped in the dark shadow that Nazism casts backward into the late nineteenth century. Certainly Hitler's crude bombast recalls the very worst of Social Darwinism, and the analogies between extermination camps and the twisted dreams of earlier pseudoscientific prophets are all too obvious. However, the common historical treatment of German Social Darwinism as a theoretical rehearsal for Nazism is a mistake.[2] Reading history "backward" may have its rewards: only the full horror of the Nazi experience could expose the true dangers that lurked beneath the surface of the nineteenth century's biologistic thinking. But such insights are likely to be bought at the price of distorted perspective. Cast in the role of proto-Nazism, Social Darwinism almost inevitably takes on not only a malevolence, but also a prominence, coherence, and direction that it lacked in reality.

Viewed from the perspective of its own time, Social Darwinism appears as a diffuse cluster of social theories sharing but a single premise: that human society is a fierce struggle for existence with victory going to the fittest. The terms, of course, suggest Darwin; but the problem with Social Darwinism as a tool of historical analysis is that the rhetoric of struggle could, and often did, exist without reference to Darwin. Hobbesian visions of the dog-eat-dog world, the *bellum omnium contra omnes*, long predated Darwin and survive to this day in the vocabulary of football coaches, drill sergeants, and self-made men. In the late nineteenth century, such views were often thinly disguised self-justifications for those who had profited from the capitalist system. But the successful bourgeois did not need Darwin to convince him of his natural superiority over the toiling masses. At most, he might borrow a few poorly understood Darwinian phrases, but these would hardly change the substance of his argument. He already knew that radical social movements had to be crushed. As the oft-quoted lines from Viktor von Scheffel's epic poem of 1854 said: "Denn der Grosse frisst den Kleinen/und der Grösste frisst den Grossen,/also löst in der Natur sich/einfach die soziale Frage!"[3] Here was "Social Darwinism" without Darwin. (Roughly translated: "For the big eat the little and the biggest eats the big, and so in nature the social question is easily solved." The poem went through 168 editions by 1900.)

Nor did the champions of national struggle need Darwin's authority. Many old-fashioned militarists, nationalists, and imperialists have been tagged with the label "Social Darwinist" solely by virtue of the fact that their bellicose utterances succeeded the publication of Darwin's *Origin*. (We might dub this the fallacy of "Post Darwin, ergo propter Darwin.") Von Moltke and Treitschke come immediately to mind. Their glorifications of war and the power state are only very superficially Darwinian. When Treitschke remarks in his *Politics* that "Brave peoples alone have an existence, an evolution or a future; the weak and the cowardly perish, and perish justly," we are reminded of Darwin by the choice of words.[4] But Treitschke does not depend on or elaborate on Darwinism; rather, he merely restates the ancient "might makes right" argument in contemporary language. Even many liberals, such as Max Weber, availed themselves of similar imagery in arguing for an aggressive foreign policy.[5]

At most, the Darwinian content of these arguments consisted of a few oblique allusions. For example, the term Lebensraum, often batted about by nationalists, originated in a book by that title written by Friedrich Ratzel in 1901. Ratzel was talking only about plants and animals competing for space; but the term Lebensraum soon escaped its Darwinian moorings and became a free-floating slogan on the destiny of the German people.[6] Yet even oblique Darwinian allusions are not as easy to find in the militant nationalist literature as we might expect. The collections of aggressive German statements compiled by Anglo-Saxon propagandists during World War I illustrate this point nicely. These lexicons of bellicosity, ingeniously culled from innumerable prewar sources, are strikingly lacking in Darwinian rhetoric.[7] General Friedrich von Bernhardi is the sole exception to the rule. His *Deutschland und der nächste Krieg* (*Germany and the Next War*, 1912) drew on Darwinism as one more "proof" of the ancient maxim that "war is the father of all things." Even Bernhardi's book would be changed only slightly in tone and not at all in content if all references to Darwin were dropped.[8]

Thus, in analyzing the rhetoric of struggle, it is useful to distinguish between those who occasionally appropriated a Darwinian phrase or two and those who undertook a sustained and detailed application of Darwinism to human society. The first group—those vast ranks of saber-rattlers, socialist-baiters, and self-righteous rich who happened to live in a Darwin-conscious age—can be called Social Darwinian only in the loosest sense of the word. The second group contained the true Social Darwinists, men who believed that Darwin alone held the key to understanding human society. Their ranks were actually rather small and their reading audience very limited. The widely read Darwin popularizers, who shaped the public perception of Darwinism, were not part of the mainstream of Social Darwinism. Rather, they had given German Darwinism a radical, anticlerical reputation, as witness its exclusion from the schools and the revulsion it stirred among conservatives in the Prussian Diet. Under such circumstances, it was virtually impossible for advocates of the conservative power state to embrace Darwinism in any form. Darwinism was, after all, inescapably a theory of change. Treitschke and others blamed Darwinism for the assassination attempts on the kaiser in 1878; they were, then, in no position to turn around and say that Darwinism was the new all-encompassing social theory. Moreover, the alliance of throne and altar further lessened the appeal of any Darwinian argument to the established classes. The very religious would not tolerate a biological view of social relations;[9] and those who were not religious themselves still perceived an attack on religion (such as Darwinism was presumed to be) as an attack on the state.

Before turning to the Darwin popularizers, it will be helpful to sketch the broad outlines of the true Social Darwinism. Social Darwinism may be divided into a moderate and a radical phase. The moderate phase, which predominated before the 1890s, was essentially a biologistic sociology; the later radical phase was characterized by eugenic proposals to save the nation or race. Unfortunately, the excesses of radical Social Darwinism have given the earlier Social Darwinism a bad press and make it very difficult to evaluate fairly. There are, to be sure, similarities between the two, but, as will become clear, radical Social Darwinism is in no way an inevitable extension of its moderate precursor. The two share a method more than anything else; both believe that human society can be explained by analogies from the nonhuman organic world. They are both, paradoxically, nonsocial social theories in that they try to subsume human events into a larger pattern of natural laws, thus implicitly denying the peculiarly human character of society. They differ in their assessment of how man ought to use his knowledge of nature. The earlier, moderate Social Darwinists were content merely to describe and to wait passively in the confidence that nature would do its work. Not so the later radical Social Darwinists, who feared that man's superior intelligence might be protecting him in the short run from the full effect of natural laws at the expense of his long-range welfare. Therefore, they argued, man ought to use that superior intelligence by helping nature "enforce" its laws.

Both the moderate and radical Social Darwinisms have often been viewed as elaborate justifications for the status quo of competitive capitalism. Although there is obviously some truth to this generalization, there are many exceptions, especially among the radical Social Darwinists, who are often hard to categorize ideologically. Moreover, it should be clear that as a reactionary ideology, Social Darwinism led a very precarious existence. To be sure, subsuming human society into a natural system entails a determinism that lends a certain inevitability to whatever is, thus tending to justify the status quo as a value-free product of nature. On the other hand, consistency demands that radical social movements that seek to change the status quo be granted the same legitimacy as inevitable natural products. The more perceptive Social Darwinists, such as the Austrian sociologist Ludwig Gumplowicz, were aware of this dilemma,[10] but many Social Darwinists were not. Unlike Gumplowicz, they blinded themselves to the "subversive" side of Darwinism, overemphasizing fierce struggle while ignoring that the inevitable Darwinian result of that struggle was a change of the status quo.

The massive tomes of "complete" social theories from the 1870s and 1880s are probably the best examples of moderate Social Darwinism. Here we find the nature analogy applied with an extraordinary thoroughness and literalness. For instance, Paul von Lilienfeld's five-volume *Gedanken über die Sozialwissenschaft* (Thoughts on social science, 1873–81) was a kind of social physiology. Everything human, including religion, could be explained in this system by analogy to an organic object or process. Individuals were cells, and societies were organisms with embryological developments. Other natural histories of human society, like Julius Lippert's *Kulturgeschichte der Menschheit* (*The Evolution of Culture*, 1886–87), were also based on the premise that today's society was a result of natural selection that went back as far as the animal world. For these thinkers, struggle was the single all-powerful explanation of everything. In their works the phrase *Kampf ums Dasein* becomes an almost mystical incantation. Friedrich Hellwald, the Austrian cultural historian, positively reveled in contemplating the giant battle he saw all around him. His *Culturgeschichte in ihrer natürlichen Entwicklung bis zur Gegenwart* (Cultural history in its natural development to the present, 1876), a book dedicated to Ernst Haeckel, was filled with derision toward those who believed in the ideal of peace. Peace conferences, he claimed, always ended in fistfights. But such was man's fate; struggle would continue until man's ultimate extinction.[11]

Not all Social Darwinists were as crude as Hellwald. Albert Schäffle painted a more figurative picture of the *Kampf ums Dasein* in his four-volume *Bau und Leben des socialen Körpers* (Structure and life of the social body, 1875-78). According to Schäffle, human struggle became less brutal as it advanced. What had been physical battle gradually metamorphoses into a refined struggle of ideas. Instead of being wiped out, the losers in Schäffle's system change jobs, emigrate, or simply enjoy less luxury than the winners. Although this sounds like a celebration of the liberal "marketplace," Schäffle was opposed to complete laissez-faire. He advocated a "practical socialism" of moderate reform and limited collectivization. Unbridled capitalism, he thought, was base and materialistic and did not bring out man's nobler characteristics. Schäffle is thus a good example of the limitations of the common view that Social Darwinism is merely an apology for the worst aspects of capitalism.[12]

Indeed, moderate Social Darwinism could easily shade into a vague liberal humanism. Gumplowicz, who is always one of the first to be mentioned in discussions of Social Darwinists, was highly critical of both Schäffle and Lilienfeld for their contention that human and natural struggles were analogous. Although he thought that radical social movements might be wrong in some of their details, Gumplowicz still argued that all such movements revealed a natural impulse to organize society on a fairer basis. In Darwinian terms, this impulse might be expressed as a drive to convert fierce group struggle into refined individual competition.[13] Similarly, Max Nordau—though not labeled a Social Darwinist—was a firm believer in the power of natural and sexual selection to improve and edify man. Nordau had no faith in equality, but he did think that if allowed to do its work, nature would produce a race of happy, loving, and cultured humanists.[14] Thus the moderate Social Darwinism could have both a bright and a dark face.

In the 1890s, Social Darwinism began to undergo some ominous changes. The old moderate Social Darwinism had shared Darwin's view that man was a product of the interaction of heredity and environment. As it was assumed that acquired positive traits would be inherited, this old view at least implicitly held out the possibility of changing man by improving his environment. By the 1890s, however, many Darwinists had come under the influence of August Weismann's germ plasm theory. Weismann challenged the influence of environment, arguing that life was a continuous stream of germ plasm, unaffected by outside influences; Darwin was wrong, he said, in assuming that acquired traits would be inherited. Ignoring the ambiguities of Weismann's evidence, many of the younger Social Darwinists concluded that man was a prisoner of heredity. Each individual was seen as a prepackaged given, whose life was predetermined by his innate talents and limitations.

With the collapse of environmentalism, the road was open to the newer radical Social Darwinism. No longer was there any reason to improve society; all effort had to go into preserving the "best" germ plasm. Here was the intellectual foundation for eugenics; but, of course, the question of who had the best germ plasm was largely a matter of opinion—that is, it was determined by the political climate. Weismann's views came very opportunely for those who were increasingly anxious about the security of their own class or race. Socialism was expanding rapidly in the 1890s and staking out well-argued claims in Darwinian territory. Why not try to discredit socialism by attributing bad germ plasm to the lower classes? The same argument could be used against the "lower races." Racism had originally come from France with the theories of Joseph Arthur de Gobineau, but by the 1890s it had found a new home in the works of native Germanic critics who feared that "superior" Aryan stock would be swamped by the "inferior" peoples of the East. Neither racism nor Social Darwinism needed the other; they had arisen independently, and the fusion between the two was never complete; but in the 1890s there was a good deal of cross-fertilization because racism and Social Darwinism shared the same fears.[15]

An important transitional figure between the moderate and the radical Social Darwinism was Otto Ammon. His numerous anthropological and political essays during the 1890s were an overt defense of class and racial privilege. Taking his stand firmly against social democracy, Ammon argued that the class system was a very accurate reflection of innate natural abilities. Socialists, such as August Bebel, who wanted to do away with the class system, would destroy society by eliminating essential competition. The people at the bottom of society, Ammon contended, by and large deserved to be there; if they had any ability they would rise socially. Any animal breeder was aware of these facts and could set the socialists straight! There was also an undercurrent of racism in Ammon's work. His measurements of army recruits in Baden convinced him that the "long heads" represented the superior intellectuality of old Aryan stock, whereas the "round heads" were descendants of inferior Asiatics.[16] Like most of the later Social Darwinists, Ammon had no faith in education to increase talent. Heredity was destiny; yet unlike some of the other later Social Darwinists, he shrank back from eugenics. Christian love compelled man to protect the unfit. Only criminals should be disposed of.[17]

The work of Alfred Ploetz was another bridge to radical Social Darwinism. Ploetz was troubled by the ethical problems raised by eugenics. In his book of 1895, *Die Tüchtigkeit unserer Rasse und der Schutz der Schwachen* (The fitness of our race and the protection of the weak), Ploetz argued that the white race was confronted with a profound moral dilemma: within the foreseeable future it would be possible for society to shield all its members, no matter how unfit, from the Darwinian struggle for life. Although the best ideals of modern civiliza-

tion demanded humane treatment of all men, it was biologically inevitable that such treatment would result in the degeneration of the
race. Crudely put, humanitarianism would save individual cripples at
the expense of crippling the entire race. Ploetz then developed a model
of the perfect racially hygienic state. All children would be examined at
birth by a team of doctors, and those found unfit would receive a fatal
morphine dose. Another examination at puberty would determine the
intellectual and moral qualities of the young person; this time, those
found wanting would not be permitted to marry. Every detail of society
would be so regulated that natural selection would work with the same
effectiveness that it had in nature. Everyone, rich and poor alike, would
enter the social competition with an equal start. Those who failed would
be left to starve. Ploetz was horrified by the grim utopia he had con-
jured up and suggested that a more humane alternative would be to
move the struggle for life from society back into the sperm so that there
would be a preselection of the best babies. Thus only healthy people
would be encouraged to engage in sexual relations; but, as Ploetz conceded, this was a vague and feeble proposal.[18]

The full dehumanizing brutality of radical Social Darwinism becomes
evident in the work of Alexander Tille, who was unmoved by the
moral qualms that so affected Ammon and Ploetz. Humanism, equality,
Christian ethics, democracy, socialism—all these are just the delusions
of the unfit, said Tille. To this Social Darwinist, the horrors of slums
were actually good because they purged the nation of useless citizens.
But "passive" selection was not enough for Tille. He wanted to intervene actively to "help" nature by killing the cripples and lunatics and
by giving more food to the gifted members of society. Significantly,
Tille was the deputy business director of the Organization of German
Industrialists in Berlin and later a representative of several industrial
associations in Saarbrücken. His work may be seen, then, as a conscious attempt to give a scientific justification to what many denounced
as the evils of capitalist society.[19]

Other industrialists were also eager to exploit Social Darwinism. In
1900, the steel magnate Alfred Krupp offered the enormous sum of
10,000 marks for the best essay on the question "What can we learn
from the theory of descent with regard to domestic political development and state legislation?" Wilhelm Schallmeyer, a Munich physician,
won the prize with an essay entitled *Vererbung und Auslese im Lebenslauf
der Völker* (Heredity and selection in the life course of peoples). The
book was only an indirect defense of capitalism. Schallmeyer's main
interest was to demonstrate the necessity of the *Daseinskampf* for all of
social and political life. Any interference with struggle would cause the
white race to degenerate to a level even lower than that of the Aus-
tralian aborigines. Accordingly, the state had to take an active role in
preserving the best racial elements. For example, marriage laws ought

to encourage the racially superior upper classes to marry earlier and have more children.[20]

Some sixty essays were entered in the Krupp contest, but they ought not to be taken as a cross-section of educated opinion on the social meaning of Darwinism. Despite the claims that the essays would be judged without regard to party, the explanations accompanying the contest question severely limited the answers that would be considered. Contest organizers (among them Ernst Haeckel) laid down as a premise to the question the "fact" that heredity was of great importance in analyzing social relations; they further stated that any social changes were therefore necessarily slow and had to be in accordance with the "flesh and blood" of the people. For the many people who would have questioned these premises, participation in the contest was futile. The two or three essays that did challenge the premises, arguing that Darwinism taught nothing about society, were summarily dismissed by the judges.[21]

Although the Krupp essays do not show that the educated middle class generally favored Social Darwinism, they do provide an interesting portrait of those who did. As Heinrich Ziegler, one of the judges, pointed out, the essays showed that Darwinism was not necessarily a "danger to the state" as had been generally presumed. Nonetheless, advocates of unrestrained capitalism would have been disappointed. Most of the essayists advocated a moderate state socialism, calling for a regulated economy with an expansion of worker protection laws, sickness and old-age insurance, and other forms of social welfare.[22] These responses attest to the well-known weakness of German liberalism, but they also call into question the conventional view of Social Darwinism as a bourgeois defense of the free-enterprise system. Moreover, it is clear from the Krupp essays that the harsh visions of such radical Social Darwinists as Tille did not strike a responsive chord in the middle class. Despite their biologistic thinking, most remained committed to humanitarian values. This is an important point to keep in mind when drawing parallels between Social Darwinism and Nazism. The extreme opinions of a few isolated figures should not be confused with a climate of opinion.

Just as Social Darwinism's relation to capitalism is problematic, so, too, is its relation to racism. Clearly, some Social Darwinists were racists and some racists were Social Darwinists, but neither position logically entailed the other. On the one hand, there were Social Darwinists like Ludwig Woltmann—author of one of the most impressive essays in the Krupp contest—who clearly used Darwinism as a prop for racism. Woltmann had been a Marxist, but under the influence of Darwin he transformed the class struggle into a biological struggle to bring the best Aryan stock to the forefront of the nation.[23] On the other hand, many Social Darwinists rejected racism, especially anti-Semitism. The

German Society for Racial Hygiene, a group of eugenicists founded by Alfred Ploetz in 1904, did not mention race in its founding statutes. Ploetz believed that the white race was indeed superior but that it included both Jews and Frenchmen. Another of the society's leading members, Fritz Lenz, contended that it was impossible for a eugenicist to be an anti-Semite. Articles in Ploetz's *Archiv für Rassen-und Gesellschafts Biologie* often referred to Jews as Aryans.[24]

Nor were all racists unqualified supporters of Darwin. Most of the *völkisch* prophets of Aryan beauty and spiritual depth found Darwin shallow and materialistic. Adolf Stöcker, as we have seen in chapter 4, rejected Darwinism outright because he thought natural selection and man's animal origin destroyed Christian morality. Julius Langbehn, whose *Rembrandt als Erzieher* (Rembrandt as educator, 1890) was the sensation of the early 1890s, voiced a common opinion when he chided Darwin for suppressing his artistic and poetic instincts. Darwin, he said, was typically English in that he merely accumulated facts without grasping the totality of nature.[25] Büchner, in turn, accused Langbehn of promoting mysticism and decadence.[26] One gets the impression that had Darwin been born a German he probably would have fared much better with the *völkisch* prophets, for it was often the attempt to define a peculiarly German spirituality that excluded him. In his *Die Grundlagen des XIX. Jahrhunderts (Foundations of the Nineteenth Century,* 1899), Houston Stewart Chamberlain flirted with Darwinism as a "proof" of the importance of race. But in the end Chamberlain's mystical concept of race precluded a total acceptance of Darwin's English empiricism.[27] Another prominent *völkisch* writer, the president of the Pan-German League, Heinrich Class, did not mention Darwin or use Darwinian language. Class's well-known book *Wenn ich der Kaiser wär* (If I were emperor, 1912) pushed a program of aggressive anti-Semitism and national expansion; but by defining materialism as specifically un-German, Class effectively excluded any Darwinian base for his argument.[28] Like many others, *völkisch* prophets used the rhetoric of struggle without being Darwinists.[29] (Nietzsche, too, though by no means a *völkisch* thinker, sometimes sounded Darwinian. Some readers probably interpreted the superman as a higher stage of evolution, although that was not Nietzsche's intention.[30])

Social Darwinism, in whatever form, never achieved a mass popularity. There were a few popular writers, like Langbehn, who talked of struggle and race, but their connection to Darwinism is so tenuous and ambiguous that it would be absurd to call them Social Darwinists. As long as Darwinism was perceived as a danger to the state (*staatsgefährlich*)—and this remained true down to World War I—there was no way that Social Darwinism could catch on as an ideology of the established classes. Support from either radical leftists or the religious was also out of the question because both groups rejected biological determinism. By a process of elimination, we are left with the conclusion that the only potential mass audience for Social Darwinism would have been a lower middle class with weak religious ties. This was indeed the group that most succumbed to the crude rhetoric of racial anti-Semitism; but, as has been suggested, such rhetoric is difficult to trace back to Socal Darwinism, not to mention popular Darwinism.

The truth is that most Darwin popularizers either ignored or opposed Social Darwinism. Magazine and encyclopedia articles almost never touched the subject, and books did so only tangentially. Nor did those clamoring for the inclusion of Darwinism in the school curriculum make an issue of Social Darwinism. By sticking to the argument that Darwinism was important because science was important, school reformers probably missed a good opportunity. School authorities might have been more sympathetic to Darwinism had it been presented as a boon to state authority. On those few occasions when the popularizers did stray outside of biology, they tended to be vague and philosophical. Moleschott, for example, inferred the inevitablity of socialism from the materialistic premise that force must follow matter in any social exchange.[31] What this meant in practical terms is not clear, but the vagueness was typical of the popularizers. Aside from their opposition to clerical influences in society, few popularizers had any concrete political proposals. What really counted to most of them was the victory of scientific rationality. Even those popularizers with socialist leanings, or whose works were published by socialist presses, kept their politics in the background, implying that the victory of socialism was but a part of the victory of science. (See chapter 7.)

The popularizers were, to be sure, very eager to root man in the animal world. But they did so not as advocates of a reactionary politics. Rather, the animal analogy was a weapon for routing Christianity and preparing the way for a naturalistic ethics. Unlike the Social Darwinists, the popularizers did not believe that social struggle was exactly analogous to animal struggle. Following Darwin more closely than the Social Darwinists, the popularizers looked back to the animal past as a source of hope that bitter struggle would lessen. Darwin had argued that positive traits like cooperation and altruism had been selected for in nature. To a man, the popularizers agreed; over time, they said, competition would become ever more refined, eventually evolving into cooperation. As Wilhelm Preyer put it, love and justice were man's "weapons" in the struggle for existence.[32] The "necessity of altruism," as Carus Sterne called it, would replace crude competition.[33] This optimism reflected the popularizers' close ties to the secular humanism exemplified by Strauss and Nordau. These men envisioned a golden future opened up by man's evolving ethical and intellectual potentials.

The popularizers accepted inequality as a fact of nature that, to some degree, would always remain with mankind. What they could not accept—and here again they reveal their progressive outlook—was the inclination of many Social Darwinists to view existing elites, as well as the very mechanisms that formed those elites, as inevitable natural products. "To live is to struggle," Dodel asserted. But, he added, without opportunity to rise (or fall) in society, that struggle is meaningless. Any fixed aristocracy was totally unnatural; for whatever talent that happened to reside in it would rot in the absence of competition and new blood.[34] Like all the popularizers, Dodel believed that better education for the lower classes would open up the class system by giving everyone a chance to compete. Thus the popularizers stressed the immense possibility of the future; in contrast, the Social Darwinists made their version of a struggling animalistic past into a moral imperative for the present. Whereas the Social Darwinists were ever more inclined to view man as a prisoner of heredity, the popularizers built their case for secular humanism on a firm foundation of environmentalism. Weismann's denial of the inheritance of acquired traits never achieved any popularity through his own works or indirectly through the popularizers. The popularizers remained firm in their belief that improvements would be passed on to succeeding generations. As long as there was no popular Weismannism, there could be no popular Social Darwinism.

Of all the popularizers, Büchner articulated anti-Social Darwinism in the most political form. He began—as did the other popularizers—with the premise that there was an immense difference between natural and social struggle. Struggle in nature was unconscious and admitted no exceptions, whereas man's struggle was conscious and therefore could be changed to suit man's special needs. Because there was so much misery in society, said Büchner, people had become inured to suffering and had jumped to the false conclusion that to suffer was natural and unalterable. Actually, man was in a transitional stage during which reason and justice were only beginning to regulate struggle. The lower levels of violence among the cultured and educated classes were supposedly proof of this contention. While those having no opportunity to participate in society's riches wallowed in a state of animalistic poverty and violence, the upper classes were advancing to a higher evolutionary stage. But how could such inequity be overcome, Büchner asked? His answer:

Here again science, and especially natural science gives the right clue. For if, as has already been shown, the true task of humanity or of human progress in opposition to the rude natural state consists in the struggle *against* the struggle for existence, or in *the replacement of the power of nature by the power of reason*, it is clear that this object must above all be attained by the greatest possible equalization of the circumstances and means under which and with which each individual has to fight out his struggle for existence and to carry on the competition for the preservation of his life. . . . If in politics we have long since come to replace the old system of oppression and domination by the now generally recognized principle of *equal rights* and *equal duties*, we must likewise socially replace the system of mutual plunder, which has hitherto prevailed, by the principle of equal means or equal circumstances.[35]

This sounds like the beginning of a plea for socialism, but Büchner was opposed to socialism. He thought that it was too narrowly focused on a worker takeover of the state and that many of its goals were unattainable given the present high level of egotism.[36] Instead, he hoped for a redistribution of wealth within the capitalist system, or, as he put it, to achieve "*FREEDOM, CULTURE AND PROSPERITY FOR ALL.*"[37] To realize this lofty goal, Büchner set forth three concrete proposals: (1) the abolition of all ground rents and the return of land to the community; (2) the gradual increase of restrictions on the right to leave inheritances to descendants; and (3) the establishment of state insurance against old age, illness, accident, and death.[38] These three reforms, said Büchner, would bring out the best of capitalism by breaking the strangleholds of interest and monopoly and allowing all to obtain some capital. No state of perfect equality would be reached because men varied in their interests and talents. There would still be a working class, whose reproduction Büchner actually wanted to encourage in order to bring more happiness and prosperity to all. But even with only partial equality, everyone would see the intimate connection between his own well-being and that of the community: "Such a state really resembles an organism in which all the juices flow constantly and in uninterrupted streams from the circumference to the center, to flow back again immediately from the center to the different parts and furnish them with strength and health."[39] What is notable here is that Büchner incorporated an organic view of society—usually seen as a monopoly of the *völkisch* Right—into his progressive, scientific social critique. His work is a good reminder of how much caution is needed in labeling people in an era of complex and shifting ideological perspectives.

Nowhere is this need for "caution in labeling" more evident than in the case of Haeckel. At first glance, Haeckel seems to be an important exception to the rule that there were no popular Social Darwinists. Was not Haeckel a sponsor of the Krupp essay contest, a supporter of pan-Germanism, and the inspiration for many eugenicists and racists? Undoubtedly, yes. And did not Haeckel, in his reply to Virchow's Munich speech, deliver the classic Social Darwinist attack on socialism? Again, yes. But these facts must be put into perspective; we need to know the public impression that Haeckel created. If he was a Social Darwinist, as conventional historical wisdom now has it, why was he consistently attacked by conservatives as a danger to public order? Certainly his anticlericalism is part of the explanation. But a better answer is that Haeckel, like all popular Darwinists, was viewed in his day as a spokesman of the radical spirit of 1848. A recent book on Haeckel, which portrays him as the central figure both in Social Darwinism and *völkisch* racism, concedes this important point, almost in passing: "On the surface, therefore, he [Haeckel] remained a spokesman for progress, optimism, modernism, and science."[40] Indeed! And in dealing with a popularizer, what can be more significant than the surface impression?

In short, Haeckel's Social Darwinism has been blown out of proportion. Consider, for example, that oft-quoted passage in *Freedom in Science and Teaching* where Haeckel argued that Darwinism was aristocratic: "Socialism demands equal rights, equal duties, equal possessions, equal enjoyments for every citizen alike; the theory of descent proves, in exact opposition to this, that the realization of this demand is a pure impossibility, and that in the constitutionally organized communities of men, as of the lower animals, neither rights nor duties, neither possessions nor enjoyments have ever been equal for all the members alike nor ever can be. . . . The theory of selection teaches that in human life, as in all animal and plant life everywhere, and at all times, only a small and chosen minority can exist and flourish, while the enormous majority starve and perish miserably and more or less prematurely."[41] This is certainly the language of Social Darwinism, but almost in the same breath Haeckel disavowed Social Darwinism. It was "dangerous," he said, to apply science to politics; and those who did produced nothing of "objective value."[42]

An examination of Haeckel's popular books shows that he usually followed his own advice. Occasionally, there are hints of Social Darwinism, but they are minor asides and do not affect the general tone or substance of his work. In *The History of Creation*, for example, he remarks that competition is necessary for social improvement, that capital punishment is needed for criminal types, and that a knowledge of ontogeny is necessary for public welfare.[43] But he discusses the artificial selection practiced in ancient Sparta without advocating it; comments that modern medicine saves people who formerly would have died, without advocating the abolition of medicine (not unlike Darwin himself, who mused that vaccinations would save the unfit[44]); and says nothing at all about the pros and cons of social welfare. The "artificial selection" he favors most is education so that struggle can become more and more refined.[45] Nor is the pattern in *The Riddle of the Universe* any different. There he touched on politics "but lightly," stopping only to blast the "reactionary" state for flinging itself into the arms of a "reactionary" church. Again, education in modern science was the panacea; it did not really matter whether the constitution was aristo-cratic or democratic as long as the citizenry was enlightened.[46] And because Haeckel opposed Weismann and accepted the inheritance of acquired traits, he had faith that the benefits of enlightenment would accrue to future generations.

Haeckel liked to see himself as a kind of common man's philosophe, and he is probably best judged as such. As he got older, he became more nationalistic, but he never lost his old democratic zest for tak-ing on the forces of "darkness and reaction." Like any long-lived and prolific writer, he was contradictory; one can quote him selectively to support almost any position. But it is pointless to search for the "true Haeckel," whose private intentions reveal themselves only in little-publicized actions or minor, largely unread books. People knew Haeckel by his *History of Creation*, his *Riddle of the Universe*, and his anticlerical speeches. Since Social Darwinism played only the tiniest role in these, Haeckel ought not to be labeled a Social Darwinist.

If Haeckel was somewhat ambiguous about Social Darwinism, his friend and disciple, Bölsche, was not. In his popular biography of Haeckel, Bölsche took his mentor to task for suggesting that Darwinism was aristocratic. Darwinism, Bölsche cautioned, yielded only the most vague and general conclusion if applied to society, namely, that "all stationary or reactionary politics are in irreconcilable contradiction to the theory of evolution."[47] Beyond that, there was nothing political to be learned from Darwin. This wariness on Bölsche's part may seem odd in light of his general inclination to use Darwinism as a universal explanation. He seems to have been bothered not so much because Darwinism was being applied outside of biology, but rather because Social Darwinists drew some unpleasant inferences. Bölsche yearned to tie his cosmic optimism to a concrete social optimism. Thus, while the Social Darwinists made the most of brutal struggle, Bölsche did just the opposite. Love and cooperation, not struggle, became the standards of what was "natural."

These themes were evident in Bölsche's work even before he had turned to serious popularization. As early as 1889, Bölsche criticized the social reformer Alfred Loth in Gerhart Hauptmann's sensational play *Before Dawn*. Loth, a character modeled on Alfred Ploetz, was a fanatical Social Darwinist, a firm believer in the power of heredity, and a devotee of human improvement. He rejected Helene, the girl he loved, because alcoholism "ran in her family." This sacrifice, done in the name of scientific principle, led to Helene's suicide. To Bölsche, Loth's behavior was unconscionable because sympathy—that noble trait inherited from the animals—was the highest human principle and should have taken precedence. If Loth's principles were to become social policy, Bölsche contended, the end result would be the cold-blooded slaughter of everyone who did not measure up to some arbitrary standard of hereditary excellence.[48] Bölsche continued this line of thought when he reviewed Ploetz's book on eugenics for *Die Neue Deutsche Rundschau*. Though admitting Ploetz's honesty and courage in asking hard questions, Bölsche shrank back in horror from Ploetz's racial utopia. Who is to say who is fit, he asked. Ploetz's team of eugenicists might well kill a Goethe or a Darwin. And what about generally fit people who are temporarily disabled? Humanity would be "rapidly ruined" by the Ploetz plan.[49] Even voluntary genetic control made Bölsche uneasy.

Yet Bölsche was troubled by the question Ploetz had raised, and he returned to it repeatedly as though it were a thorn in the side of his optimistic Weltanschauung. Could sympathy for one's fellowman be justified scientifically? He stated the problem eloquently in his essay on mutual aid in nature: "In former times if I gave a poor man a coat I no longer needed, I was considered a good person. Today it is possible that a learned and thoughtful person would raise the question of whether such sympathy and help are at all justified from an evolutionary perspective."[50] Bölsche answered this challenge by disputing the major premise of Social Darwinism. The struggle for existence in nature, he contended, had no exact analogy in human society. In nature, individual animals competed on two levels: first, with other individuals of the same species; and second, with the common environment. Lower animals protected only the whole species without regard for the individual. But higher up on the evolutionary scale, the individual became increasingly important, and cooperation began to replace struggle. At the human level, the richness and diversity of the individuals actually made any crude intraspecific struggle counterselective. No one could be sure what subtle and complex variations might prove useful for survival. Cooperation had thus become a positive variation, because the only real physical struggle left to human beings was the common struggle with the environment. For man, intraspecific competition retained value only in higher, more abstract forms—the "battle" of ideas.[51]

Bölsche conceded that there were individuals who were obviously unfit by any standard; but the solution was not simply to kill them. Rather, efforts should be directed toward eliminating the causes of unfitness, efforts that would go hand in hand with the creation of every possible opportunity for each person to develop his full potential. How well the unfit were treated was a test of how civilized a society was. To concentrate on the minor burden of caring for the unfit, instead of the great problem of unrealized potential, was misguided and truly anti-Darwinian: "From the perspective of natural selection, the loss of great talent through economic accident, lack of education, and the general chaos of our cultural life is a thousand times worse than the maintenance of a few cripples and lunatics."[52] This profoundly anti-Social Darwinian sentiment sums up Bölsche's views on the subject.

If Social Darwinism found little favor among the popularizers, racism is another matter. There is no doubt that by today's standards most of the popularizers—though not Bölsche—held racist opinions. Although they were not anti-Semites, the popularizers did firmly believe in the superiority of the "white race" over the "colored races," particularly black Africans. It is important to stress here that this conviction was in no way unique to the Darwin popularizers. The belief in white superiority was deeply ingrained in European culture; it predated Darwin, and it transcended every ideological and class boundary. As Büchner put it, "And who does not know the innate mental inferiority of the black race, and how it is and must ever remain as an infant compared to the white?"[53] Even the socialists—the group most committed to an environmentalist view of man—accepted white superiority as a matter of course. August Bebel, the most popular socialist author, took for granted the lower intelligence of black Africans in his *Die Frau und der Sozialismus* (*Woman and Socialism*, 1879).[54] Aveling, popular as a socialist as well as a Darwinian, used his *Die Darwin'sche Theorie* to explain in detail the apelike structure of the Negro skeleton.[55] Given the atmosphere they worked in, it would have been remarkable indeed if the Darwinians had not been racists.

Ironically, the works of Darwin himself were relatively free of racism. When he talked of the "favored races" in the subtitle of *The Origin* he merely meant varieties of plants and animals. Later, in his *Descent of Man*, Darwin did deal with the various races of man, but, unlike racists, he found the differences between the races superficial: "Although the existing races of man differ in many respects, as in color, hair, shape of skull, proportions of the body, etc., yet if their whole organization be taken into consideration, they are found to resemble each other in a multitude of points."[56] More than likely, it was Darwin's extensive travel that had opened his mind to a cultural relativism that was still fairly uncommon in his day. In *The Descent of Man* he mentions several Fuegeans and a full-blooded Negro of his acquaintance, all of whom were very similar to himself. A few pages later, Darwin notes that civilized nations tend to destroy barbarous ones, but he does not include biological superiority among the reasons. And certainly there was no anti-Semitism in Darwin's biology.[57]

But racist appeals to Darwin were not entirely groundless. Occasionally Darwin did refer to higher and lower races of man and to the superiority of the English; but of more importance to racism was his evidence on the frequent detriments of crossing different varieties. Again, Darwin was referring to plants and animals, but racists applied his arguments to people. Usually racists put more emphasis on human racial differences than did Darwin, thus exaggerating the dangers of mixing. Carl Vogt, in his *Lectures on Man*, argued that there was no single origin of man, that in fact man was several different species. He compared the "German type" to the Negro, finding that in every respect the Negro was closer to the apes.[58] Most did not agree with Vogt that the races were separate species, but there was general agreement that the lower races had more in common with the apes than they did with the cultured men of higher races.

Mental and spiritual qualities were said to depend upon measurable physical qualities. Hand and foot shape, limb proportions, facial angle, skull volume, even genital size—all these determined the potential for cultural development. And in every case the black man came out on the bottom as a kind of ape man. Both Büchner and Haeckel claimed that Negro feet retained the primitive apelike capacity to grip tree branches. Some tribes actually still lived in trees, according to Büchner;[59] and Haeckel's *Evolution of Man* (1874) contained an illustration showing the similarities between a Bushman's brain and ape brains. "No wooly haired nation," said Haeckel in his *History of Creation*, "has ever had an important history."[60] Such statements had little relationship with Darwinism. Since the language of racism was already in existence, it was not necessary to deduce racism from evolution. In fact, most discussions of race in popular works actually tended to be poorly integrated into the overall explanation of evolution. By making so much of the gulf between the higher and lower races, the popularizers were perhaps unconsciously taking some of the sting out of the ape theory. The lower races were made to bear the greater part of the burden of animal descent, thus sparing cultured whites some of the humiliation of being no more than higher apes.

When the popularizers spoke of the higher races, they usually meant white people in general. Haeckel divided mankind into twelve groups, with "Mediterranean man" on the top. The Germanic races, by which he meant the peoples of northwestern Europe and their North American cousins, were the most advanced within this subgroup. It was they who were "laying the foundation for a new era of higher mental culture, in the recognition of the monistic theory of evolution."[61] But neither Haeckel nor any of the other popularizers believed (as did the *völkisch* thinkers) that the Germans themselves were a special superior subgroup of the whites. Perhaps their tremendous devotion to their English mentor precluded a German nationalist racial mystique. Nor was there any attempt to exclude the Jews from the ranks of the superior race. The occasional hints of anti-Semitism in Haeckel's works are not racial; rather, they are a spin-off of his anti-Christianity. Unlike the *völkisch* thinkers, the popularizers used the black man, not the Jew, as the countertype to the superior race. Büchner attacked the anti-Semites for making the Jews a scapegoat for economic woes. If such a tiny fraction of the population really did have so much influence, Büchner pointed out, then they would have to be superior in some way. To Büchner, the "Jewish problem" was no different than the "Christian problem." The Jews, he said, ought to give up their obsolete religion, become freethinkers, and intermarry with the Gentiles. (Hardly a *völkisch* solution!)[62] Dodel went even further. He argued that the Jews definitely were superior to the Gentiles because the long history of persecution had thinned the ranks of unfit Jews.[63]

Remarkably, some popularizers completely escaped the great current of racism. Bernhard Langkavel's *Der Mensch und seine Rassen* (Man and his races, 1892), a book greatly admired by socialist workingmen, preached a thoroughgoing cultural relativism. Different peoples, Langkavel said, are like particles on a rough sea. The surface is relatively level, but at a given moment some particles are higher than others. Who could say what will be the most "advanced" culture in five hundred years? To Langkavel, racism was an expression of arrogant self-interest. One had to be just as "fit" to live in nature as to live in a civilized land. In fact, a case could be made, he said, that the Europeans were the closest, not the furthest, from the ape![64]

Bölsche, too, was little affected by racism, especially *völkisch* nationalism. The white man, he agreed, was culturally more advanced than the other races; but this fact, he insisted, was not necessarily permanent. Man, as a part of nature, was in a constant state of flux. *Völkisch* stress on the eternal verities of German superiority was thus irreconcilable with evolution. That much-heralded spiritual unity of the German people was but a stage in the evolution of love, which had begun with the primeval sympathy of matter and would end with universal brotherhood. Love proceeded "beyond the *Volk* to a community of all cultured men and finally to mankind in general."[65] Not even World War I could induce Bölsche to abandon his ideals. Unlike many other prominent German writers, he never enlisted in the spiritual battle against Germany's enemies. Instead, he continued to hammer away on his same themes, stressing that no matter how terrible the present, nature still gave a sense of perspective, inner peace, and optimism. The struggle among nations was a vestige of the struggle among animals; in the short run it was indeed horrible, but in the long run the drive toward love and harmony was inexorable. In short, for Bölsche, Darwinian monism implied a humanitarian internationalism, not a racist nationalism.[66]

This internationalist outlook was firmly entrenched in the institutions of the free-thought movement. A good illustration is the textbook for the youth of the Berlin Free Religious Congregation. The book's editor was Berlin's most prominent free-thought organizer, Bruno Wille, who was an intimate friend of Bölsche and a fellow Darwin enthusiast. In each of its songs, poems, fables, and aphorisms, the text celebrates a high-minded love of nature, science, brotherhood, and humanity. Here is a stanza from a typical song, called *Vorwärts* (Forward):

> Lasst das Licht des Geistes strahlen,
> Dass die Herzen es durchglüht,
> Und die reine Menschenliebe
> Überall auf Erden blüht!
> Dass kein finstrer Hass die Völker
> Ferner von einander trennt,
> Dass man gern in jedem Menschen
> Seinen Bruder anerkennt.[67]

(Roughly translated: "Let the light of spirit shine, so it burns in every heart, and the pure love of man blossoms everywhere on earth! So that no darker hate divides the peoples further from each other, so that each is happy to see in every man his brother.") These values, which are deemed appropriate for the young, are a good indication of deeply held adult values. And it should be kept in mind that the free-thought movement was the closest popular Darwinism ever got to any institutional expression.

Why, then, in light of this relatively benign record, has popular Darwinism frequently been linked to Nazism? The reason is that historians seeking the roots of Nazism have failed to make some crucial distinctions. They have falsely associated popular Darwinism with radical Social Darwinism and racist anti-Semitism. Unfortunately, such loose reasoning is typical of the general character of most quests for the ideological origins of Nazism. The enormous obstacles to proving anything substantial have tended to mire the whole subject in vagueness, overly facile generalizations, questionable causal reasoning, and sheer guessing masquerading as evidence. Too often we find very different thinkers lumped together as "precursors" who exercise some kind of "influence" on the future. As suggested earlier, the problem starts back with the analysis of pre-World War I nationalism. For example, Alfred Kruck's study of the Pan-German League asserts that the Pan-Germans were the "children" of a Darwinian age and that Heinrich Class's organic theory of the state had its "strongest roots" in Darwin's natural selection.[68] But do such tenuous attributions really mean anything, especially in light of Class's antimaterialism? How easy it is for Darwin to become a precursor of a precursor, ad infinitum! Even so fine a book as Karl Bracher's *The German Dictatorship* traffics in such causal vagueness. There we learn that biological anti-Semitism "paralleled the emergence of Social Darwinism" and that radical Social Darwinism "helped shape the racial-biological, pseudo-scientific theories of National Socialism and culminated in the breeding and extermination policies of the Third Reich."[69] Since we are not told exactly who is doing what to whom, nor exactly when or how, we are left with the false impression that there must have been a mass, undifferentiated social movement of Social Darwinian anti-Semitism—a movement that everyone knew about and drew inspiration from.

Now it is always easy to criticize the shorthand language of general historical accounts. Consider a statement such as "It [facist ideology] was inspired by the fashionable contemporary doctrine of Social Darwinism, with lurid overtones of Nietzsche's *Will to Power*" (from A. J. Ryder's *Twentieth Century Germany*).[70] Ordinarily, one would simply pass over such key words as "inspired" and "fashionable" and not ask what they really mean. After all, the historian must write the language of everyday common sense. It would be pedantic and absurd to ask for precise definitions at every step. But it is neither pedantic nor absurd to point out that general statements, such as the one above, may contain assumptions that are so obvious that they go unexamined. In this case, the "obvious" assumptions (leaving aside the phrase about Nietzsche) are that many people were Social Darwinists and that they or their ideas somehow "caused" or were responsible for Nazism. If we examine these assumptions more closely in the works of those who set them forth in more detail, we see that they crumble. And if they do not stand up in their details, they certainly cannot stand up as general statements.

Consider the case of Haeckel and the Nazis. Günter Altner, in seeking the "intellectual background" of Nazi racism, sees Haeckel's role as central. He notes that Haeckel's *Riddle of the Universe* was very popular, that Haeckel subordinated ethics to an aristocratic causal law of nature, and that several Social Darwinists found inspiration in Haeckel's work.[71] But what, then, is the real meaning of Haeckel's influence? There was in fact little trace of Social Darwinism in *The Riddle of the Universe*, so Haeckel exerted no mass influence as a Social Darwinian. If he was an inspiration for radical Social Darwinists, this would make him at most a proto-Nazi once removed; and even this is questionable because, as has been seen, the radical Social Darwinists were not racial anti-Semites as were the Nazis.

Similar problems plague Daniel Gasman's book on Haeckel and the Monist League, *The Scientific Origins of National Socialism*. Seizing upon every hint of Social Darwinism and racism in Haeckel's works—mostly ones that were scarcely read—Gasman turns Haeckel into a *völkisch* prophet. Every racist and Social Darwinist in the Monist League is said to be elaborating on the general guidelines laid down by the master, Haeckel. Not only does this greatly exaggerate the role of Social Darwinism and nationalism in Haeckel's own thought, it also ignores the rational, liberal, and humanitarian side of monism. If anything, monism tilted to the left. After all, Bölsche, Carl von Ossietzky, Helene Stöcker, and Magnus Hirschfeld were among the most prominent monists. The league's president, Wilhelm Ostwald, wanted to keep the league apolitical, but as he admitted, "The orientation of every monist must necessarily be *against the right*, that is against conservatism, orthodoxy, and ultramontanism in all their forms."[72] Many monists actually wanted an alliance with Social Democracy. If Haeckel and the Monist League can be forerunners of Nazism, then so can most any other thinker or organization. Once blame has been distributed so widely, it begins to lose its meaning.[73]

By the same overly casual reasoning, Bölsche, too, has been turned into a proto-Nazi. Hermann Glaser, in his *The Cultural Roots of National Socialism*, argues that organic monism is indistinguishable from *völkisch* thought. The Nazi "blood and soil" philosophy is a fusion of Bölsche and Goebbels, says Glaser. Bölsche furnishes the sensual organic base and Goebbels the political propaganda necessary for mass success. The "evidence" for this rather strained interpretation is the famous passage on the day flies at the beginning of Bölsche's *Love-Life*. As will be recalled, in this passage Bölsche depicts the swarm of flies as they mate and die, killed by the "lightning of love." Glaser sees in Bölsche's description of the orgy of sex and death a foreshadowing of the Nazi "breeding marriages." He adds: "The bubbling, grinding and orgasmic activity is such that one does not know whether the 'sacrificial death of a mother' is of a folkish heroine or a protozoan, whether the 'new melody' accompanies the mating of racially akin humans or the love tale of the bee (but not the tapeworm because this creature 'cannot experience the majesty of love, the tête-à-tête.')"[74] This is indeed reading history backward!

Others have tried to link Bölsche directly to Hitler. Henry Picker, editor of a book of Hitler's table talk, asserts, without proof, that Hitler studied and admired Bölsche's books and that Bölsche was part of the "intellectual circle" from which Hitler emerged.[75] Similarly, the Hitler researcher, Werner Maser, lists Bölsche as a key source of Hitler's ideas about race. Bölsche's essay collection, *Vom Bazillus zum Affenmenschen* (From bacillus to apeman, 1900), is said to be the inspiration of Hitler's conception of the Jew as a vermin whose extermination is necessary to save the Aryan race.[76] The book in question is a typical Bölsche celebration of the advance of life; certainly no anti-Semitism can be read into it. Nor is there evidence that Hitler read it; and even if he did, it is hard to imagine what sort of influence the book could have exerted. Apparently, Hitler did know of Bölsche, but disapproved of him. Hermann Rauschning quotes Hitler as saying to Goebbels in conversation: "No, not in the big city, Goebbels! There we get into the godless propaganda of the Marxists: Bölsche, love-life in nature and such absurdities."[77]

As usual, the Führer's remarks are somewhat garbled, but his basic sentiment was in tune with Nazi ideology. When all is said and done, there was no way that the Nazis could fully accept Darwinism. Darwinism, after all, entailed a common primitive beginning for all men, and above all it stressed change. Acceptance of evolution by the Nazis would have been tantamount to a denial of the eternal, immutable superiority of the German race. As a newspaper headline on the nobility of the Aryan race proclaimed in 1936, "Race Unchanged through Thousands of Years."[78] Thus celebrations of Haeckel's one hundredth (1934) and Bölsche's seventy-fifth (1936) birthdays were very muted, even though these two men were among the most well known and admired of all Germans.[79] In fact, the popular Darwinists were officially out of favor. When the Nazi Propaganda Ministry issued its guidelines of acceptable and unacceptable literature in 1935, popular Darwinism appeared as one of the categories of "expunged books," defined by the guidelines as "writings of a philosophical and anthropological character, whose content is the false scientific enlightenment of a primitive Darwinism and monism (Haeckel)."[80] Nor is it an accident that neither Bölsche, Haeckel, nor any other popular Darwinist appears on the party-sponsored recommended lists for libraries.[81] Surely, the most popular pre-1933 nonfiction authors would appear if they were at all acceptable to Nazi ideology. Any attempt to connect Nazism to popular Darwinism must run aground on these hard facts. This is not to suggest that there are no connections between Darwinism (Social, popular, or otherwise) and Nazism, but only that those connections are far more tenuous, indirect, and problematic than is commonly assumed.

On the whole, then, the Darwin popularizers remained faithful to the old cosmopolitan and humanitarian tradition of popular science. Even their racism—which never loomed large in their overall output— was little more than an updated version of the old travel literature on exotic peoples. In no way could the popularizers be considered opinion leaders in racist anti-Semitism of the sort that appealed to the Nazis. That role was left to *völkisch* nationalists like Chamberlain, men who rejected Darwinism as un-German. Nor were the popularizers the major source of radical Social Darwinism. That stemmed from little-known and largely unread figures far from the mainstream of the popular science tradition. Neophilosophes that they were, the popularizers could accept neither the pessimism of radical Social Darwinism nor the narrow-mindedness and mysticism of *völkisch* racism. Their commitment to an optimistic rationalism, to a revival of the Enlightenment, by and large estranged the popularizers from the political Right. As the old liberal spirit of 1848 weakened at the end of the century, it was more and more the socialists who found popular Darwinism their natural ally.

Chapter 7

Darwin, Marx, and

the German Workers

No one needs to pay more attention to popularization than the historian of the working class. If the workers are cast in an important role as historical actors, then we must know what they read and thought in order to understand why they acted—or failed to act—as they did. Certainly, the German working class in the generation before World War I was overwhelmingly socialist in its political outlook. But what did socialism mean on a popular level? Learned Marxist theoreticians formulated the ideology of the Social Democratic party. Yet studies of these thinkers, whom the average worker neither read nor understood, are likely to mislead the historian. The most we could infer from such studies is that the workingman's view of socialism was a dim, oversimplified reflection of sophisticated ideology—a kind of clichéd Kautskyism or thirdhand Marxism. And this assumption would be wrong. Marxist socialism did not simply "trickle down" to the workers, reaching them only in a dilute and vapid form. Rather, on its way "down" to the workers Marxism changed radically because it mixed with another momentous system of ideas—Darwinism.

In fact, as will be seen, by the time Marxism reached a popular level, it had practically ceased to be recognizable as Marxism at all and had become instead a vague Darwinian monism. The reasons for this ideological metamorphosis are fairly obvious. The Darwin popularizers were, as we have seen, peddling not simply a biological theory but rather a comprehensive philosophy of life—a Weltanschauung. As this term suggests, popular Darwinism made monopolistic religiouslike claims that threatened the integrity of other systems of beliefs. And, of course, Marxism—also a theory of change—made similar claims to totality. One of the two—either Darwinism or Marxism—had to yield to the other; and the outcome of the contest was almost a foregone conclusion. Whereas Marxist political and economic theory was difficult, abstruse, and forbidding, and good popularizers were scarce, Darwinism was relatively simple and alluring, and good popularizers abounded. Stated in Darwinian terms, Darwinism and Marxism were closely related and therefore competing species of ideas in the popular arena; but Darwinism was fitter, so it survived, whereas Marxism perished. If the image is a bit overdrawn, the outcome is still clear: the German work-ingman saw his future in Darwinian terms. He was, in short, a natural evolutionist rather than a political revolutionist.

This popular substitution of Darwin for Marx was preceded on a high theoretical level by a subtle infusion of Darwinian terminology into Marxist ideology. At Marx's funeral in 1883, Engels could think of no higher praise for his departed friend than to compare him to Darwin: "Just as Darwin discovered the law of evolution in organic nature, so Marx discovered the law of evolution in human history."[1] Marx probably would have been proud of the company Engels placed him in. Although he found Darwin philosophically crude, Marx admired the biologist and was quick to sense that Darwinism would set the intel-lectual style of the age.[2] Evolution, struggle, nature—these concepts were "scientific" and could lend added prestige to any argument. Why not exploit them?

Thus Marx acquiesced when, as early as the 1870s, Engels began to "Darwinize" Marxism. Superficially, the boundary between the two thinkers' territories was clear: Darwin was master of the organic, Marx of the historical. But once the comparison had been made—and it was inevitable that it would be—could the two domains be kept sepa-rate? Did not invoking Darwin imply that human society was somehow linked to natural history? Engels was especially prone to the Darwinian analogy when he described bourgeois society: "It is the Darwinian struggle for individual existence carried over from nature with added fury into society. The natural condition of the animal appears as the climax of human society."[3] Of course, Engels believed that socialism would abolish these barbaric conditions and thus bring man out of the animal world to a truly human state. But how? If Darwin accurately described bourgeois society, then did he not also describe the process of change that would transcend that society? And here is where the confusion began. By at least partially accepting the support of Darwin, Engels turned Marxist thought into a kind of scientism. Nature tended to replace history as the engine of change. Instead of being a conse-quence of the dialectical interplay of thought and action, the future became for Engels a necessity of natural law. In effect, Engels was dephilosophizing the foundations of Marxism, dethroning Hegel in favor of Darwin. The unavoidable result was a neutralization of dialec-tical materialism and a muddling of the meaning of the transformation to a socialist society. As George Lichtheim has aptly put it, Marxist thought in the years 1840 to 1880 moved "from Hegel to Haeckel."[4]

It was partly through Engels—the chief guardian of Marx's personal legacy—that the Darwinian ambiguity entered the mainstream of the Social Democratic movement. But other theoreticians were also caught in the Darwinian web. Karl Kautsky, the "pope" of Marxism, came to Marx by way of Darwinism. In his memoirs, Kautsky tells of his early fascination with Haeckel and Büchner; in the 1870s he even sketched a book on the evolutionary history of mankind.[5] Until the late 1880s, Kautsky believed that Marx's ideas could be absorbed into Darwinism. Only in 1890 did he clearly separate Darwin's nature from Marx's history, arguing that the two had nothing to do with each other—a position he held throughout the 1890s. Writing in 1894, he remarked: "Trying to prove the necessity of socialism through natural law rather than through particular historical conditions is anything but Marxist."[6] Later, in 1902, Kautsky actually dismissed Darwinism as antisocialist because of the slow, imperceptible pace of change evolution entailed. Yet Kautsky could shake off neither Darwin nor biologistic thinking; by 1909 he had resurrected Darwinism, hooking it to a catastrophe theory of change that gave new natural support to sudden revolutionary upheaval. And in his late work of 1927, *Die materialistische Geschichtsauffassung* (The materialistic conception of history), Kautsky still clung to Darwinism as a prop of socialism. He even reprinted his early evolutionary history, causing one critic to scoff that Kautsky's view of history came straight out of *Brehms Tierleben*.[7]

Part of the reason for the nature/history confusion among socialists was that the terms of discussion were often set by opponents of socialism who refused to recognize such a distinction. "Scientific" proofs of the impossibility of socialism were frequent in Social Darwinist literature. Heinrich Ziegler and Otto Ammon, for example, argued that society was by nature competitive rather than cooperative and that socialism was therefore unnatural. Sometimes this critique—done under the guise of objectivity—was little more than mudslinging, which of course made it all the more provocative. Ammon even contended that Social Democratic functionaries were degenerate failures who in former times would have committed suicide.[8] Fearing that Darwin, and thus the immense prestige of science, would be appropriated entirely by the enemy, Social Democrats were forced to make claims on Darwin that they might have had second thoughts about under less pressing circumstances.

Accordingly, instead of taking to heart Kautsky's advice of 1890 that Darwin and Marx had nothing to do with each other, many socialist thinkers went about the thankless task of sorting out the implications of Darwinism for socialism. Unfortunately, this task was made more difficult by the widespread ignorance in the party of the Hegelian roots of Marx's thought.[9] Without Hegel, Marxism appeared to lack a theoretical engine of change. Darwinism was attractive because it could serve as a kind of ersatz engine, a role that gave Darwinism an exaggerated relevance for socialists. Since struggle was a key to change in both Darwinism and socialism, it was tempting for socialists to adapt Darwinian struggle to their own needs. In order to do this, they had to avoid the Social Darwinists' obviously "bourgeois" conclusion that an individualistic free-for-all was the natural state of human society. But there were ingenious ways to evade this trap and convert Darwinian struggle into a force promoting socialism. Most who tackled the problem began with the premise—laid down by Marx—that man was more than a mere biological creature. Ludwig Woltmann, the prominent revisionist who later converted to racism (see chapter 6), argued in an influential book published in 1899 that man's tools, techniques, and culture set him apart from animals. Animals, he said, act purely instinctively, struggling merely to leave the most progeny; man engages in a more refined struggle for goods, profits, and prestige. What is more, this human struggle tends to be social rather than individual, that is, internally cooperative groups struggle with each other and with a common environment. The advantage of this view, which was embraced by many socialists, was that it preserved the pivotal concept of history as class struggle without conceding that man was an inherently competitive animal. The pattern of intraclass cooperation already revealed an advanced state of evolution that held out the promise of total social cooperation in the classless society. Thus man evolved through intergroup struggle to a higher stage of existence.[10]

Another line of argument, which often existed uneasily alongside the first, met the Social Darwinists on their own ground. Struggle and natural selection, so many socialists contended, would be effective only in a socialist society, when all had a real chance to compete equally and could rise according to natural ability. Woltmann went so far as to suggest that socialism would thus realize the ideals of liberalism.[11] But since most socialists felt awkward with the idea of individual struggle, they stressed its future refinement and benevolence, in contrast to the unfair cruelty of capitalist society. Indeed, as with most socialist thought, the emphasis here was not on the future but on the shortcomings of the present. Under capitalism, the idiot son of a factory owner had a better chance than the brilliant son of a factory worker. That was hardly natural. As Anton Pannekoek, a prominent spokesman for the party's left wing, pointed out, the workers did not take part in the so-called competitive society; they merely sold their labor to those few who did. Moreover, Pannekoek insisted, the struggle among that small group of competing capitalists would advance only their predatory and immoral instincts. There was no way for society to advance biologically and morally until all participated.[12] As Woltmann observed, under capitalism only the machines would get better.[13]

It is tempting to suggest that acceptance of organic evolution translated directly into evolutionary socialism or revisionism. But this would be a misleading equation. As Kautsky's own waverings suggest, there was no clear lineup of forces in the Social Democratic party on the meaning and significance of Darwinism. To be sure, such evolutionary socialists as Edmund Fischer sometimes argued openly that slow organic evolution proved the unnaturalness of revolution.[14] And the leader of the revisionists, Eduard Bernstein, seemed at times to imply that socialism was the natural culmination of biological evolution.[15] But, on the whole, revisionism was based not on an appeal to natural science, but on an economic critique of Marx's predictions. Bernstein and other revisionists were really saying that socialism was not historically inevitable. This did indeed open the way to Darwinism as another source of inevitability, but generally revisionists were willing to forsake inevitability in favor of the argument that socialism was an ethical necessity. Sometimes it appeared that revisionists wanted both natural evolution and ethics as the engine of history leading to socialism. Of course, there was a contradiction here, but it was no worse than the nature/history confusion that infected the entire party. Like everyone else, socialists twisted Darwinism to suit their own needs.

George Lichtheim has suggested that the scientism or Darwinism that permeated Social Democracy was a necessary adaptation "to the rather modest intellectual requirements of the labour movement."[16] This would seem to imply that the party knowingly passed on to the masses a distorted Darwinized Marxism, believing it to be the only popularly understandable Marxism. Actually, the effects on the masses were more indirect. What happened was more like the following. The workers tended to bypass Marx (or popularizations of him) altogether and to go directly to popular Darwinism; and because of their philosophical leanings (or perhaps better, their confusion), the party leaders usually acquiesced. A wealth of evidence on workers' reading habits shows that they were far more interested in science than in economics or politics. And science usually meant Darwinism, the workingman's favored subject. As we have seen, popular Darwinism in Germany had always had an antiestablishment tone. It was certainly no coincidence that when the future socialist leader, August Bebel, was in prison in the early 1870s, his reading list included Darwin's *Origin*, Haeckel's *History of Creation*, Büchner's *Force and Matter*, and Liebig's *Familiar Letters on Chemistry*.[17] These interests would set the tone for succeeding generations. Many, even such liberals as Rudolf Virchow, actually feared that Darwinism could "lead to" socialism and ought to be kept out of the public arena. ("What a foolish idea seems to prevail in Germany on the connection between Socialism and Evolution through Natural Selection," Darwin mused.[18]) And, of course, the successful exclusion of Darwinism from the schools only served to enhance the attractive, forbidden aura about it. Moreover, the ban on much socialist literature during the formative years of the movement in the 1880s, probably had much to do with focusing the workers' attention away from Marxism. Science (or culture generally) was "safer" and could serve as a substitute radicalism.[19]

In any case, the pattern of interest in Darwin rather than Marx was clearly established by the 1890s and persisted throughout the next generation. As Paul Göhre, a young theologian who worked in a machine factory in Chemnitz, reported in 1891, the workers knew little of socialist theory, but they were fascinated by the popular scientific, "materialistic" literature.[20] Göhre's impressions are confirmed by all of the available surveys of workers' libraries. With the exception of Bebel's *Woman and Socialism*, popular Darwinism dominated worker nonfiction reading. As *Die Neue Zeit* reported in 1894 (on the basis of statistics from a Social Democratic club in a south German city), political literature was not in demand. After Bebel, the most popular nonfiction authors were Arnold Dodel, Oswald Köhler, and Edward Aveling—all Darwin popularizers. *Die Neue Zeit* speculated that the workers lacked political interest because they already had political brochures.[21]

The results of the most impressive reading survey at the turn of the century cast doubt on this explanation. In 1899, A. H. T. Pfannkuche placed an ad in *Die Neue Zeit* asking the librarians of workers' libraries to send him lists of the most popular books. Pfannkuche published the results the next year in a short book entitled *Was liest der deutsche Arbeiter?* (What does the German worker read?) Although Bebel's *Woman and Socialism* headed the list of nonfiction, four out of the top ten books in this category were of the genre Darwiniana. (And this prior to the publication of Haeckel's *Riddle of the Universe* and Bölsche's many books!) Workers were also very fond of the bourgeois family magazines like *Gartenlaube*; for their fiction reading they preferred Zola above all others, as well as *Die Neue Welt*, which came with most socialist newspapers as an entertainment supplement. Typically, librarians lamented their patrons' lack of political interests. Pfannkuche concluded that the number of political and economic titles was inflated because the librarians pushed the "right kind" of books.[22] Many were probably returned unread.[23] It was wrong to argue, he said, that the political curiosity of the workers was already met by party newspapers, for these papers also followed science. Clearly, the fascination with science was deep and genuine. What concerned the workers most could be summarized by the title of Dodel's popular book, *Moses or Darwin?*[24]

The same patterns emerge from other surveys after 1900. For example, questionnaires distributed to workers taking evening courses in Berlin from 1904 to 1908 showed "knowledge of nature" as their main interest, with economics and politics lagging far behind.[25] Similarly, Adolf Levenstein, who did a sociological survey of workers in metals, textiles, and mining from 1907 to 1911, found that workers usually listed popular science books as their favorite reading, the names Bölsche and Haeckel appearing repeatedly.[26] Further, *Der Bibliothekar*, a monthly magazine for workers' libraries, is a gold mine of statistical reports. Everywhere the story was the same: workers liked exciting fiction and science. Except for *Woman and Socialism*, books on economics and politics remained largely unread. Haeckel, Bölsche, Bommeli, Aveling, Köhler, and even Darwin were the nonfiction authors in demand. Zola, Edward Bellamy, the German classics, and cheap escape literature (E. Marlitt, Karl May, and the like) remained the fiction favorites.[27] These interests were stable and persistent, lasting beyond World War I. A questionnaire distributed to Leipzig workers taking evening courses in the early 1920s revealed that Bölsche was by far the favorite nonfiction author.[28]

Workingmen's memoirs, of which there are several dozen for the period before World War I, are another source of information on reading habits. Rarely do the memoirs mention reading Marx or even Kautsky. More typically, the road to political awareness (if there is any) went via popular science. Thus, Moritz Bromme, whose recently reissued *Lebensgeschichte eines modernen Fabrikarbeiters* (Life story of a modern factory worker, 1905) is probably the best-known worker memoir, reports reading among others Darwin, Bebel, Vogt, and Bommeli.[29] Likewise, Nikolaus Osterroth, a brickworker, tells eloquently of the great impression Dodel's *Moses or Darwin?* made on him.[30] Wenzel Holek, a Czech worker who learned German so he could read Darwinian literature, boasted that his personal collection contained volumes by Vogt, Büchner, Ferdinand Lassalle, Haeckel, and Bölsche. Holek recommended Bölsche as a starting point for workers studying science. He once loaned a fellow worker who had been a little puzzled by Haeckel a copy of Bölsche's *Vom Bazillus zum Affenmenschen*. "That pleased him; he understood it," Holek recalls.[31] Nor are these reading lists isolated cases; they are typical.

Care must of course be taken not to generalize too much from the workers' memoirs. But they are at least typical of a small, articulate minority of self-educated workingmen. Just how large this articulate reading minority was cannot be determined with any precision. The mere fact that in 1914 only 2,156,014 books were checked out of workers' libraries in all of Germany suggests the minority status of reading workers.[32] The workers' memoirs are filled with complaints that most fellow workers are ignorant and unread. Bromme, who worked in a machine factory in Gera, refers to himself and his small circle of reading friends as "We Enlightened" and suggests that they were the only ones who read anything better than trash.[33] Wives and mothers may have been one inhibiting influence, for women were usually more closely tied to traditional values and frequently regarded serious reading as unChristian or impractical.[34] There is even some evidence that interest in serious reading was declining in the generation before World War I. Data from the woodworkers' library in Berlin for the period 1890 to 1913 show a dramatic drop in the relative interest in science in favor of escape fiction.[35] It is also suggestive that after the war Bölsche was most popular among older workers.[36]

But this is not the whole story. In some areas, workers made up as much as half of the patrons of city libraries;[37] in the year 1906, for example, four hundred thousand workers took out some 1.6 million books from public libraries in big cities.[38] The high circulation figures (several hundred thousand in the cases of Haeckel, Bölsche, Zola, and Bellamy), combined with low prices of many editions, suggest that some workers owned a small personal library. Moreover, many workers were avid readers of the party or union papers, *Die Neue Welt*, and the various calendars for working-class homes. In 1900, Social Democratic newspapers had a total circulation of about four hundred thousand,[39] by the eve of the war about one million,[40] and each copy probably reached four or five readers. Most workers at least claimed to be readers. In the survey by Levenstein mentioned above, only 4.5 percent of the metalworkers, 13.6 percent of the textile workers, and 26 percent of the miners admitted to not having read a book.[41]

Given the great diversity of the working class, it is, of course, very difficult to make generalizations about reading habits. Still, a few patterns do emerge. The more skilled a worker, the more he read, printers being the most avid readers. Big city workers read more than small town workers and those in the western part of the country more than those in the east. Women workers read a lot of cheap fiction but almost no serious books. Reading for all groups tended to increase in the winter and in bad economic times.[42] In 1891, Göhre estimated that the intellectually aware workers in the machine factory where he worked comprised about 4 percent of the total. The rest he dismissed as ignorant.[43] Levenstein, writing twenty years later, was a bit more generous. On the basis of some five thousand detailed questionnaires, he estimated that the truly "intellectual strata" of workers was 5.9 percent and the "mass strata" 64.1 percent. The rest of the workers fell somewhere in between. But there were great variations: whereas Silesian miners were 88 percent "mass" and only 1.2 percent "intellectual," Berlin metalworkers were only 24.6 percent "mass" and 14.7 percent "intellectual."[44]

Taking all the evidence into account, it is safe to say that there was a small but significant minority of self-educated workingmen who knew their popular Darwinism. These men were numerous enough to have been present in many, if not most, work places, and their influence as leaders of local opinion was probably far beyond their numbers. If we can judge from the memoirs, these serious readers were treated with respect and seen as a source of authority. Some were called "Herr Professor" by their comrades.[45] Moreover, the views of these literate few may well have represented the vague, inarticulate opinions and desires of the "mass strata."[46] To understand the impact of socialism on the working classes, it is therefore essential to appreciate the view of reality afforded by the Darwinian books that the articulate minority so eagerly read. For, as we shall see, the average workingman's Weltanschauung was a close replica of the content of these books.

It is significant that Bebel's *Woman and Socialism*, the single most widely read nonfiction book among the workers, was in the form of a popular anthropological tract. Bebel's aim was to make socialism comprehensible to the masses, a task that would elude Kautsky. Yet, unlike Kautsky in his Erfurt program, Bebel began not with an economic analysis of capitalist society, but rather with man's (or woman's) primitive past. Elsewhere, Bebel insisted on a clear distinction between natural and historical law,[47] but in *Woman and Socialism* that distinction was blurred and history was firmly rooted in natural evolution. Change was an eternal part of human history, because change was part of the entire animal world, of which man was but a part. Bebel largely ignored Marx, not to speak of dialectical change. Nor did he speculate on how the transformation to socialism would occur. The most obvious inference was that socialism was simply another stage in the natural history of the earth. Indeed, the political and economic change to socialism had a natural justification. Under capitalism, said Bebel, the class structure inhibited natural selection; those at the top were protected from competition and those at the bottom had no real chance. Only socialism could restore the natural balance: "The point in question, then, is, so to arrange social conditions that every human being will be given an opportunity for the untrammeled development of his nature; that the laws of development and adaptation—called Darwinism after Darwin— may be consciously and expediently applied to all human beings. But that will only be possible under socialism."[48] Bebel's analysis of capitalism (it was similar to Kautsky's) was tacked onto the anthropology, splitting the book clumsily into two poorly related parts. Given what we know of working-class reading habits, it is fair to ask how many readers got through the later, more tedious sections of the book.

Turning to the Darwinian literature as such, two names stand out above all others: Bölsche and Haeckel. That Bölsche, a socialist sympathizer who had developed his style talking to workers, should be so popular is only natural. But why should Haeckel, a vehement opponent of Social Democracy, find so much favor among workers? The answer, as has been suggested in the last chapter, is that Haeckel's political convictions were not much in evidence in his popular works. What came through in *The Riddle of the Universe*—the book through which most workers knew Haeckel—was not a clear political line, but rather an attack on so-called reactionary forces that conspire to suppress scientific enlightenment. Haeckel brandished an aggressive, even intolerant, rationality against social institutions, especially church and school, that were already suspect in the workingman's eye. It was probably this negative, polemical side of Haeckel that so endeared him to working-class readers. Reading Haeckel, one gained the impression that Darwin was a freedom fighter against superstition and oppression. This was not only Haeckel's message but also that of the other favored Darwinists—Aveling, Bommeli, Dodel, and Köhler.[49] All of these authors were published by the Social Democratic Dietz Verlag and were heavily advertised in socialist newspapers. Like other popular Darwinists, they believed that science, especially Darwinism, was intentionally being kept from the people in order to protect oppressive institutions. Once enlightenment was spread to the masses, it was implied, justice could not be far behind. Darwinism, as Bölsche was fond of pointing out, was not just a set of facts—it was a progressive Weltanschauung that put those who understood it in tune with the course of nature. Certainly none of the popularizers intended to provide a direct and concrete political message. Yet presented (essentially without serious competition) as an all-encompassing Weltanschauung, Darwinism inevitably colored political perceptions.

By tying man's future to the interminably slow process of natural evolution, the popularizers obviated a political discussion of how any real transition to a cooperative future might come about. With the exception of Bölsche and Aveling (who was Marx's son-in-law), none of the popularizers had any clear identification with socialism. And even in these two cases their Darwinism clearly overshadowed their socialism. Bölsche could not conceive of socialism except as a form of Darwinism and had no clear political vision of the future.[50] What the popularizers were really envisioning was a worldly alternative to the Christian heaven. Theirs was a future of secularized Christian love. Typically, they had forged their views in opposition to Christian theology, not the capitalist class struggle. As Dodel put it in his *Moses or Darwin?* Christianity has had two thousand years to help the poor, and it has failed. Now it must make way for the real hope of Darwinism: "With overwhelming power of an uncontrollable force the conception of a *realizable and desirable happiness of ALL mankind during our LIFE-TIME, not beyond the grave,* has taken root, spread and become an intrinsic part of the moral ideal of this age."[51] Significantly, Dodel had reached the last page of his book when he made this extraordinary claim. He had come to an intellectual dead end.

The workingman was also exposed to popular Darwinism in fiction. Zola's works are a prime example. Gripped by evolutionary thought, Zola saw man as primarily a biological being, a pawn of heredity and environment. This view is most striking in *Germinal*, a book always near the top of the German workingman's list of favorite fiction. Étienne, the hero of *Germinal*, who leads the great strike of coal miners in northern France, is an avid student of Darwin, or rather popular Darwinian tracts. The idea of struggle fills him with a religiouslike fervor that overshadows his intellectual endeavors to understand the socialism of the First International. For Étienne, the survival of the fittest means the ultimate triumph of the robust proletariat over the effete bourgeoisie. When the strike collapses and the men of the International are discredited, Étienne still retains his faith in revolution, but not for economic reasons; rather, he believes that new, vigorous blood will naturally and inevitably overwhelm degeneracy. As Étienne leaves the scene at the end of the novel, the miners are back at work underground, but all around him nature is bursting out in the first flush of eternally recurrent spring. Here again, hope for the workingman springs not from historical action, but from nature herself.

Nor was a reading of Edward Bellamy's utopian novel *Looking Backward, 2000–1887* (1888)—probably the best-loved novel among working people—likely to promote revolutionary consciousness. Translated as *Im Jahre 2000*, the novel appeared in serial form in many socialist newspapers. It tells the story of a middle-class Bostonian, Julian West, who wakes in the year 2000 after sleeping since 1887. During the hero's 113-year sleep, industrial society has managed to solve all its social and economic problems. The state is now a gigantic cooperative that perfectly and harmoniously meets all needs. After a period of pleasurable social service, each individual is totally free to pursue his own personal interests. West's hosts explain that the great transition came about peacefully and naturally. All saw it coming and agreed on its desirability—there is no class conflict here.

In fact, Bellamy leaves the reader quite in the dark about the specifics of historical change. According to his postscript, the forecast is "in accordance with the principles of evolution."[52] Bellamy's great historical evolution entails a shift from a "bad Darwinian" society to a "good Darwinian" society. In 1887, society was a cruel free-for-all, demeaning man, stifling real opportunity. Now, in the year 2000, the Darwinian struggle has narrowed to a purely sexual selection and works toward the ultimate refinement of the race. All marry for love (a great boon to sustaining romantic interest in the story). The invisible hand of biological evolution, rather than historical action, has liberated man. There is nothing for man to do but to wait passively for the future to come.

Kautsky was quick to see that Bellamy's evolutionary vision in effect lifted the burden of struggle from the proletariat. In his review of *Looking Backward* for *Die Neue Zeit* he took Bellamy to task for his totally unMarxist view of history. Where was the all-important class struggle? he asked. Yet Kautsky recommended the book highly because its entertaining view of a noncapitalist future would stimulate the working-class reader to further study. The worker would see through Bellamy's limitations, Kautsky predicted.[53] (Probably wishful thinking!) But this attitude was typical. In spite of the obvious threat to revolutionary consciousness posed by such literature, the Social Democratic party itself actually did much to promote it. The very first volume of the party's own low-priced *Internationale Bibliothek* (1886) was a Darwinian book, *Die Darwin'sche Theorie* by Edward Aveling. Three more such books followed in the same series.[54] *Die Neue Zeit* (originally conceived as a popular monthly, though it never achieved that goal) also paid close attention to Darwinism. At its founding in 1883, Kautsky wrote that Darwinism would be central to the journal's political message. "The name itself is already a program," he said of Darwin.[55] Although Kautsky himself later decided that Darwinism and socialism had nothing to do with each other, *Die Neue Zeit* continued to follow popular science. Bölsche's *Love-Life* was very favorably received, though the reviewer was a bit taken aback by the "tone of an uncle in the nursery."[56] Even Haeckel's *Riddle of the Universe* found a sympathetic reception in the pages of *Die Neue Zeit*. Franz Mehring, the party's chief cultural critic, acknowledged that Haeckel was no friend of social democracy, but he praised Haeckel for unwittingly rendering service to the proletariat. Haeckel was a good educator of the masses, Mehring said, even though his naturalistic materialism lacked a historical dimension.[57] The implication was that the proletarian reader could make the conceptual leap from natural history to human history—a dubious assumption. As popularizers go, Haeckel was fairly difficult.

Other socialist publishers were equally keen to cater to the working-class taste for Darwinism. In 1908, the Vorwärts Verlag published Eduard David's *Referentenführer*, a list of recommended books needed to acquire political consciousness. Typically, David had especially high praise for Bölsche.[58] A similar pattern is evident in a brochure put out by the Verlag der Leipziger Buchdruckerei in 1914. This was a guide for workers who wanted to acquire their own inexpensive libraries. The basic twenty-six-book, fifty-mark collection included five popular science works.[59] One of these, Curt Grottewitz's guide for Sunday afternoon nature walks for workers (originally published by Vorwärts Verlag in 1905), contained a revealing introduction by Bölsche. Alienation from nature, he argued, was the great crisis of the time; therefore, an emotional yet informed "feeling for nature" was the closest the modern worker could come to liberation. In effect, what Bölsche was doing—with tacit party sanction—was locating the origins of the worker's problems in his urbanization rather than in class oppression. The worker would recover his lost humanity by returning to and comprehending nature, not by changing society politically. Bölsche saw a golden future, but the key to it was held by Darwin, not Marx.[60]

Of course, not everyone wanted or could afford a fifty-mark book collection (about two weeks' wages for the average worker). But almost every serious social-democratic household subscribed to one of the various workers' calendars. Among the little inspirational messages ("Golden Words") in the pages of these calendars, quotations from

Darwin popularizers like Büchner and Haeckel were as frequent as those from Marx, Lassalle, or Engels. *Die Neue Welt Kalendar* for 1909, for example, advised its readers that the theory of evolution "fills us with a happy confidence, insofar as it lets us hope that all the irrationality, injustice, and inadequacy that we find everywhere, but especially in our social order, will not continue forever; rather these are only steps in the development to higher, more complete forms of human community."[61] This is pure Bölsche, the apolitical optimism of popular Darwinism that would form the core of the workers' view of progress. And the calendars were not alone. The entertainment supplement *Die Neue Welt* (with its 550,000 circulation[62]) brought a flood of popular science into working-class homes every week.

The party's promotion among the masses of such evolutionary non-Marxist thought reflected its larger failure to develop real alternatives to bourgeois culture. In theory, knowledge was supposed to be directly revolutionary. "Knowledge is power, power is knowledge,"[63] Wilhelm Liebknecht had asserted back in 1872. But a glance through the pages of *Die Neue Welt* is enough to belie these fighting words; it differed hardly at all from the "bourgeois" *Gartenlaube*. The simple fact was that the party was living off the progressive elements of bourgeois culture, of which popular Darwinism was an integral part. That this was true not only in the case of popular Darwinism, but also of naturalist literature and workers' education generally, reveal the breadth of the party's cultural problem.[64] On one side were party regulars who wanted direct politicization through art and education ("dramatized Marx," one naturalist scoffed[65]); on the other were bourgeois radicals, often on the fringe of the party, who wanted to use art and education for the cultural elevation of the masses. The schism in the free theater movement in Berlin was a typical symptom of this divisiveness. In 1892, party regulars forced the expulsion of the Freie Volksbühne's founders, Bruno Wille (also an avid Darwinist) and Bölsche, because under them the theater had offered mere educational entertainment, rather than revolutionary agitation.[66]

The same question came up again at the 1896 SPD Congress. *Die Neue Welt*'s editor, Edgar Steiger, came under attack for printing so much naturalist literature, which some delegates found not only offensive in a family magazine but also unrevolutionary. Steiger's reply was significant: he argued that naturalism dissected reality with the tools of Darwinian materialism that all socialists certainly accepted.[67] With Bebel's support, Steiger kept his job. It was no accident that Bölsche, the apostle of Darwinism, was on the side of cultural uplift rather than agitation. His own novel, *Die Mittagsgöttin*, had been serialized in *Die Neue Welt* in 1892 and was itself an example of the failure of Darwinism to translate into a coherent political program. Science was identified with progress and social justice, but it was never clear exactly how.

Bölsche believed that the enlightenment of the proletariat would somehow bear its own fruits.

However much some in the party might deplore the "mere education" that popular Darwinism represented, or the nonrevolutionary thought it implied, they seemed unwilling and powerless to stop it. Engels protested that *Die Neue Welt* was a bore, that science never scared anyone[68]; but the number of science articles increased, while references to Marx were almost impossible to find. Every issue of *Vorwärts* was filled with ads for workers' education, often including courses on evolution. Aveling called the workers' educational organizations "temples" of evolution.[69] Bölsche and others lectured and showed their slides to packed assemblies of workers.[70] There was little centralization of any of this activity because, even after 1906 when it set up a Central Education Committee, the party still had no coherent policy on workers' education. Was it to be agitation or mere enlightenment? Yet, left to themselves, local clubs, unions, and education committees sponsored an impressive array of courses. By 1913, there were 791 local education committees that offered 420 courses and 599 individual lectures. Altogether over 220,000 workers took part that year, and this represents only a part of the total educational effort.[71] Those involved in workers' education felt a special need to cover science because it was slighted in the regular schools.[72] Thus, a typical cycle of lectures, aiming at both general and political education, was that sponsored by the Berlin lithographers in 1911. Before turning to history and economics, the lectures considered "The Wonder of the Cosmos" and "From Primeval Animals to Man," thus hooking society onto nature. Well-known scientists shared the platform with prominent socialists, including both Eduard Bernstein and Rosa Luxemberg.[73]

Although the events that were held appear impressive, there was an obvious drawback to teaching Darwinian science. So complex was the theoretical relationship between Darwinism and Marxism that there was no practical way to make the distinction between them clear to the masses. Even those who, like Engels, Kautsky, and Bebel, were usually careful to separate Darwin's natural history from Marx's human history, were neither consistent nor really aware of how much their own thought was imbued with Darwinism. When Ludwig Woltmann told the party Congress in 1899, "In our political agitation, let us replace the 'dialectic' with the much more precise and richer concept of 'evolution,' which is much more comprehensible to the workers,"[74] he was actually advocating what had already taken place in practice. And why not? After all, most popular Darwinism taught rationality, struggle, skepticism of Christianity, and the inevitability of change—all virtues in the eyes of socialists. Breaking the church's hold on the workers' minds and hearts was a prerequisite for the success of socialism. With the prestige of science running so high at the end of the nineteenth century, it seemed to make good practical sense—at least in the short run—to exploit the workingman's interest in evolution.

But those who wanted to link science directly to politics had a nearly impossible task. An amusing and revealing example of such an attempt is an 1897 article in *Die Neue Welt* on the canals of Mars, then thought to be artificial. The author remarked that these stupendous engineering achievements required an intelligence and technology far in advance of man's—which was only natural because Mars was older and life there had had more time to evolve. He then told his working-class readers that until capitalism was abolished, man would have no chance to catch up with the Martians.[75] Clearly, they were already socialists! (One has visions of an Interplanetary Workingmen's Association.) The clumsiness of the image demonstrates how difficult it was to enlist science in the class struggle. Lenin himself might extol Haeckel's *Riddle of the Universe* as a "weapon in the class struggle,"[76] but revolutionary socialism paid a high price for this weapon. Science was imperious; it would not simply lend its prestige to socialism without bringing along a dangerously independent world view. Thus the sifting of Marxism through a Darwinian filter in the process of popularization meant that the consciousness of the masses was inevitably rather different from what the party might have wished.

Indeed there is little evidence that the SPD imparted any real understanding of economics and politics to the workers before 1914. Max Weber was probably right when he remarked in 1895 that politically the workers were "far less mature than left-wing journalists would make them believe they are."[77] The caution and expediency of socialist politicians at the top of the party were reflected by an almost complete lack of revolutionary consciousness at the bottom. Workers' memoirs rarely mention Marx or the possibility of revolution; more frequently they pay tribute to Bellamy's influence.[78] Even those who later became party functionaries or journalists admit that it took them years to achieve any understanding of socialist theory.[79] When Levenstein did his poll from 1907 to 1911, he found a very low level of class consciousness. Only a small minority told Levenstein that they ever thought about political or organizational questions. When asked what they would do with more time, their favorite answer was not party or union work, but self-education. Workers were more interested in nature than politics; they liked to walk in the woods, and their dream of what they would do with more money was to build a little house in the country.[80] Earning more money was actually more important to them than the victory of socialism![81] In short, their values were "petty bourgeois."[82]

The above analysis of workers' reading suggests that the wide diffusion of popular Darwinism may have played an important role in shaping these values. Marxism was tedious and difficult, even in simplified forms, and the conspicuous failure of its popularization left an intellectual and emotional vacuum which Darwinism rushed in to fill. To be sure, reading was only one of many influences on the workingman, but it is nonetheless striking to note how closely his values paralleled those of the Darwinian literature. Obviously, popular Darwinism struck a resonant chord in the workers' experiences. The world as the worker saw it was indeed a *Kampf ums Dasein*, a struggle for jobs and for money, a struggle just to live through a 60-hour week or to keep up with the brutal demands of piecework. No doubt the worker could also experience exploitation (*Ausbeutung*) on a daily basis, but it was hard to integrate this experience into the complex theoretical system of Marxism. The advantage of the Darwinian *Kampf ums Dasein* was that it was not only concrete but also comprehensible within the relatively simple theoretical schema of evolution. In Darwinism it was easy to move back and forth between mundane reality and theory; in Marxism only the very sophisticated could do so. Granted, most workers said they were social democrats, but they meant it in a Darwinian rather than a Marxist way. Many had come to socialism via a destruction of their Christianity, prompted by Darwinism. For them the gripping question had been, as Dodel phrased it, "Moses or Darwin?" not "Moses or Marx?" Having chosen Darwin, they often went no further, being either unaware of Marx or unable to distinguish him from Darwin. Their Weltanschauung remained grounded in the familiar anti-Christian evolutionary monism.[83] Socialism became for them a peculiar mixture of science and emotional commitment to a brighter future. Countless workers referred to their socialism as a religion or a "new gospel."[84] Marxist socialism already had a pseudoreligious strain that the infusion of popular Darwinism could only deepen and broaden.

When the workingman spoke of the future, he used the emotional, yet naturalistic, language of popular Darwinism. Here Levenstein is an invaluable source, for he encouraged the workers to give their philosophy in their own words. Many wrote sizable essays—sometimes inarticulate, sometimes eloquent, frequently both. One metalworker wrote movingly, "O, I think so deeply, but writing, that I can't do."[85] Levenstein found that hopes for the future were almost invariably vague—dignity, justice, love, brotherhood, and the like. But all was in "the foggy-gray distance," as one young miner put it. Another was content to die in a "social democratic sense!" But the future did not seem to be within the grasp of these men. It was, in a sense, not a tangible result of progress, but rather a formless cosmic development. It would inevitably, as that almost magic word had it, "evolve." "Everything evolves," said one miner. And therein lay the hope. Not a few had succumbed to the despair of a hard life, but another young miner spoke for the many who still had hope: "Yes, it will get better because the whole of evolution is pointed toward something great, the realization of a higher stage of culture when we will finally separate from the animal kingdom."[86] Here speaks the marriage of Marx and Darwin.

Not only did nature give hope for the future, it also was an object of worship in the present. Most workers denied to Levenstein that they believed in God, but it is clear that they meant the Christian God. They referred repeatedly to the God in nature so beloved by Haeckel and especially by Bölsche. "I believe in Nature," remarked one metalworker. "I profess the monistic world view," said another.[87] These men saw the purity and promise of nature as an antidote to the misery and ugliness of city life. Their views were romantic and sentimental, not surprising perhaps, because the rural life was for many only far enough in the past to be enveloped in an idealized glow. Somehow evolution would bring that little house in the country for their descendants. That such views persisted into the 1920s is a tribute to the power of popular Darwinism. Gertrud Hermes's study of the workers taking workingmen's courses in Leipzig in the early 1920s reveals continuing faith in Darwinian science as a substitute religion: "The core of their world of thought is the theory of evolution. It is the beginning and end of the workers' natural philosophy; it recurs in the most varied forms as a leitmotif in their testimonies,"[88] writes Hermes. Their faith in the future, she adds, comes not from Marx, but from Darwin—as befits a group whose favorite nonfiction author was Bölsche. Similarly, Paul Piechowski, who surveyed Berlin workers in 1927, found that when workers were asked their Weltanschauung, they would often reply "Darwinism," "pantheism," or "monism." He concluded from his questionnaires that a "scientific pantheism meets us at every turn: God-Nature."[89]

Such deification of Darwinian nature inevitably had a debilitating effect on revolutionary consciousness. Darwinism offered no political solution to the proletariat's problems. It could just as easily be used to support as to undermine bourgeois society. But even if interpreted as a theory of radical change, Darwinism tended to obscure the role of praxis in the Marxist revolutionary equation. Seen from a Darwinian perspective, the proletariat no longer worked in tandem with inexorable historical forces to create its own destiny. Rather, the focus of change was shifted away from human relationships—and thus out of human control—onto nature at large. Man's development, in this Darwinian view, was no longer a result of class struggle, but only a small facet of an ever-improving universe. Once human history was subsumed by cosmic evolution, the vision of a greater future receded into oblivion and the will to revolutionary action atrophied. This is not to suggest that popular Darwinism blocked the understanding of economic exploitation or class interests, but only that it interfered with a full understanding of the meaning of socialist liberation. Thus there is little doubt that the wide and deep diffusion of popular Darwinism tended to work in favor of the moderating forces within German Social Democracy. As did the exigencies of parliamentary politics, popular Darwinism helped to push the party in the direction of an idealistic radical democracy.

The playwright Karl Sternheim dramatized this point very nicely in his *Tabula Rasa* (1916), which treats Darwinian monism as a force that bourgeoisifies socialism. In the play, Sternheim contrasts a revolutionary firebrand with a humanitarian, moderate socialist as the two compete for the sympathies of workers in a glass factory. The latter, Artur, is an avid Bölsche fan; in fact, he regards Bölsche as a kind of demigod and prophet of the coming age. Reading *Love-Life* (with his fiancée), he exclaims, "If anything could be dearer to me than the ideal of social democracy, it would be monism."[90] Artur pleads for the establishment of a huge workers' library that would help raise everyone up to the bourgeois level. His political philosophy seems to be the only logical application of Bölschean principles to the social struggle. Change will come, says Artur, "but not by violence, rather by the peaceful path of evolution. The citizen with equal rights will take over the place of the privileged. Social democracy does not destroy the present society and reduce all its members to the proletariat; rather it raises the worker from the position of a proletarian into that of a citizen and universalizes the bourgeoisie."[91] Here indeed is the ultimate blow to the revolution: the transformation of evolution into upward mobility. Perhaps Sternheim has overstated his case, but the basic point is sound. It was no accident that those articulate workingmen who wrote memoirs typically were Majority Socialists after the war.[92] The heavy dose of bourgeois culture that these men had absorbed while educating themselves took its toll on their radicalism.

Clearly, then, Darwinian monism was a poor ally of revolutionary Marxism. On a strictly theoretical level, the two did not mix well; indeed, the monism peddled by Haeckel and Bölsche actually precluded Marxism, if only for the obvious reason that monism was by definition undialectical. But there were other, more practical obstacles to an alliance. However much popular Darwinism might resemble socialism on the surface, it resisted conversion to a political ideology. It was just as easy for the Right to stake out a claim in Darwinian territory as for the Left. The closest Darwinian monists could get to even pseudopolitical organizational forms were the ethical culture and free-thought movements. Both advocated a rational culture based upon secular humanism, and both aroused the suspicion of socialists. If Darwinism had an ideological role to play on the Left, it was as a weapon against antiscientific, antimodern opponents of the progressive bourgeoisie. To the extent that socialism still had a vested interest in the outcome of this battle, Darwinism was a needed ally. But to the extent that socialism had to go beyond this battle, Darwinian views among the masses could only be an ideological drag.

Epilogue

I N retrospect, the most striking feature of German popular Darwinism was its long-term success. For over fifty years a host of popularizers drew inspiration from a single scientific theory, the essence of which could be stated in a few simple sentences. Popular Darwinism seemed to have the secret of perpetual youth. One can leap over the decades, from one best-seller to the next, with scarcely a jolt. The same familiar arguments are there to guide the way: bringing science to the people is essential to democracy; Darwin has redefined man by connecting him to nature; Darwin has proved progress; man is freed from the old gods; science is the new religion. That such propositions could so dominate the nonfiction reading of millions for so long is a true cultural phenomenon. Recalling some of the reasons for Darwinism's German success is perhaps the best way to summarize the preceding chapters.

Doubtless, a certain continuity of personnel had something to do with the stability of German popular Darwinism. Both Haeckel and Büchner, who did so much to set the original tone of popularization, remained models until after the turn of the century. They and others reissued or rewrote the same books, recycling the tried and true formulas. In the early years, the success of these formulas might be attributed simply to faddishness. There was something exciting and new about Darwinism, especially the idea of man as ape. Without descending into sensationalism, the popularizers could still cleverly exploit the "spicy" side of Darwinism. Such men as Haeckel, Büchner, and Vogt might be tagged with the epithet *"Affenprofessoren"*; but it was hard for anyone not to listen when they spoke out. Yet the appeals of shock and fad are by their very nature fleeting, and we are back with our original question: What was it that sustained the interest in popular Darwinism?

To answer this question, we must look beyond Darwinism itself. Surely, if the popularizers had merely given cut-and-dried descriptions of Darwinism as one more scientific theory, they would have attracted little attention. Popular Darwinism was a sensation in Germany because it was sucked into some of the deep cultural currents of the day. It became a force larger than itself, a Weltanschauung, not dependent on a particular thinker, book, or intellectual fad. The revolutionary spirit of 1848—to which many popularizers had personal commitments—was of pivotal importance in turning Darwinism into a Weltanschauung. The failure of that revolutionary spirit sent German progressives running for cover—sometimes literally—in the 1850s. Those who had based their radical democracy on a philosophical idealism found that intellectually they had nowhere to hide. Their only political alternatives were to join the reaction or to turn inward, away from politics. On the other hand, those forty-eighters who had armed themselves with a social critique based on scientific materialism could, as Feuerbach pointed out, continue the fight on a new front—science. Their strategy was to erode the unquestioned authority of state and church by preaching scientific rationality. Thus it was no accident that materialists were both political radicals and scientific popularizers.

When Darwinism arrived in Germany in the early 1860s, it found its natural home within this matrix of materialism, radicalism, and scientific popularization. Because Darwinism dispensed with any external spirit guiding nature and because it seemed to prove that progress was natural, materialists eagerly took it up as a weapon against authority. What better way to subvert a reactionary church and state than to spread among the people the idea that science had disproved both political reaction and the Christian God? Why not hook Darwinism onto that long tradition of popular Enlightenment going back through von Humboldt all the way to Fontenelle? Nor surprisingly, church and state responded by trying to quarantine Darwinism. They denounced Darwinism as atheistic, socialistic, and immoral, and they backed up their fears by excluding it from the schools. Such responses would have been absurd had Darwinism been no more than an isolated scientific theory. But, like everyone else, the guardians of the social order soon learned that Darwinism had become a competing Weltanschauung. There seems little doubt that popular Darwinism profited from this antiestablishment image. As Goethe once said, a little censorship may actually stimulate intellectual activity. So long as Darwinism was avoided in the schools and frowned upon by the upholders of public morality, its continued healthy existence was all but assured. There was always a new constituency, whether middle-class progressives, opponents of the church, partisans of science, the youth, or the workers.

It was not only the political atmosphere that promoted the growth of Darwinism in Germany. Darwinism was also fortunate in arriving at a time when the prestige of science was riding high. Before about 1860, the impact of science on everyday life was relatively small. But the later phases of the industrial revolution, in which Germany led the way, witnessed the marriage of science and industrial technology. In everything from electric motors to fertilizers to drugs, the average layman could see and share in the progress of science. Though Darwinism was without any immediate practical effects, it was able to borrow some of this prestige. Of course, most people associated both Darwinism and science in general with materialism. Among professional scientists and philosophers, the old materialism of the 1850s had begun to seem increasingly naive after about 1870, but the public was largely unaffected by this shift. Popular materialism (in tandem with Darwinism) continued unabated, probably because the results of science were most easily perceived in the machine, that is, as usable power in a tangible object ("force and matter" in the old Büchner terminology). Moreover, the abandonment of materialism by the more advanced thinkers was a complex process, too sophisticated for popularization. In any case, the public's continuing love affair with its own version of scientific materialism could only benefit Darwinism.

As scientists took on the role of new priests, it was inevitable that the influence of the old priests would wane. And here, too, Darwinism benefited. The erosion of Christian beliefs—to which Darwinism would later contribute—had begun in the 1830s with the Bible criticism of Strauss and had been continued in the 1840s and 1850s by Feuerbach and other materialists. By the time Darwinism arrived on the scene, educated people had already been exposed to the unsettling ideas that the Bible was myth, that God was a projection of man's own needs, and that there were no spiritual forces. Beginning in the 1870s, socialist leaders had their own good reasons to spread these ideas among the working class. With the ground so well prepared, the inferences drawn from Darwinism were far less likely to be rejected out of hand. If the Bible was a myth and man just a form of carbon, then it was not so shocking to hear the popularizers say that Genesis was untrue, that there was no purpose in nature, and that man was a kind of ape.

Even with all these advantages, the wave of popular Darwinism might have run its course by the 1880s had it depended only on a progressive bourgeoisie for its audience. As the forces of liberalism waned, popular Darwinism had either to adapt or find new audiences if it was to continue expanding. Tied as it was to the spirit of 1848, popular Darwinism could not express the values of an illiberal society. Instead, popular Darwinism found a new mass audience in the working class, whose leaders embraced it as a weapon in the class struggle. This descent of Darwinism into the lower classes was made possible by increased literacy and the falling prices of books, magazines, and newspapers. Not that popular Darwinism at the turn of the century had become completely a working-class phenomenon, for it had not. A sizable middle-class audience still was especially fond of Bölsche, whose peculiar charms cut across all class lines and marked the final spectacular flowering of popular Darwinism. In the years before World War I, Bölsche's incredibly prolific output of articles and books was so widely scattered that anyone who read at all knew his work.

On the whole, it is probably true that, in the words of a recent intellectual history, "Sceptical good sense, the best of the Enlightenment tradition, has not won a mass audience."[1] But German popular Darwinism deserves to be counted as an exception to this rule. There is no doubt that the popularizers reached a mass audience—millions in the case of Bölsche. And certainly they preached rationality, tolerance, progress, optimism, and skepticism of Christianity. They were, in short, neophilosophes, vulgar philosophes perhaps, but nonetheless the recognizable heirs of the eighteenth-century encyclopedists. Their work stands as a testimony to the qualitative as well as quantitative potential of mass culture.

Vital as it was in Germany in its day, popular Darwinism has completely vanished. Although some Darwinists were still popular in the 1920s, especially among workers, they were already a voice from the past. Deeply rooted as it was in the peculiarities of pre-1914 culture, popular Darwinism had little future in the twentieth century, for it was not a good time for philosophes. In part, popular Darwinism was simply a victim of its own success. The great battles against church and school, which had given the genre its fighting spirit, had been won. After World War I nobody felt threatened enough by Darwinism to bother to fight it. Left without a benighted enemy, popular Darwinism lost much of its raison d'être. Indeed, the genre began to appear increasingly bland and naive. Its simple optimism, unified vision of the world, and belief in progress were ill-adapted to a generation glutted on horrors and suffering and buried under mountains of confusing new knowledge. Increasingly, popular Darwinism became a historical curiosity, an escape to the past, rather than a guide to the future. The need for scientific popularization had probably never been greater than in the 1920s, but no one of the stature of Haeckel or Bölsche rose to the occasion.

Ultimately, obscurity is the fate of every popularizer, particularly popularizers of science. Most of what the popular Darwinists said is now hopelessly out-of-date. Today, if a person wanted to learn about evolution, it would be ridiculous for him to turn to the likes of Haeckel or Bölsche, where he could find nothing about modern genetics or any of the major discoveries of the last two generations. Inevitably, the advance of knowledge outdistances the popularizer; there is no way that his reputation can hold up after his death, for unlike the encyclopedia, his works are not continually revised. But the historian should not be misled by the rapid decline of reputations. Many of those who now have great reputations had little or no influence in their own time.

The German Darwin popularizers, to be sure, have not aged well, but in their day they commanded the respect of millions. Surely they—and other popularizers—merit the attention of the historian. If intellectual history is to remain vital, it must move beyond a preoccupation with seminal ideas to an analysis of the social fates of those ideas.

Notes

CHAPTER 1

1. H. Stuart Hughes, *Consciousness and Society*, p. 9.
2. Jacques Barzun, "Cultural History as a Synthesis," *The Varieties of History*, ed. Fritz Stern (Cleveland, 1956), p. 396.
3. See, for example, the extensive bibliographies at the end of Wolfgang Langenbucher, *Die Aktuelle Unterhaltungsroman: Beiträge zu Geschichte und Theorie der Massenhaft Verbreiteten Literatur* (Bonn, 1964). See also, Rudolf Schenda, *Volk ohne Buch*; Rolf Engelsing, *Analphabetentum und Lektüre*; and Walter Schatzberg, *The Scientific Themes in the Popular Literature and the Poetry of the German Enlightenment, 1720–1760*.
4. In his study of articles on Darwinism in the British press in the 1860s, Alvar Ellegard argues that the orientation of a journal is a good reflection of the opinions of the readers. Here again, however, we are left in doubt as to the depth and breadth of real influence. See Ellegard's *Darwin and the General Reader*. The same problems arise in regard to lectures. We hear of them only if they were printed or reported in periodicals. Rarely do we know the size of the audience or the reception accorded the lecturer.

CHAPTER 2

1. Walter D. Wetzels, "Versuch einer Beschreibung populärwissenschaftlicher Prosa in den Naturwissenschaften," pp. 76–77.
2. Immanuel Kant, "What is the Enlightenment?" Crane Brinton, ed., *The Portable Age of Reason Reader*, p. 300.
3. Bernard le Bovier de Fontenelle, *Conversations on the Plurality of Worlds*, Brinton, ed., *Portable Age*, p. 312.
4. Alexander von Humboldt, *Ansichten der Natur*, pp. vii–x.
5. Ernst Glaser, *Kann die Wissenschaft verständlich sein?* pp. 55–56.
6. Helmut Hiller, *Zur Sozialgeschichte von Buch und Buchhandel*, pp. 21–22.
7. Johann Goldfriedrich, *Geschichte des deutschen Buchhandels*, 4:211.
8. Quoted by Hiller, *Zur Sozialgeschichte*, pp. 94–95. All translations from German sources are my own.
9. Carlo M. Cippola, *Literacy and Development in the West*, pp. 91, 115, 85.
10. Hiller, *Zur Sozialgeschichte*, p. 103.
11. Rolf Engelsing, *Analphabetentum und Lektüre*, pp. 127–29. Many memoirs of people from a peasant background tell of encountering resistance to their reading. See, for example, Franz Rehbein, *Gesinde und Gesindel*, p. 120, and Emil Unger-Winkelried, *Von Bebel zu Hitler*, p. 27.
12. Hiller, *Zur Sozialgeschichte*, p. 95.

13. Rolf Engelsing, "Die Perioden der Lesegeschichte in der Neuzeit," p. 972; Goethe quoted on p. 985.
14. Stephen F. Mason, *A History of the Sciences*, pp. 580–81.
15. Von Humboldt, *Ansichten*, p. xv.
16. Quoted by Theodor Heuss, *Justus von Liebig*, p. 77.
17. Ludwig Büchner, *Force and Matter*, p. vii.
18. Engelsing, *Analphabetentum*, pp. 119–20.
19. Hans A. Münster, *Geschichte der deutschen Presse in ihrer Grundzügen dargestellt*, p. 103.
20. A. H. T. Pfannkuche, *Was liest der deutsche Arbeiter?* p. 10.
21. Engelsing, *Analphabetentum*, p. 136.
22. See chapter 7.
23. Münster, *Geschichte*, pp. 95, 138, quote on p. 97.
24. On Reclam see the centennial volume, *100 Jahre Reclams Universal Bibliothek*.
25. Engelsing, *Analphabetentum*, p. 127.
26. The exact circulation of *Gartenlaube* is a matter of dispute. One estimate is as high as 460,000 in 1873; see Heinrich Wuttke, *Die deutschen Zeitschriften und die Entstehung der öffentlichen Meinung*, p. 76. Eva-Annemarie Kirchstein puts the high point at 382,000 (in 1875); see her *Die Familienzeitschrift*, pp. 88–89. My estimates of the total readership come from Engelsing, *Analphabetentum*, pp. 119–20.
27. Quoted by Wilmont Haake, *Feuilletonkunde*, 1:131.
28. Quoted by Wilmont Haake, *Handbuch des Feuilletons*, 1:140–41.
29. Quoted by Kirchstein, *Die Familienzeitschrift*, p. 92.
30. Quoted by Magdelene Zimmermann, *Die Gartenlaube als Dokument ihrer Zeit*, p. 12.
31. Mason, *History*, pp. 580–81.
32. Hermann Misteli, *Carl Vogt*, pp. 156–203.
33. On this theme see Hermann Lübbe, *Politische Philosophie in Deutschland*, especially pp. 130–40; Dieter Wittich, *Vogt, Moleschott, Büchner*, introduction; and Werner Bröker, *Politische Motive naturwissenschaftlicher Argumentation gegen Religion und Kirche im 19. Jahrhundert*, pp. 246–56.
34. Lübbe, *Politische Philosophie*, p. 130; and Wittich, *Vogt*, p. liv.
35. William M. Montgomery, "Germany," p. 85.
36. Wittich, *Vogt*, p. xliii. See also Emmanuel Radl, *Geschichte der biologischen Theorien*, 2:162; and Frederick Gregory, *Scientific Materialism in Nineteenth Century Germany*, pp. 96–97.
37. Kirchstein, *Die Familienzeitschrift*, p. 94.
38. E. A. Rossmässler, *Mein Leben und Streben*, pp. 131–35.
39. Quoted in Gregory, *Scientific Materialism*, p. 8.
40. On Rossmässler see Karl Friedel and Reimar Gilsenbach, *Das Rossmässler Büchlein*.
41. Quoted in Gregory, *Scientific Materialism*, p. 105.
42. Ludwig Feuerbach, "Die Naturwissenschaft und die Revolution," pp. 350–51.
43. Ibid., pp. 366–67.
44. See Mason, *History*, pp. 349–62; also Alexander Gode-von Aesch, *Natural Science in German Romanticism*.
45. Radl, *Geschichte*, 2:158 ff. See also Ernst Krause, *Charles Darwin und sein*

Verhältnis zu Deutschland; Pierce C. Mullen, *The Preconditions and Reception of Darwinian Biology in Germany, 1800–1870;* and Gregory, *Scientific Materialism,* pp. 174–88.

46. Francis Darwin, ed., *The Life and Letters of Charles Darwin,* 2:71.

47. Heinrich Bronn, "Schlusswort des Übersetzers," appendix to German translation of Darwin's *The Origin (Über die Entstehung der Arten),* pp. 503–4.

48. Darwin, ed., *Life and Letters,* 2:139, 232–33.

49. Montgomery, "Germany," p. 82.

50. Ibid., pp. 83–89.

51. Darwin, ed., *Life and Letters,* 2:270.

52. Ibid., 2:243, 401.

53. Ernst Haeckel, *Gemeinverständliche Vorträge und Abhandlungen aus dem Gebiete der Entwicklungslehre,* 1:4–5, 30.

54. Friedrich Ratzel, *Sein und Werden der organischen Welt,* p. v.

55. Krause, *Charles Darwin,* p. 149.

56. "Darwin und Darwinismus," *Illustrierte Zeitung* 50 (1868): 323–26.

57. Georg Buchmann, *Geflügelte Worte* (1871 ed.), p. 84.

58. Friedrich Luft, ed., *Facsimile Querschnitt durch die Berliner Illustrierte Zeitung,* pp. 47–49. Readers thought that only encyclopedias and the Bible were more influential than *The Origin.* After Darwin's *The Origin,* the most influential books were said to be Marx's *Kapital,* August Bebel's *Die Frau und der Sozialismus,* Bismarck's *Gedanken und Erinnerungen,* and Bertha von Suttner's *Die Waffen nieder.*

59. Charles Darwin, *The Origin of Species,* p. 447.

60. Ernst Haeckel, *Natürliche Schöpfungsgeschichte,* foreword.

61. Ernst Haeckel, *The History of Creation,* l:xvi, 4. A better translation of the title would be the natural history of creation.

62. Erik Nordenskiöld, *The History of Biology,* p. 515.

63. Ibid., p. 519. See also Ernst Cassirer, *The Problem of Knowledge,* p. 163; and Niles R. Holt, "Ernst Haeckel's Monistic Religion," pp. 265–80.

64. Nowhere in his popular works does Haeckel give a unified summary of his Darwinian monism. My account here is based on his *The History of Creation* and *The Riddle of the Universe at the Close of the Nineteenth Century.* The standard English translation is in error; it should be plural, *Riddles.* The reference is to Emil Du Bois-Reymond's famous riddles which he believed science could never solve. Haeckel, of course, thought otherwise. Other statements of Haeckel's monism can be found in his *Freedom in Science and Teaching* and *Monism as Connecting Religion and Science.*

65. Haeckel, *The History of Creation,* 2:380–401.

66. Darwin, ed., *Life and Letters,* 2:251, 286.

67. Haeckel, *The History of Creation,* 1:204. Italics in original.

68. Ibid., 1:184.

69. Darwin, *The Origin,* p. 450.

70. Haeckel, *The History of Creation,* 1:230–31.

71. Haeckel, *The Riddle,* pp. 177, 225.

72. Ludwig Büchner, *Sechs Vorlesungen,* pp. 164–67.

73. Wilhelm Preyer, *Der Kampf um das Dasein,* pp. 7–11.

74. Edward Aveling, *Die Darwin'sche Theorie,* pp. 44–45.

75. Büchner, *Sechs Vorlesungen*, p. 42.
76. "Darwinismus," in Supplement to 11th ed. (1872) of *Brockhaus Konversations-Lexikon*, 1:476.
77. Darwin, *The Origin*, p. 88.
78. Büchner, *Sechs Vorlesungen*, p. 42.
79. Darwin, *The Origin*, p. 75.
80. Aveling, *Die Darwin'sche Theorie*, pp. 18–19.
81. Jakob Moleschott, *Der Kreislauf des Lebens*, pp. 159–60.
82. *Brockhaus Konversations-Lexikon*, 1:476.
83. Alfred Brehm, *Illustriertes Tierleben*, l:ix.
84. Aveling, *Die Darwin'sche Theorie*, p. 3.
85. Moritz Wagner, "Darwinistische Streitfragen," pp. 45–53.
86. Carl Vogt, "Einige Darwinistische Ketzereien," pp. 481–91.
87. Otto Zacharias, "Charles R. Darwin," pp. 356–57.
88. Büchner, *Sechs Vorlesungen*, pp. 96, 98, 122, 153–64.
89. Gregory, *Scientific Materialism*, p. 120.
90. Carus Sterne, "Menschliche Erbschaften aus dem Tierreiche," pp. 266–68.
91. Otto Zacharias, "Die Popularisierung der Naturwissenschaft," p. 380.
92. Brehm, *Illustriertes Tierleben*, 2:132–33.
93. On the question of Darwin's popularity see the interesting articles in *Ausland*, "Was Macht Darwin Populär?" and Georg Seidlitz, "Erfolge des Darwinismus."

CHAPTER 3

1. Wilhelm Bölsche, "Humboldt frei! Gedanken zur volkstümlichen Wissenschaft," *Freie Bühne* 1 (1890):1017.
2. "Die Verbreitung der naturwissenschaftlichen Literatur," pp. 162–64. This is not the old *Kosmos* of the 1870s but a new popular magazine put out by the Society of the Friends of Nature in Stuttgart.
3. Albert Weidner, "Wilhelm Bölsche als Sechziger," unlabeled newspaper clipping, Bölsche Archive, Munich.
4. It is notoriously difficult to obtain hard circulation figures. The estimates presented here are based on information from the *Kosmos Verlag* in Stuttgart as well as the relevant volumes of the *Deutsches Bücherverzeichnis*. At the turn of the century in Germany, the first edition (*Auflage*) of a nonfiction book might run from one thousand to as many as ten thousand copies (in a few rare cases, more).
5. Rudolf Magnus, *Wilhelm Bölsche*, pp. 1–18.
6. Wilhelm Bölsche, " 'Das Liebesleben in der Natur,' aus den Werdetagen meines Buches," *Münchener Neueste Nachrichten*, 2 Jan. 1931, pp. 3–4.
7. Wilhelm Bölsche, "Die Überschwemmung im Zoologischen Garten zu Köln," *Die Gefiederte Welt* 5 (1876):126.
8. See Alfred Kelly, "Between Poetry and Science," pp. 14–16.
9. Ibid., pp. 16–18, 30–36.
10. Ibid., pp. 18–29.
11. Ibid., pp. 23–25.
12. Conversation with Bölsche's son, Karl Bölsche, 23 June 1973.

13. See note 6.
14. Quoted in Eugen Diederichs, *Selbstzeugnisse und Briefe von Zeitgenossen*, p. 93.
15. Bruno Wille, ed., *Darwins Weltanschauung*, p. xii.
16. Wilhelm Bölsche, *Hinter der Weltstadt*, p. 32.
17. Ibid., pp. 259–347.
18. Panpsychism has had something of a popular revival lately; see Peter Tomkins and Christopher Bird, *The Secret Life of Plants* (New York, 1973), which contains a section on Fechner, pp. 135–40.
19. Wilhelm Bölsche, *Die Abstammung des Menschen*, pp. 83–91.
20. Wilhelm Bölsche, *Das Liebesleben in der Natur*, 1:116–25.
21. Ibid., 2:113–40.
22. Ibid., 1:90.
23. Ibid., 1:10–15, 39, 63–75, 145–79.
24. Ibid., 2:164–65.
25. Wilhelm Bölsche, *Stirb und Werde*, pp. 135–53.
26. See Wilhelm Bölsche, "Die Humanität im Kampf mit dem Fortschritt," pp. 125–37. The article is a review of Alfred Ploetz's book *Die Tüchtigkeit unserer Rasse und der Schutz der Schwachen*.
27. See the excellent discussion of this problem in Gertrude Himmelfarb, *Darwin and the Darwinian Revolution*, chap. 16. See also Ernst Cassirer, *The Problem of Knowledge*, pp. 160–75.
28. Ludwig Büchner, *Kraft und Stoff*, p. 150.
29. Charles Darwin, *The Origin of Species*, p. 450.
30. Darwin to Asa Gray, 26 Nov. 1860, in Francis Darwin, ed., *The Life and Letters of Charles Darwin*, 2:146.
31. In his book *The Triumph of the Darwinian Method*, Michael T. Ghiselin argues forcefully that Darwin was actually a sophisticated philosopher and that he was very clearly opposed to teleology and anthropomorphism (see in particular pp. 131–59). Perhaps so. But it is fair to wonder, then, why there has been so much confusion among even very sophisticated thinkers.
32. Novalis, *Schriften*, 2:331.
33. Bölsche, *Liebesleben*, 2:v.
34. Wilhelm Bölsche, *Aus der Schneegrube*, p. 51.
35. Wilhelm Bölsche, "Über den Wert der Mystik für unsere Zeit," pp. xxii–xxv.
36. For a discussion of this problem see Alexander Gode-von Aesch, *Natural Science in German Romanticism*, pp. 89 ff.
37. Bölsche, "Über den Wert," p. xxxiv.
38. Bölsche, *Liebesleben*, 3:366, 1:359.
39. Bölsche, *Aus der Schneegrube*, p. 54.
40. Ibid., pp. 29–57; and also, Wilhelm Bölsche, *Von Sonnen und Sonnenstäubchen*, pp. 260–74.
41. Wilhelm Bölsche, *Was ist die Natur?* p. 131.
42. Wilhelm Bölsche, *Vom Bazillus zum Affenmenschen*, pp. 41–87.
43. Wilhelm Bölsche, *Der Mensch der Zukunft*, p. 41.
44. Wilhelm Bölsche, "Zukunft der Menschheit," pp. 27–40.
45. Bölsche, *Liebesleben*, 3:373.
46. Bölsche, *Stirb und Werde*, pp. 154–60; also *Die Abstammung der Kunst*, pp.

1–28. Bölsche's ideas on the artistry of nature clearly owe a great deal to Ernst Haeckel, who climaxed his career as an artist of nature with his *Kunst Formen der Natur* of 1899. At one time Haeckel even considered becoming an artist rather than a biologist. See Daniel Gasman, *The Scientific Origins of National Socialism*, pp. 71–76.

47. Bölsche, *Von Sonnen*, p. 242.
48. Bölsche, *Hinter der Weltstadt*, p. 187.
49. Bölsche, *Von Sonnen*, pp. 239–43.
50. Novalis, *Schriften*, 3:272.
51. Bölsche, *Liebesleben*, 2:263–92.
52. Ibid., 3:34.
53. Bölsche, *Was ist die Natur?* p. 132.
54. See Wilhelm Bölsche's essay *Goethe im 20. Jahrhundert*, especially pp. 43, 46.
55. Wilhelm Bölsche, *Weltblick*, p. 25.
56. Quoted in Gode-von Aesch, *Natural Science*, p. 112.
57. Bölsche, *Weltblick*, pp. 108–28.
58. Wilhelm Bölsche, *Die Eroberung des Menschen*, p. 127.
59. Bölsche, *Aus der Schneegrube*, pp. 327–46.
60. Bölsche, *Weltblick*, pp. 184–85.
61. Wilhelm Bölsche, "Zur Erinnerung an Carus Sterne," introduction to 6th edition (Berlin, 1904) of Carus Sterne, *Werden und Vergehen*, p. viii.
62. Wilhelm Bölsche, *Lichtglaube*, pp. 290–301.
63. Bölsche, *Weltblick*, p. 185.
64. Quoted in Walter Wetzels, "Versuch einer Beschreibung populärwissenschaftlicher Prosa in den Naturwissenschaften," p. 79.
65. On the *Plauderei*, see Wilmont Haake, *Handbuch des Feuilletons*, 2:241.
66. Wilhelm Bölsche, "Wie das erste Kosmosbändchen entstand," *Kosmos* 28 (1931): 24.
67. Wilhelm Bölsche, *Love-Life in Nature*, 1:3.
68. An illuminating description of Bölsche's style can be found in Dolf Sternberger, *Panorama*, pp. 144–50.
69. Bölsche, *Liebesleben*, 1:22–23.

CHAPTER 4

1. J. Norrenberg, *Geschichte des naturwissenschaftlichen Unterrichts an den höheren Schulen Deutschlands*, pp. 44, 66.
2. Ernst Haeckel, "Über die heutige Entwickelungslehre im Verhältnisse zur Gesammtwissenschaft," pp. 14–22.
3. Rudolf Virchow, "Die Freiheit der Wissenschaft im modernen Staat," pp. 65–77. For a short discussion of the Haeckel-Virchow debate see John R. Baker, "The Controversy on Freedom in Science in the Nineteenth Century."
4. Virchow, "Freiheit," pp. 68–69.
5. Ernst Haeckel, *Freedom in Science and Teaching*, pp. 38, 88–98; quotation on p. 90.
6. Quoted in Walther May, *Ernst Haeckel*, p. 109.
7. Carl Vogt, "Pope and Anti-Pope," pp. 324–25.

8. Ludwig Büchner, *Nature et science*, pp. 52–54.
9. Jakob Moleschott, *Der Kreislauf des Lebens*, p. 121.
10. May, *Ernst Haeckel*, p. 100.
11. See, for example, the articles in the journal *Paedagogium*, A. W. Grube's "Der Darwinismus und seine Consequenzen," and Ad. Jos. Pick's "Die Darwinsche Weltanschauung und die Schule."
12. Heinrich von Treitschke, "Der Socialismus und der Meuchelmord," *Preussische Jahrbücher* 44 (1879):638.
13. Ernst Haeckel, "Freie Wissenschaft und freie Lehre," *Gemeinverständliche Vorträge*, 2:204–5.
14. See *Kosmos* 4 (1878–79):234, 357–58.
15. This account of the details of the Müller affair follows the exhaustive study by Philipp Depdolla, "Hermann Müller-Lippstadt (1829–1883) und die Entwicklung des biologischen Unterrichts." See also the unpublished article by Fritz Bolle, "Der Fall Müller-Lippstadt und der deutsche Monistenbund"; and Emil Strauss, *Die Hypothese in der Schule und der naturwissenschaftliche Unterricht in der Realschule zu Lippstadt*.
16. Quoted by Depdolla, "Hermann Müller-Lippstadt," p. 286.
17. Wilhelm Breitenbach, "Hermann Müller-Lippstadt und der biologische Unterricht," pp. 43–48.
18. E. Dennert, "Die Entwicklungslehre als Lehrgegenstand der höheren Schulen," pp. 333–34.
19. Quoted by Depdolla, "Hermann Müller-Lippstadt," p. 292.
20. *Stenographische Berichte über die Verhandlungen der durch die Allerhöchste Verordnung vom 3. Nov. 1878 einberufenen beiden Häuser des Landtages, Haus der Abgeordneten*, 1:606.
21. Ibid.
22. Ibid., pp. 682–83.
23. Ibid., pp. 682–85, 732–33.
24. Depdolla, "Hermann Müller-Lippstadt," pp. 311–12.
25. *Zentralblatt für die gesammte Unterrichts-Verwaltung in Preussen, 1882*, pp. 244, 258–59.
26. Depdolla, "Hermann Müller-Lippstadt," p. 318.
27. Karl Adolf Schmid, *Geschichte der Erziehung vom Anfang an bis auf unsere Zeit*, 5, no. 1:496–508, and 5, no. 2:79–103.
28. *Zentralblatt, 1882*, pp. 256–62.
29. See, for example, the 1901 plan, *Lehrpläne und Lehraufgaben für die höheren Schulen in Preussen*, pp. 61–69.
30. Schmid, *Geschichte*, 5, no. 1:428.
31. K. A. Schönke, *Naturgeschichte*, pp. 4–5.
32. Johannes Leunis, *Analytischer Leitfaden für den ersten wissenschaftlichen Unterricht in der Naturgeschichte*, p. iii.
33. Ibid., pp. vi–x.
34. Carl Baenitz, *Lehrbuch der Botanik in populärer Darstellung*, p. 260.
35. Samuel Schelling, *Grundriss der Naturgeschichte des Thier-Pflanzen-und-Mineralreichs*, 20th ed., Part III, pp. 75–86.
36. Oscar Schmidt, *Thierkunde*, p. 73.
37. Otto Schmeil, *Der Mensch*, p. 1.
38. Carl Baenitz, *Lehrbuch der Zoologie in populärer Darstellung*, p. 275.

39. Schönke, *Naturgeschichte*, p. 13.
40. Schelling, *Grundriss*, 14th ed., p. 14.
41. Schelling, *Grundriss*, 22d ed., p. 37.
42. Johannes Leunis, *Synopsis der drei Naturreiche*, Part I, pp. 82–84.
43. H. Wettstein, *Leitfaden für den Unterricht in der Naturkunde an Sekundär-und Bezirksschulen, sowie unteren Gymnasien*, Part I, p. 233.
44. Schmidt, *Thierkunde*, p. 115.
45. *Stenographische Berichte über die Verhandlungen der durch die Allerhöchste Verordnung vom 2. November 1882 einberufenen beiden Häuser des Landtags, Haus der Abgeordneten*, 2:848–49, 917–20.
46. Ibid., p. 849.
47. Ibid., pp. 918, 920.
48. Ibid.
49. Ibid., pp. 921–25.
50. Ibid., pp. 925–28.
51. Arnold Dodel, *Moses or Darwin?* pp. 134–76.
52. Otto Schmeil, *Über die Reformbestrebungen auf dem Gebiete des naturgeschichtlichen Unterrichts*, p. 67.
53. See, for example, the remarks from *Natur und Glaube*, cited by Hermann Josef Dörpinghaus, *Darwins Theorie und der deutsche Vulgärmaterialismus im Urteil deutscher katholischer Zeitschriften zwischen 1854 und 1914*, pp. 167–68.
54. J. Reinke, "Was heisst Biologie?" pp. 452–53; also J. Reinke, *Haeckels Monismus und seine Freunde*, pp. 9–15.
55. Dennert, "Die Entwicklungslehre," pp. 332–43.
56. Friedrich Paulsen was one of many who exposed the futility of excluding Darwinism from the classroom. See his "Die Biologie im Unterricht der höheren Schulen," p. 26; also, Bastian Schmid, "Dringen durch die modernen Naturwissenschaften materialistische Ideen in die Schulen?" p. 4; and Walter Schoenichen, *Die Abstammungslehre im Unterrichte der Schule*, p. 12.
57. Wilhelm Bölsche, "Naturwissenschaftlicher Unterricht in den Schulen," *Die Freie Bühne* 4 (1893):38. This article was originally a speech before the Ethical Culture Society.
58. Ibid., p. 32.
59. Wilhelm Bölsche, "Der Jugendunterricht und die Tatsachen der Embryologie," *Die Freie Bühne* 2 (1891):257–61, 310–14.
60. Bölsche, "Naturwissenschaftlicher Unterricht," p. 34.
61. *Verhandlungen über Fragen des höheren Unterrichts*, p. 782.
62. Ibid., pp. 27, 28.
63. "Verhandlungen über den biologischen Unterricht an höheren Schulen," pp. 145–52.
64. Karl Kraepelin, *Leitfaden für den biologischen Unterricht in den oberen Klassen der höheren Schulen*, p. iv.
65. Karl Kraepelin, *Einführung in die Biologie zum Gebrauch an höheren Schulen und zum selbst Unterricht*, pp. 276 ff.
66. Depdolla, "Hermann Müller-Lippstadt," p. 238.

CHAPTER 5

1. Ernst Haeckel, *The Riddle of the Universe*, p. 308.
2. Ernst Haeckel, "Über die Entwicklungstheorie Darwins," *Gemeinverständliche Vorträge und Abhandlungen aus dem Gebiete der Entwicklungslehre*, 1:4.
3. David Friedrich Strauss, *The Old Faith and the New*, 1:107.
4. Quoted by Emmanuel Radl, *Geschichte der biologischen Theorien*, 2:162.
5. John Dewey, *The Influence of Darwin on Philosophy*, p. 12.
6. Quoted by Gertrude Himmelfarb, *Darwin and the Darwinian Revolution*, p. 397.
7. Cited by Roy Pascal, *From Naturalism to Expressionism*, p. 167.
8. Charles Darwin, *The Origin of Species*, p. 443.
9. Ibid., p. 450.
10. See Himmelfarb, *Darwin*, pp. 380–87; and Neal C. Gillespie, *Charles Darwin and the Problem of Creation*, esp. pp. 134–45.
11. Edward Aveling, "Charles Darwin und Karl Marx," pp. 754–55.
12. *Brockhaus Konversations-Lexikon*, 11th ed. Supplement, 1:479.
13. Friedrich Rolle, *Ch's Darwin's Lehre von der Entstehung der Arten im Pflanzen- und Thierreich in ihrer Anwendung auf die Schöpfungslehre*, p. 274.
14. Alfred Brehm, *Illustriertes Tierleben*, p. xxxii.
15. Carl Vogt, *Lectures on Man*, pp. 461–62.
16. Himmelfarb, *Darwin*, pp. 397–411.
17. Strauss, *The Old Faith*, 2:119.
18. Max Nordau, *The Conventional Lies of Our Civilization*, pp. 362, 364; see also pp. 26, 30, 57.
19. Friedrich Ratzel, *Sein und Werden der organischen Welt*, pp. 1–6, 479–80.
20. Wilhelm Preyer, *Der Kampf um das Dasein*, pp. 9, 30–31.
21. See Oswald Köhler, *Weltschöpfung und Weltuntergang*, esp. pp. 292, 385–86, 387–94; and Rudolf Bommeli, *Die Geschichte der Erde*, pp. 616–44.
22. Ludwig Büchner, *Force and Matter*, pp. 167, 183–84. Italics in original.
23. Ludwig Büchner, *Sechs Vorlesungen*, pp. 194–96.
24. Ludwig Büchner, *Man in the Past, Present and Future*, p. 220. See also pp. 211–17.
25. Arnold Dodel, *Moses or Darwin?* quotation on p. 60; see also pp. 74–97.
26. Ibid., pp. 98–133 and 323–26.
27. Haeckel, *The Riddle*, p. 201.
28. Ibid., pp. 289–91.
29. Ibid., p. 337.
30. Otto Zacharias, "Charles R. Darwin," p. 357.
31. Carus Sterne, *Werden und Vergehen*, 1:vii–xii and 2:548–60.
32. Gottfried Riehm, "Darwinismus und Christentum," pp. 129–42.
33. See, for example, C. Bock, "Die Anmassung des sogenannten 'natürlichen Verstandes' oder des 'gesunden Menschenverstandes,'" *Die Gartenlaube* 21 (1873):372–74.
34. Rudolf Sendel, "Zur Aussöhnung mit dem Darwinismus," pp. 361–77.
35. Wilhelm Bölsche, *Die Abstammung des Menschen*, p. 8.
36. Wilhelm Bölsche, *Auf dem Menschenstern*, p. viii.
37. Ibid., p. 129.
38. Wilhelm Bölsche, et al., *Im Kampf um die Weltanschauung*, p. 38.

39. Novalis, *Hymns to the Night and Other Selected Writings*, p. 71.
40. Wilhelm Bölsche, *Die Schöpfungstage*, p. 5.
41. Wilhelm Bölsche, *Das Liebesleben in der Natur*, 1:20.
42. Ibid., 1:128–29.
43. Bölsche, *Die Schöpfungstage*, p. 5.
44. Wilhelm Bölsche, *Naturgeheimnis*, p. 253.
45. Bölsche, *Liebesleben*, 1:33.
46. Ibid., p. 30.
47. Wilhelm Bölsche, *Hinter der Weltstadt*, p. 273.
48. Wilhelm Bölsche, *Aus der Schneegrube*, p. 19.
49. Bölsche, *Liebesleben*, 1:37.
50. See, for example, Wilhelm Bölsche, *Stirb und Werde*, pp. 148–53.
51. Wilhelm Bölsche, *Goethe im 20. Jahrhundert*, p. 7.
52. Bölsche, *Liebesleben*, 2:7.
53. Wilhelm Bölsche, "Über den Wert der Mystik für unsere Zeit," p. xvi.
54. Ibid., pp. i–v.
55. Ibid., p. xl.
56. Wilhelm Bölsche, "Sonne und Seele," *Die Woche* 11 (1909):826.
57. Wilhelm Bölsche, *Die Neuen Gebote*, no page.
58. Wilhelm Bölsche, introduction to Rudolf Penzig, *Ohne Kirche*, pp. ix–xviii.
59. Dolf Sternberger, *Panorama*, pp. 143–44.
60. Norbert Falk, "Bölsche am Vortragspult," unlabeled Berlin newspaper, 1910.
61. *Die Freigeistige Bewegung*, p. 79. The other essential source of the free-thought movement is Max Henning's *Handbuch der freigeistigen Bewegung Deutschlands, Österreichs und der Schweiz*.
62. Wilhelm Bölsche, "Vom ethischen Konzil zu Berlin," p. 1194.
63. Ibid., p. 1197.
64. Ibid., p. 1194.
65. Hermann Lübbe, *Politische Philosophie in Deutschland*, esp. pp. 146–72.
66. Bölsche, "Vom ethischen Konzil," p. 1201.
67. Ernst Haeckel, *Die Welträtsel*, pp. 462–63.
68. Such, at least, is the tone of a letter from Haeckel to Bölsche, 11 Nov. 1905; see Georg Uschmann, *Ernst Haeckel*, p. 258.
69. J. Reinke, *Haeckels Monismus und seine Freunde*, pp. 9–15.
70. Johannes Hemleben, *Ernst Haeckel in Selbstzeugnissen und Bilddokumenten*, pp. 132–33.
71. Oron J. Hale, *The Great Illusion, 1900–1914*, pp. 122–23.
72. Hermann Josef Dörpinghaus, *Darwins Theorie und der deutsche Vulgär-materialismus im Urteil deutscher katholischer Zeitschriften zwischen 1854 und 1914*, pp. 44–45.
73. Ibid., pp. 31–37.
74. *Allgemeine Zeitung*, Supplement to no. 105 (1875):1645.
75. "An unsere Leser," *Daheim* 1 (1866):1.
76. Victor von Strauss, "Die Darwinsche Hypothese," pp. 630–32.
77. Frederick Gregory, *Scientific Materialism in Nineteenth Century Germany*, pp. 41–42.
78. J. Vetter, *Darwinismus oder Christentum*, pp. 25, 28.
79. Dörpinghaus, *Darwins Theorie*, esp. p. 176.

80. Ludwig Plate, ed., *Ultramontane Weltanschauung und moderne Lebenskunde, Orthodoxie und Monismus,* passim.
81. Albert Wigand, *Der Darwinismus,* pp. 93–110.
82. Ibid., p. 102.
83. See, for example, G. P. Weygoldt, *Darwinismus, Religion, Sittlichkeit,* pp. 135–53; Joseph Kuhl, *Die Descendenzlehre und der Neue Glaube,* pp. 202–29; Georg Friedrich Hertling, *Der Darwinismus, eine geistige Epidemie,* pp. 43–72; and August Trümpelmann, "Seelenverwandtschaft der Monisten und Socialisten."
84. Kuhl, *Die Descendenzlehre,* p. 225.
85. Wigand, *Der Darwinismus,* pp. 115–22.
86. E. Dennert, *At the Deathbed of Darwinism,* p. 32.

CHAPTER 6

1. There is a German reference to "Social Darwinism" as early as 1906, but the term entered the historian's vocabulary largely through Richard Hofstadter's *Social Darwinism in American Thought.* The major studies of German Social Darwinism are Hedwig Conrad-Martius, *Utopien der Menschenzüchtung;* Hans-Günter Zmarzlik, "Social Darwinism in Germany, Seen as a Historical Problem"; Daniel Gasman, *The Scientific Origins of National Socialism;* Hans-Ulrich Wehler, "Sozialdarwinismus im expandierenden Industriestaat"; Fritz Bolle, "Darwinismus und Zeitgeist"; Georg Lukacs, *Die Zerstörung der Vernunft;* and Loren R. Graham, "Science and Values."
2. Examples of such treatment are Karl Bracher, *The German Dictatorship,* pp. 13–16; Lukacs, *Die Zerstörung,* esp. pp. 537–50; Wehler, "Sozialdarwinismus"; and above all, Gasman, *Scientific Origins.*
3. Quoted by Eda Sagarra, *Tradition and Revolution,* p. 262.
4. Heinrich von Treitschke, *Politics,* 1:28.
5. Bolle, "Darwinismus und Zeitgeist," p. 173.
6. Alfred Kruck, *Geschichte des Alldeutschen Verbandes, 1890–1939,* p. 223.
7. See, for example, Wallace Notestein and Elmer Stoll, *Conquest and Kultur.*
8. See General Friedrich von Bernhardi, *Germany and the Next War,* esp. pp. 18–19.
9. Catholic periodicals, for example, were usually critical of Social Darwinism when they did rarely mention it. Hermann Josef Dörpinghaus, *Darwins Theorie und der deutsche Vulgärmaterialismus im Urteil deutscher katholischer Zeitschriften zwischen 1854 und 1914,* p. 215.
10. Especially later in his career, Gumplowicz backed off from a crude Social Darwinism; see his article from 1895, "Darwinismus und Soziologie," pp. 30–31.
11. Friedrich Hellwald, *Culturgeschichte in ihrer natürlichen Entwicklung bis zur Gegenwart,* 2:739–42.
12. Schäffle summed up his view of the social uses of Darwinism in an essay entitled "Darwinismus und Socialwissenschaft."
13. Ludwig Gumplowicz, *Outlines of Sociology,* pp. 102–6; and "Darwinismus und Soziologie."

14. Max Nordau, *The Conventional Lies of Our Civilization*, esp. pp. 26, 119, 364.
15. On racism see George L. Mosse, *Toward the Final Solution*, esp. pp. 73–82.
16. Otto Ammon, *Die natürliche Auslese beim Menschen.*
17. Otto Ammon, *Die Gesellschaftsordnung und ihre natürlichen Grundlagen;* the best summary of his ideas is *Der Darwinismus gegen die Sozialdemokratie.*
18. Alfred Ploetz, *Die Tüchtigkeit unserer Rasse und der Schutz der Schwachen,* pp. 144–47.
19. Bolle, "Darwinismus und Zeitgeist," pp. 168–69.
20. Wilhelm Schallmeyer, *Vererbung und Auslese im Lebenslauf der Völker,* esp. pp. 326–44.
21. Heinrich Ernst Ziegler, *Einleitung zu dem Sammelwerke Natur und Staat,* pp. 1–10.
22. Ibid., pp. 10–21.
23. For a good discussion of Woltmann, see George L. Mosse, *The Crisis of German Ideology,* pp. 99–103.
24. Mosse, *Toward the Final Solution,* pp. 80–81.
25. Julius Langbehn, *Rembrandt als Erzieher,* pp. 136–37.
26. Frederick Gregory, *Scientific Materialism in Nineteenth Century Germany,* p. 260.
27. Houston Stewart Chamberlain, *Foundations of the Nineteenth Century,* 1:17–27, 261, 277, 284, and 2:216–17. Chamberlain was an Englishman who adopted Germany as his homeland.
28. Daniel Frymann, (Heinrich Class), *Wenn ich der Kaiser wär,* esp. pp. 131–33.
29. The only writer who might possibly be viewed as a bridge between popular *völkisch* thought and popular Darwinism is Friedrich Ratzel. His geography books, which were widely known at the turn of the century, romanticized the German landscape in a *völkisch* style. But these books had little connection to Ratzel's Darwinism or to national struggle. On Ratzel see Mosse, *The Crisis of German Ideology,* p. 18.
30. On this issue, see Walter Kaufmann, *Nietzsche,* pp. 270, 284.
31. See Gregory, *Scientific Materialism,* pp. 191–92.
32. Wilhelm Preyer, *Der Kampf um das Dasein,* pp. 30–38.
33. Carus Sterne, *Werden und Vergehen,* 2:552.
34. Arnold Dodel, *Moses or Darwin?* pp. 266, 289–302.
35. Ludwig Büchner, *Man in the Past, Present and Future,* pp. 175–76.
36. Ibid., pp. 186–92. See also Büchner's *Darwinismus und Sozialismus.*
37. Büchner, *Man,* p. 230.
38. Ibid., pp. 178–79; and Büchner, *Darwinismus und Sozialismus,* pp. 22–47.
39. Büchner, *Man,* pp. 179–80.
40. Gasman, *Scientific Origins,* p. 22. For other views of Haeckel as a Social Darwinist see Wehler, "Sozialdarwinismus," p. 141; Günter Altner, *Weltanschauliche Hintergründe der Rassenlehre des Dritten Reiches,* pp. 20–27; and Dietrich Bronder, *Bevor Hitler kam,* pp. 291 ff.
41. Ernst Haeckel, *Freedom in Science and Teaching,* pp. 91–93.
42. Ibid., p. 94.
43. Ernst Haeckel, *The History of Creation,* 1:166, 178, 338.
44. Michael Ruse, *The Darwinian Revolution,* p. 264. Ruse sees a hint of Social Darwinism running through Darwin's works.

45. Haeckel, *The History of Creation*, 1:175–79.
46. Ernst Haeckel, *The Riddle of the Universe at the Close of the Nineteenth Century*, pp. 7–11.
47. Wilhelm Bölsche, *Ernst Haeckel*, p. 212.
48. The review is reprinted in Bölsche's *Hinter der Weltstadt*, p. 92.
49. Wilhelm Bölsche, "Die Humanität im Kampf mit dem Fortschritt," p. 135.
50. Wilhelm Bölsche, *Stirb und Werde*, p. 135.
51. Ibid., pp. 135–53.
52. Ibid., p. 148. The same points are made several other places in Bölsche's works. See, for example, *Das Liebesleben in der Natur*, 2:196–97; and *Der Mensch der Zukunft*, p. 75.
53. Ludwig Büchner, *Force and Matter*, p. 222.
54. August Bebel, *Woman and Socialism*, p. 249.
55. Edward Aveling, *Die Darwin'sche Theorie*, pp. 184–222.
56. Charles Darwin, *The Descent of Man and Selection in Relation to Sex*, 1:223.
57. Ibid., pp. 223, 229, 231. Darwin notes that Europeans differ more from Hindus than from Jews, even though Jews are supposedly different "stock."
58. Carl Vogt, *Lectures on Man*, Lecture 7, and pp. 461–62.
59. Ludwig Büchner, *Sechs Vorlesungen*, pp. 203–4.
60. Haeckel, *The History of Creation*, 2:415.
61. Ibid., 2:445.
62. Ludwig Büchner, *Fremdes und Eignes aus dem geistigen Leben der Gegenwart*, pp. 201–8.
63. Dodel, *Moses or Darwin?* p. 279.
64. Bernhard Langkavel, *Der Mensch und seine Rassen*, pp. 1–6, 92–96.
65. Bölsche, *Liebesleben*, 1:31; also his "Die Schule und die Sprache," *Sozialistische Monatshefte* 7 (1901):983.
66. See, for example, the foreword to Bölsche's *Von Wundern und Tieren*; and the afterword to his *Der Mensch der Zukunft*.
67. Bruno Wille, *Lehrbuch für den Jugendunterricht freier Gemeinden*, Part 1, p. 70.
68. Kruck, *Geschichte*, pp. 4, 181.
69. Bracher, *The German Dictatorship*, pp. 13, 14. For a similarly loose association of Social Darwinism and Nazism, see Hannsjoachim Koch, *Der Sozialdarwinismus*, pp. 154–57.
70. A. J. Ryder, *Twentieth Century Germany*, p. 283.
71. Altner, *Weltanschauliche Hintergründe*, pp. 20–21.
72. Quoted by Hermann Lübbe, *Politische Philosophie in Deutschland*, p. 162.
73. Niles R. Holt takes the more subtle position that monists "very indirectly" contributed to Nazism. In an article called "Monists and Nazis," Holt argues that the monists unintentionally abused the great trust put in them by the German middle classes. Most monists were indeed pacifist liberals, but by insisting "that science was the source of all value," they in effect undercut their own humanitarianism. It was never too clear what that much-touted enlightened scientific elite would bring in the way of actual social reform. Thus when the Nazis made a mockery of humanitarian social reform, the middle classes were left without any critical ethical defenses. Holt suggests that science popularizers should pay more attention to the

relation between science and ethics, rather than setting up science as an absolute standard. The last point is perhaps well taken, but again, the question arises: If people whose values are opposite those of the Nazis are somehow guilty, then who is not guilty? Nor is it clear how all of this relates to popular Darwinism. Holt does not even mention the most widely read monist, Bölsche.

74. Hermann Glaser, *The Cultural Roots of National Socialism*, p. 186.
75. Henry Picker, ed., *Hitlers Tischgespräche im Führerhauptquartier, 1941–1942*, pp. 84, 114.
76. Werner Maser, *Adolf Hitler*, p. 253. See also pp. 166, 190, 200, 228, 233, 279, where Bölsche's influence is repeatedly stressed.
77. Hermann Rauschning, *Gespräche mit Hitler*, p. 56.
78. Quoted by Mosse, *Toward the Final Solution*, p. 31.
79. Bölsche was, of course, still alive, living in retirement in a small Silesian town. He no longer published, and no new editions of his earlier works were appearing. His attitude toward the Nazis is not easy to establish. In 1934, he gave a speech in Breslau, praising the new order for bringing science to the people. Later he lapsed into silence, hinting in letters that it was no longer possible for him to publish. The honors he was paid on his seventy-fifth birthday were strictly local and minor, such as the naming of a fish pond after him.
80. Quoted by Dietrich Strothmann, *Nationalsozialistische Literaturpolitik*, p. 144.
81. See, for example, the *Reichsliste für kleinere städtische Büchereien* (Leipzig, 1936); the second edition of the same list in 1939 did mention Alfred Brehm's *Tierleben*. Also lacking popular Darwinian literature were *Unsere Bücherei: Ein Verzeichnis ausgewählter Bücher schöner und belehrender Literatur aller Gebiete* (Munich, 1938) and the *Reichsliste für Dorfsbüchereien* (Leipzig, n.d.).

CHAPTER 7

1. Quoted by Gertrude Himmelfarb, *Darwin and the Darwinian Revolution*, p. 349.
2. It was long believed that Marx had tried to dedicate either the second volume or the English translation of *Kapital* to Darwin and that Darwin had refused because he did not want to be publicly associated with atheism. It has recently been shown, however, that the Darwin letter on which this inference was based was actually not to Marx but to Edward Aveling, who wanted to dedicate his *The Student's Darwin* to Darwin. See Lewis S. Feuer, "The Case of the 'Darwin-Marx' Letter."
3. Friedrich Engels, *Herrn Eugen Dührings Umwälzung der Wissenschaft*, p. 337.
4. George Lichtheim, *Marxism*, p. 244. On the relationship between Marxism and Darwinism see also Dieter Groh, "Marx, Engels und Darwin"; Erhard Lucas, "Marx' und Engels' Auseinandersetzung mit Darwin"; and Hans-Josef Steinberg, *Sozialismus und deutsche Sozialdemokratie*, pp. 43–60.
5. Karl Kautsky, *Erinnerungen und Erörterungen*, pp. 172, 212–16.
6. Karl Kautsky, "Darwinismus und Marxismus," p. 710.

7. My account of Kautsky's wavering follows that of Steinberg in his *Sozialismus*, pp. 48–53.

8. Otto Ammon, *Der Darwinismus gegen die Sozialdemokratie*, p. 78. See also Heinrich Ziegler, *Die Naturwissenschaft und die Socialdemokratische Theorie*. The question also arose at the 1878 meeting of the Association of German Scientists and Physicians where Oskar Schmidt argued that socialism was unscientific; see his address in *Tageblatt der 51. Versammlung Deutscher Naturforscher und Aerzte in Cassel 1878* (Cassel, 1878), pp. 178–85.

9. On this issue, see Steinberg, *Sozialismus*, pp. 56–60.

10. See Ludwig Woltmann, *Die Darwinsche Theorie und der Sozialismus*, a book that contains selections from the writings of several socialists and Darwinists; Woltmann summarized his ideas in *Die Neue Zeit* 17, no. 1 (1898–99): 246–49. See also Eduard Bernstein, "Ein Schüler Darwin's als Vertheidiger des Sozialismus," and Heinrich Cunow, "Darwinismus contra Sozialismus," an article that gives a good summary of the issues.

11. Woltmann, *Die Darwinsche Theorie*, p. 357.

12. Anton Pannekoek, *Marxismus und Darwinismus*, pp. 19–26.

13. Woltmann, *Die Darwinsche Theorie*, p. 30.

14. Edmund Fischer, "Der Entwickelungsgedanke," p. 576.

15. See Bernstein's "Ein Schüler Darwin's," p. 172.

16. Lichtheim, *Marxism*, p. 243.

17. August Bebel, *Aus meinem Leben*, 2:263–64.

18. Francis Darwin, ed., *The Life and Letters of Charles Darwin*, 2:413.

19. Wilhelm Bock, *Im Dienst der Freiheit*, p. 35; and Wilhelm Keil, *Erlebnisse eines Sozialdemokraten*, 1:79–80.

20. Paul Göhre, *Drei Monate Fabrikarbeiter und Handwerkbursche*, p. 212.

21. J. S. and E. F., "Was lesen die organisierten Arbeiter in Deutschland?" p. 154.

22. A. H. T. Pfannkuche, *Was liest der deutsche Arbeiter?*, foldout appendix, p. 59. The other books on the top ten were: Corwin's *Pfaffenspiegel*, Ferdinand Lassalle's *Reden und Schriften*, Blos's *Französische Revolution*, Zimmermann's *Deutscher Bauernkrieg*, and Simon's *Gesundheitspflege des Weibes*.

23. Wilhelm Nitschke, "Wie und nach welcher Richtung entwickelt sich das Lesebedürfnis der Arbeiterschaft?" p. 366. Friedrich Stampfer recalls taking Kautsky's *Erfurt Program* out of a workers' library. The first twenty pages were well worn, but the rest of the book was untouched. See Friedrich Stampfer, *Erfahrungen und Erkenntnisse*, p. 14.

24. Pfannkuche, *Was liest*, pp. 8, 9, 60. A survey done in Leipzig at the same time yielded the same favorite authors. See Konrad Haenisch, "Was lesen die Arbeiter?" pp. 691–96.

25. E. Graf, "Die Bildung der Berliner Arbeiter," p. 22.

26. Adolf Levenstein, *Die Arbeiterfrage*, pp. 388–403.

27. See, for example, the article "Statistisches über die Bildung Berliner Arbeiter," pp. 168–69. See also Deubner, "Das Lesebedürfnis der gewerblichen Arbeiter," p. 260. In Vienna, the story was the same—only 2–3 percent of all books lent were socialist literature; the figures are cited by Günther Roth in his article "Die kulturellen Bestrebungen der Sozialdemokratie im kaiserlichen Deutschland," p. 361.

28. Gertrud Hermes, *Die geistige Gestalt des marxistischen Arbeiters und die Arbeiterbildungsfrage*, pp. 317–23.

29. Moritz Bromme, *Lebensgeschichte eines modernen Fabrikarbeiters*, p. 287.

30. Nikolaus Osterroth, *Vom Beter zum Kämpfer*, p. 149.

31. Wenzel Holek, *Vom Handarbeiter zum Jugenderzieher*, p. 103.

32. Manfred Häckel, "Arbeiterbewegung und Literatur," p. 395.

33. Bromme, *Lebensgeschichte*, p. 287. See also Otto Buchwitz, *50 Jahre Funktionär der deutschen Arbeiterbewegung*, p. 47; and August Winnig, *Frührot*, p. 310.

34. Bromme, *Lebensgeschichte*, p. 287; Bruno Bürgel, *Vom Arbeiter zum Astronomen*, p. 42; and Günther Roth, *The Social Democrats in Imperial Germany*, p. 218. Adelheid Popp tells of the astonishment she aroused by her serious reading; see her *The Autobiography of a Working Woman*, p. 102.

35. Nitschke, "Lesebedürfnis der Arbeiterschaft," p. 366. The high percentage of escape fiction may reflect the desires of the workers' wives and daughters. See Roth, "Die kulturellen Bestrebungen," p. 361. A recent study of workers' readings suggests that the decline in serious reading was general throughout Germany. See Dieter Langewiesche and Klaus Schönhoven, "Arbeiterbibliotheken und Arbeiterlektüre im Wilhelminischen Deutschland," esp. pp. 166–99.

36. Hermes, *Die geistige Gestalt*, pp. 317–23.

37. Deubner, "Das Lesebedürfnis," p. 259. Pfannkuche estimated that the workers made up 25 percent of the *Volksbibliothek* clientele; see *Was liest*, p. 10. See also Langewiesche and Schönhoven, "Arbeiterbibliotheken," p. 148–55.

38. Langewiesche and Schönhoven, "Arbeiterbibliotheken," p. 151.

39. Friedrich Apitzsch, "Die deutsche Tagespresse unter dem Einfluss des Sozialistengesetzes," pp. 100–101.

40. Roth, *The Social Democrats*, p. 247.

41. Levenstein, *Die Arbeiterfrage*, pp. 382–405.

42. Pfannkuche, *Was liest*, p. 19; Deubner, "Das Lesebedürfnis," p. 259; Levenstein, *Die Arbeiterfrage*, pp. 388–403; and Langewiesche and Schönhoven, "Arbeiterbibliotheken," pp. 137–42.

43. Göhre, *Drei Monate Fabrikarbeiter*, p. 111.

44. Levenstein, *Die Arbeiterfrage*, p. 113.

45. Bürgel, *Vom Arbeiter*, p. 36; and Count Stenbock-Fermor, *My Experiences as a Miner*, p. 67.

46. This seems a reasonable assumption. When discussing the Levenstein survey, Barrington Moore, Jr., makes the same case. See his book, *Injustice*, p. 195.

47. See Bebel's review of Woltmann's *Die Darwinsche Theorie* in *Die Neue Zeit* 17, no. 1 (1898–99):484–89.

48. August Bebel, *Woman and Socialism*, p. 249.

49. Rudolf Bommeli, it will be recalled, was the author of *Die Geschichte der Erde* and Oswald Köhler was known for his *Weltschöpfung und Weltuntergang*.

50. See Bölsche's article, "Sozialismus und Darwinismus," pp. 267–77.

51. Arnold Dodel, *Moses or Darwin?* pp. 324–25. Italics in original.

52. Edward Bellamy, *Looking Backward, 2000–1887*, p. 272.

53. Karl Kautsky, "Die jüngste Zukunftsroman," *Die Neue Zeit* 7 (1889):268–76.

54. In Series 1, two out of the ten volumes were on popular Darwinism; in Series 2, two out of four.
55. Quoted by Steinberg, *Sozialismus*, p. 51.
56. *Die Neue Zeit* 21 (1902):699–700.
57. Franz Mehring, "Die Welträtsel," pp. 417–21.
58. Eduard David, *Referentenführer*, p. 19.
59. Häckel, "Arbeiterbewegung," pp. 389–99.
60. Wilhelm Bölsche, "Zur Erinnerung an Curt Grottewitz," foreword to Curt Grottewitz, *Sonntage eines Großstädters in der Natur*.
61. Quoted by Steinberg, *Sozialismus*, p. 141.
62. See the article "Die Neue Welt" in *Lexikon Sozialistischer Deutscher Literatur*, pp. 380–82. The first volume of *Die Neue Welt* in 1876 had a picture of Darwin and two articles on him.
63. This was the title of his speech at the opening ceremonies of the Dresdener Arbeiterbildungs-Verein.
64. For a good analysis of the relationship of radical intellectuals to the SPD, see Vernon L. Lidtke, "Naturalism and Socialism in Germany." Georg Fülberth summarizes the party's cultural problem in the title of his book *Proletarische Partei und bürgerliche Literatur*.
65. Lidtke, "Naturalism and Socialism," p. 25.
66. Alfred Kelly, "Between Poetry and Science," pp. 109–12.
67. *Protokoll über die Verhandlungen des Parteitages der Sozialdemokratischen Partei Deutschlands, abgehalten zu Gotha vom 11. bis 16. Oktober 1896* (Berlin, 1896), pp. 78–85.
68. *Lexikon Sozialistischer Deutscher Literatur*, p. 381.
69. Edward Aveling, *Die Darwin'sche Theorie*, p. 71.
70. Many workers recall taking such courses. See, for example, Joseph Joos, *Krisis in der Sozialdemokratie*, p. 120; Franz Bergg, *Ein Proletarierleben*, p. 56; and Keil, *Erlebnisse*, 1:79–80. Walter Ulbricht recalls reading Haeckel's *Riddle of the Universe* in a natural science course sponsored by the Socialist Workers' Youth. See Peter Klein, *Ernst Haeckel, Der Ketzer von Jena*, p. 244.
71. Langewiesche and Schönhoven, "Arbeiterbibliotheken," pp. 142–45.
72. See, for example, the remarks of Dr. Zadek in support of the Berliner Arbeiterbildungsschule, in *Vorwärts*, no. 56, Supplement 2, 8 March 1894.
73. Langewiesche and Schönhoven, "Arbeiterbibliotheken," p. 146.
74. *Protokoll über die Verhandlungen des Parteitages der Sozialdemokratischen Partei Deutschlands, abgehalten zu Hannover vom 9. bis 14. Oktober 1899* (Berlin, 1899), p. 148.
75. Th. Overbeck, "Erde und Mars," *Die Neue Welt* (1897):284–86.
76. Cited by Günter Schmidt, *Die literarische Rezeption des Darwinismus*, p. 28.
77. Quoted by Eda Sagarra, *Tradition and Revolution*, p. 263.
78. Wolfgang Emmerich, ed., *Proletarische Lebensläufe*, 1:304. On Bellamy's influence, see Bürgel, *Vom Arbeiter*, p. 50, and Keil, *Erlebnisse*, pp. 104–5.
79. See, for example, Popp, *Autobiography*, p. 87; Carl Severing, *Mein Lebensgang*, 1:34; and Alfons Petzold, *Aus dem Leben und der Werkstätte eines Werdenden*, p. 56. Men for whom class consciousness came early and easily, like Otto Buchwitz, were the exception; see Buchwitz, *50 Jahre Funktionär*, pp. 25–29. Friedrich Stampfer estimated that in 1885 in his industrial town

of Brünn, there were only a few dozen men out of a population of eighty thousand who knew anything about Marx; see Stampfer's *Erfahrungen*, p. 10. Hitler was probably right when he claimed in *Mein Kampf* (p. 372) that not one worker in a thousand understood anything of Marx's *Kapital*.

80. Levenstein, *Die Arbeiterfrage*, pp. 115, 123, 130, 187, 198, 212–13. A similar result was obtained from a 1913 questionnaire; see Langewiesche and Schönhoven, "Arbeiterbibliotheken," pp. 136–37.

81. Levenstein, *Die Arbeiterfrage*, pp. 213–42.

82. Moore makes the same point, but does not attempt to link it to the influence of Darwinism; see Moore, *Injustice*, pp. 216–17.

83. Bürgel, *Vom Arbeiter*, p. 49; Osterroth, *Vom Beter*, p. 149; and Karl Scheffler, quoted by Hermann Bertlein, *Jugendleben und soziales Bildungsschicksal*, p. 175. The same theme appears repeatedly in the testimonies given to Levenstein in *Die Arbeiterfrage* as well as in his *Aus der Tiefe*. Likewise, Fritz Bolle, who worked on construction sites in the early 1930s, recalls that discussions with the old "gelernte Sozialisten" always started from the assumption that Marx and Darwin were the same; see Fritz Bolle, "Darwinismus und Zeitgeist," p. 150.

84. Ernst Preczang, "Rückblick" (unpublished), quoted by Emmerich, *Proletarische Lebensläufe*, pp. 288–89; Otto Krille, *Unter dem Joch*, p. 96; Severing, *Mein Lebensgang*, 1:34; Keil, *Erlebnisse*, 1:79–80; and Levenstein, *Die Arbeiterfrage*, passim.

85. Levenstein, *Die Arbeiterfrage*, p. 381.

86. Ibid., pp. 288, 215, 297, 291.

87. Ibid., pp. 336, 343, 353, 348, 349.

88. Hermes, *Die geistige Gestalt*, p. 159.

89. Paul Piechowski, *Proletarischer Glaube*, pp. 188, 123.

90. Karl Sternheim, *Tabula Rasa*, in *Dramen* (Berlin, 1964), 2:231.

91. Ibid., p. 188.

92. Emmerich, *Proletarische Lebensläufe*, p. 25.

EPILOGUE

1. Michael D. Biddiss, *The Age of the Masses*, p. 17.

Bibliography

The following bibliography does not pretend to be exhaustive. I have not listed all the articles that I have read or used from journals, encyclopedias, or newspapers, including *Allgemeine Zeitung*; *Aus der Heimat*; *Ausland*; *Brockhaus Konversations-Lexikon*; *Daheim*; *Die Deutsche Rundschau*; *Die Gartenlaube*; *Grenzboten*; *Illustrirte Zeitung*; *Kosmos*; *Meyers Konversations-Lexikon*; *Die Natur*; *Die Neue Welt*; *Nord und Süd*; *Piercers Konversations-Lexikon*; *Preussische Jahrbücher*; and *Westermanns Monatshefte*. An extensive list of scholarly books on Darwin appears in Friedrich Überwegs, *Grundriss der Geschichte der Philosophie*, 4 vols. (Berlin, 1902), 4:255–76.

Altner, Günter. *Charles Darwin und Ernst Haeckel*. Zurich, 1966.

————. *Weltanschauliche Hintergründe der Rassenlehre des Dritten Reiches*. Zurich, 1968.

Ammon, Otto. *Der Darwinismus gegen die Sozialdemokratie*. Hamburg, 1891.

————. *Die Gesellschaftsordnung und ihre natürlichen Grundlagen*. 3d ed. Jena, 1900.

————. *Die natürliche Auslese beim Menschen*. Jena, 1893.

Apitzsch, Friedrich. "Die deutsche Tagespresse unter dem Einfluss des Sozialistengesetzes." Ph.D. dissertation, Leipzig, 1928.

Aveling, Edward. "Charles Darwin und Karl Marx." *Die Neue Zeit* 15, no. 2 (1896–97): 745–57.

————. *Die Darwin'sche Theorie*. Stuttgart, 1887.

Baader, Ottilie. *Ein steiniger Weg: Lebenserinnerungen*. Berlin and Stuttgart, n.d.

Baenitz, Carl. *Lehrbuch der Botanik in populärer Darstellung*. Edition B. Berlin, 1887.

————. *Lehrbuch der Zoologie in populärer Darstellung*. 6th ed. Berlin, 1884, originally published 1876.

Baker, John R. "The Controversy on Freedom in Science in the Nineteenth Century." In *The Logic of Personal Knowledge: Essays Presented to Michael Polanyi on his Seventieth Birthday, 11th March 1961*. London, 1961, pp. 89–95.

Barzun, Jacques. *Darwin, Marx, Wagner: Critique of a Heritage*. Garden City, 1958.

Bebel, August. *Aus meinem Leben*. 3 vols. Stuttgart, 1911.

————. *Die Frau und der Sozialismus*. Frankfurt, 1977, originally published 1879. Translated as *Woman and Socialism* by Meta L. Hebe-Stern. New York, 1910.

Bellamy, Edward. *Looking Backward, 2000–1887*. New York, 1951, originally published 1888.

Bergg, Franz. *Ein Proletarierleben*. Edited by Nikolaus Wetter. Frankfurt, 1913.

Bernhardi, Friedrich von. *Deutschland und der nächste Krieg*. Stuttgart, 1912. Translated as *Germany and the Next War* by Thomas Powers. New York, 1914.

Bernstein, Eduard. "Ein Schüler Darwin's als Vertheidiger des Sozialismus." *Die Neue Zeit* 9, no. 1 (1890–91):171–77.

Bertlein, Hermann. *Jugendleben und soziales Bildungsschicksal*. Hanover, 1966.

Biddiss, Michael D. *The Age of the Masses: Ideas and Society in Europe since 1870.* New York, 1977.

Blassfeldt, Wilhelm, ed. *Der erste internationale Monisten-Kongress in Hamburg vom 8.–11. Sept., 1911.* Leipzig, 1912.

Bock, Wilhelm. *Im Dienst der Freiheit: Freud und Leid aus sechs Jahrzehnten Kampf und Aufstieg.* Berlin, 1927.

Bolle, Fritz. "Darwinismus und Zeitgeist." *Zeitschrift für Religions-und Geistesgeschichte* 14 (1962):143–80.

————. "Der Fall Müller-Lippstadt und der deutsche Monistenbund." Unpublished manuscript, Bölsche Archive, Munich.

Bölsche, Wilhelm. *Die Abstammung der Kunst.* Stuttgart, 1926.

————. *Die Abstammung des Menschen.* Stuttgart, 1904.

————. *Auf dem Menschenstern: Gedanken zu Natur und Kunst.* Dresden, 1900.

————. *Aus der Schneegrube: Gedanken zur Naturforschung.* Dresden, 1903.

————. *Charles Darwin: Ein Lebensbild.* Leipzig, 1898.

————. *Entwicklungsgeschichte der Natur.* 2 vols. Berlin, 1894–96.

————. *Ernst Haeckel: Ein Lebensbild.* Leipzig, 1900.

————. *Die Eroberung des Menschen.* Berlin, 1901.

————. *Goethe im 20. Jahrhundert: Ein Vortrag.* Berlin, 1901.

————. *Hinter der Weltstadt: Friedrichshagener Gedanken zur aesthetischen Kultur.* Leipzig, 1901.

————. "Die Humanität im Kampf mit dem Fortschritt." *Neue deutsche Rundschau* 7 (1896):125–37.

————. *Lichtglaube: Stunden eines Naturforschers.* Leipzig, 1927.

————. *Das Liebesleben in der Natur: Eine Entwicklungsgeschichte der Liebe.* 3 vols. Florence and Leipzig, 1898–1902. Translated as *Love-Life in Nature: The Story of the Evolution of Love* by Cyril Brown. 2 vols. New York, 1926.

————. *Der Mensch der Zukunft.* Stuttgart, 1915.

————. *Die Mittagsgöttin: Ein Roman aus dem Geisteskampf der Gegenwart.* 3 vols. Stuttgart, 1891.

————. *Naturgeheimnis.* Jena and Leipzig, 1905.

————. *Die naturwissenschaftlichen Grundlagen der Poesie: Prolegomena einer realistischen Aesthetik.* Leipzig, 1887.

————. *Die neuen Gebote: Ein Traum.* Leipzig, 1901.

————. *Paulus: Ein Roman aus der Zeit des Kaisers Marcus Aurelius.* Leipzig, 1885.

————. *Die Schöpfungstage: Umrisse zu einer Entwicklungsgeschichte der Natur.* Dresden, 1906.

————. "Sozialismus und Darwinismus." *Der Sozialistische Akademiker* 2 (1896):267–77.

————. *Stirb und Werde: Naturwissenschaftliche und kulturelle Plaudereien.* Jena, 1913.

————. *Stunden im All: Naturwissenschaftliche Plaudereien.* Stuttgart, 1909.

————. "Über den Wert der Mystik für unsere Zeit." Introduction to Angelus Silesius, *Cherubinischer Wandersmann.* Jena, 1904.

————. *Vom Bazillus zum Affenmenschen: Naturwissenschaftliche Plaudereien.* Leipzig, 1900.

————. "Vom ethischen Konzil zu Berlin." *Die Freie Bühne* 3 (1892):1192–1200.

————. *Von Sonnen und Sonnenstäubchen: Kosmische Wanderungen.* Berlin, 1903.

————. *Von Wundern und Tieren: Neue naturwissenschaftliche Plaudereien.* Stuttgart, 1915.

————. *Was ist die Natur?* Berlin, 1907.

————. *Was muss der neue deutsche Mensch von Naturwissenschaft und Religion fordern?* Berlin, 1934.

————. *Weltblick: Gedanken zu Natur und Kunst.* Dresden, 1904.

————. *Der Zauber des Königs Arpus: Humoristischer Roman aus der römischen Kaiserzeit.* Leipzig, 1887.

————. "Zukunft der Menschheit." *Die Neue Rundschau* 15 (1904):27–40.

Bölsche, Wilhelm, et al. *Im Kampf um die Weltanschauung.* Berlin, 1908.

Bommeli, Rudolf. *Die Geschichte der Erde.* 2d ed. Stuttgart, 1898, originally published 1890.

Bracher, Karl. *The German Dictatorship.* Translated by Jean Steinberg. New York and Washington, 1970.

Brehm, Alfred. *Illustriertes Tierleben.* Hildburghausen, 1864 and following.

Breitenbach, Wilhelm. "Hermann Müller-Lippstadt und der biologische Unterricht." *Natur und Schule* 2 (1903):43–48.

————. "Zum Gedächtnis Hermann Müllers." *Natur und Schule* 5 (1906):304–9.

Brinton, Crane, ed. *The Portable Age of Reason Reader.* New York, 1956.

Brockhaus Konversations-Lexikon 11th ed. Leipzig, 1872.

Bröker, Werner. *Politische Motive naturwissenschaftlicher Argumentation gegen Religion und Kirche im 19. Jahrhundert: Dargestellt am 'Materialisten' Karl Vogt (1817–1895).* Münster, 1973.

Bromme, Moritz Th. W. *Lebensgeschichte eines modernen Fabrikarbeiters.* Jena, 1905.

Bronder, Dietrich. *Bevor Hitler kam: Eine historische Studie.* 2d ed. Marva and Geneva, 1975.

Brücher, Heinz. *Ernst Haeckels Blut-und Geistes-Erbe: Eine Kultur-biologische Monographie.* Munich, 1936.

Brüggemann, Otto. *Naturwissenschaft und Bildung: Die Anerkennung des Bildungswertes der Naturwissenschaften in Vergangenheit und Gegenwart.* Heidelberg, 1967.

Bruhns, Julius. *Es klingt im Sturm ein altes Lied! Aus der Jugendzeit der Sozialdemokratie.* Stuttgart and Berlin, 1921.

Buchmann, Georg. *Geflügelte Worte.* Berlin, 1871.

Buchner, Hans. "Darwinismus und Hygiene." *Westermanns Monatshefte* 76 (1894):313–24.

Büchner, Ludwig. *Aus Natur und Wissenschaft: Studien, Kritiken und Abhandlungen in allgemein verständlicher Darstellung.* 2 vols. 3d ed. Leipzig, 1874, 1884. Translated as *Nature et science.* 2 vols. Turin and Leipzig, 1886.

————. *Darwinismus und Sozialismus oder Der Kampf um das Dasein und die moderne Gesellschaft.* Leipzig, 1894.

————. *Fremdes und Eignes aus dem geistigen Leben der Gegenwart.* 2d ed. Leipzig, 1890.

————. *Im dienst der Wahrheit: Ausgewählte Aufsätze aus Natur und Wissenschaft.* Giessen, 1900.

————. *Kraft und Stoff, oder Grundzüge der natürlichen Weltordnung: Nebst einer darauf gebauten Moral oder Sittenlehre: In allgemein verständlicher Darstellung.* Leipzig, 1855. Translated as *Force and Matter* from the 15th German ed., reprinted from the 4th English ed. New York, 1950.

———. *Der Mensch und seine Stellung in der Natur in Vergangenheit, Gegenwart und Zukunft, oder, Woher kommen wir? Wer sind wir? Wohin gehen wir? Allgemein verständlicher Text, mit zahlreichen wissenschaftlichen Erläuterungen und Anmerkungen.* 2d ed. Leipzig, 1872, originally published 1870. Translated as *Man in the Past, Present and Future* by W. S. Dallas. London, 1872.

———. *Sechs Vorlesungen.* 3d ed. Leipzig, 1872, originally published 1868.

Buchwitz, Otto. *50 Jahre Funktionär der deutschen Arbeiterbewegung.* Berlin, 1949.

Bürgel, Bruno. *Vom Arbeiter zum Astronomen: Der Aufstieg eines Lebenskämpfers.* Berlin, 1950.

Cassirer, Ernst. *The Problem of Knowledge: Philosophy, Science, and History since Hegel.* New Haven and London, 1950.

Chamberlain, Houston Stewart. *Die Grundlagen des XIX. Jahrhunderts.* Munich, 1932, originally published 1899. Translated as *Foundations of the Nineteenth Century* by John Lees. New York, 1968.

Cippola, Carlo M. *Literacy and Development in the West.* Harmondsworth, 1969.

Conrad-Martius, Hedwig. *Utopien der Menschenzüchtung: Der Sozialdarwinismus und seine Folgen.* Munich, 1955.

Cunow, Heinrich. "Darwinismus contra Sozialismus." *Die Neue Zeit* 8 (1890):326–33, 376–86.

Dahl, Dr. Friedrich. *Die Nothwendigkeit der Religion: Eine letzte Consequenz der Darwinischen Lehre.* Heidelberg, 1886.

Darwin, Charles. *The Descent of Man and Selection in Relation to Sex.* 2 vols. New York, 1871.

———. *The Origin of Species by Means of Natural Selection or the Preservation of Favoured Races in the Struggle for Life.* New York, 1958. Translated as *Über die Entstehung der Arten* by Heinrich Bronn, with an appendix ("Schlusswort des Übersetzers"). Stuttgart, 1860.

Darwin, Francis, ed. *The Life and Letters of Charles Darwin.* 2 vols. New York, 1896.

David, Eduard. *Referentenführer: Eine Anleitung zum Erwerb des für die Sozialdemokratische Agitations-Tätigkeit nötigen Wissens und Könnens.* Berlin, 1908.

Dennert, E. *At the Deathbed of Darwinism.* Translated by E. V. O'Harra and John Peschges. Burlington, Iowa, 1904, originally published 1902.

———. *Der Darwinismus und sein Einfluss auf die heutige Volksbewegung.* 2d ed. Stuttgart, 1907.

———. "Die Entwicklungslehre als Lehrgegenstand der höheren Schulen." *Natur und Schule* 2 (1903):332–43.

Depdolla, Philipp. "Hermann Müller-Lippstadt (1829–1883) und die Entwicklung des biologischen Unterrichts." *Sudhoffs Archiv* 34, no. 5, and 34, no. 6 (1941):261–334.

Deubner. "Das Lesebedürfnis der gewerblichen Arbeiter." *Concordia* 19 (1912):256–60.

Dewey, John. *The Influence of Darwin on Philosophy.* New York, 1910.

Diederichs, Eugen. *Selbstzeugnisse und Briefe von Zeitgenossen.* Berlin, 1967.

Dodel, Arnold. *Moses oder Darwin? Eine Schulfrage.* Zurich, 1889. Translated as *Moses or Darwin?* by Friedrich Dodel. New York, 1891.

Dörpinghaus, Hermann Josef. *Darwins Theorie und der deutsche Vulgärmaterialismus im Urteil deutscher katholischer Zeitschriften zwischen 1854 und 1914.* Freiburg, 1969.

Dreyer, Max. *Der Probekandidat*. Leipzig and Berlin, 1900.

Dub, Julius. *Kurze Darstellung der Lehre Darwin's über die Entstehung der Arten der Organismen*. Stuttgart, 1870.

Du Bois-Reymond, Emil. *Über die Grenzen des Naturerkennens*. Leipzig, 1872.

Eiseley, Loren. *Darwin's Century*. Garden City, 1958.

Ellegard, Alvar. *Darwin and the General Reader: The Reception of Darwin's Theory of Evolution in the British Periodical Press, 1859–72*. Göteborg, 1958.

Emmerich, Wolfgang, ed. *Proletarische Lebensläufe: Autobiographische Dokumente zur Entstehung der zweiten Kultur in Deutschland*. Vol. I. Hamburg, 1974.

Engels, Friedrich. *Herrn Eugen Dührings Umwälzung der Wissenschaft*. Berlin, 1959.

Engelsing, Rolf. *Analphabetentum und Lektüre: Zur Sozialgeschichte des Lesens in Deutschland zwischen feudaler und industrieller Gesellschaft*. Stuttgart, 1973.

———. "Die Perioden der Lesegeschichte in der Neuzeit." *Archiv für Geschichte des Buchwesens* 10 (1970):946–1002.

Escarpit, Robert. *Das Buch und der Leser: Entwurf einer Literatursoziologie*. Cologne, 1961.

Fechner, Gustav Theodor. *Nanna, oder das Seelenleben der Pflanzen*. Leipzig, 1848.

———. *Die Tagesansicht gegenüber der Nachtansicht*. Leipzig, 1879.

Feuer, Lewis S. "The Case of the 'Darwin-Marx' Letter: A Study in Socio-Literary Detection." *Encounter* 51, no. 4 (Oct. 1978):62–78.

Feuerbach, Ludwig. "Die Naturwissenschaft und die Revolution." In *Gesammelte Schriften*, ed. Werner Schuffenhauer. 10 vols. Berlin, 1971, 10:347–68.

Fischer, Edmund. "Der Entwickelungsgedanke." *Sozialistische Monatshefte* 13, no. 1 (1909):576–83.

Franz, Victor. *Ernst Haeckel: Sein Leben, Denken und Werken: Eine Schriftenfolge für seine zahlreiche Freunde und Anhänger*. 2 vols. Jena and Leipzig, 1943.

Die Freigeistige Bewegung: Wesen und Auftrag. Mainz, 1959.

Friedel, Karl, and Gilsenbach, Reimar. *Das Rossmässler Buchlein*. Berlin, 1956.

Frymann, Daniel (Class, Heinrich). *Wenn ich der Kaiser wär: Politische Wahrheiten und Notwendigkeiten*. 5th ed. Leipzig, 1914, originally published 1913.

Fülberth, Georg. *Proletarische Partei und bürgerliche Literatur*. Neuwied and Berlin, 1972.

Gasman, Daniel. *The Scientific Origins of National Socialism: Social Darwinism in Ernst Haeckel and the German Monist League*. New York, 1971.

Ghiselin, Michael T. *The Triumph of the Darwinian Method*. Berkeley and Los Angeles, 1969.

Gillespie, Neal C. *Charles Darwin and the Problem of Creation*. Chicago and London, 1979.

Glaser, Ernst. *Kann die Wissenschaft verständlich sein? Von der Schwierigkeit ihrer Popularisierung*. Vienna, 1965.

Glaser, Hermann. *The Cultural Roots of National Socialism*. Translated by Ernest A. Menze. London, 1978.

Glass, Bentley. *Forerunners of Darwin: 1745–1859*. Baltimore, 1959.

Gode-von Aesch, Alexander. *Natural Science in German Romanticism*. New York, 1941.

Göhre, Paul. *Drei Monate Fabrikarbeiter und Handwerkbursche*. Leipzig, 1891.

Goldfriedrich, Johann. *Geschichte des deutschen Buchhandels*. Vol. 4. Leipzig, 1913.

Graf, E. "Die Bildung der Berliner Arbeiter." *Zentralblatt für Volksbildungswesen* 9 (1909):17–25.

Graham, Loren R. "Science and Values: The Eugenics Movement in Germany and Russia in the 1920s." *American Historical Review* 82 (Dec. 1977):1133–64.

Gregory, Frederick. *Scientific Materialism in Nineteenth Century Germany*. Dordrecht (Holland) and Boston, 1977.

Groh, Dieter. "Marx, Engels und Darwin: Naturgesetzliche Entwicklung oder Revolution." *Politische Vierteljahresschrift* 8, no. 4 (1967):544–59.

Grottewitz, Curt. *Sonntage eines Großstädters in der Natur*. Berlin, 1907.

Grube, A. W. "Der Darwinismus und seine Consequenzen." *Paedagogium* 1 (1879):352–63, 413–39, 492–507.

Grünewald, Chr. *Leitfaden zu einem bildenden Unterrichte in der Naturgeschichte*. Kaiserslautern, 1869 and 1872.

Gruppe, Heidemarie. *"Volk" zwischen Politik und Idylle in der "Gartenlaube,"* 1853–1914. Frankfurt and Munich, 1976.

Gumplowicz, Ludwig. "Darwinismus und Soziologie." In *Soziologische Essays*. Innsbruck, 1899, pp. 19–42.

———. *Outlines of Sociology*. Edited by Irving R. Horowitz. New York, 1963, originally published 1885.

Haake, Wilmont. *Feuilletonkunde: Das Feuilleton als literarische und journalistische Gattung*. 2 vols. Leipzig, 1943.

———. *Handbuch des Feuilletons*. 3 vols. Emsdetten, 1953.

Häckel, Manfred. "Arbeiterbewegung und Literatur." In *100 Jahre Reclams Universal Bibliothek, 1867–1967*. Leipzig, 1967, pp. 378–411.

Haeckel, Ernst. *The Evolution of Man: A Popular Exposition of the Principle Points of Human Ontogeny and Phylogeny*. 2 vols. London, 1879, originally published 1875.

———. *Freedom in Science and Teaching*. New York, 1879.

———. *Gemeinverständliche Vorträge und Abhandlungen aus dem Gebiete der Entwicklungslehre*. 2d ed. 2 vols. Bonn, 1902.

———. *Last Worlds on Evolution: A Popular Retrospect and Summary*. Translated by Joseph McCabe. New York, n.d.

———. *Die Lebenswunder*. Stuttgart, 1904.

———. *Monism as Connecting Religion and Science: A Confession of Faith of a Man of Science*. Translated by J. Gilchrist. London, 1895, originally published 1892.

———. *Die Natürliche Schöpfungsgeschichte*. 8th ed. Berlin, 1889, originally published 1868. Translated as *The History of Creation* by Sir E. Ray Lankester. 2 vols., New York, 1914.

———. "Über die heutige Entwickelungslehre im Verhältnisse zur Gesammtwissenschaft." *Amtlicher Bericht der 50. Versammlung deutscher Naturforscher und Aerzte in München vom 17. bis 22. September 1877*. Munich, 1877, pp. 14–22.

———. *Die Welträtsel: Gemeinverständliche Studien über monistische Philosophie*. Bonn, 1899. Translated as *The Riddle of the Universe at the Close of the Nineteenth Century* by Joseph McCabe. New York and London, 1900.

Haenisch, Konrad. "Was lesen die Arbeiter?" *Die Neue Zeit* 18, no. 2 (1899–1900):691–96.

Hale, Oron J. *The Great Illusion, 1900–1914*. New York, 1971.

Hamann, Otto. *Die Abstammung des Menschen: Eine Darstellung der neueren Ergebnisse der Anthropologie*. Berlin, 1909.

Heberer, Gerhard, and Schwanitz, Franz, eds. *Hundert Jahre Evolutionsforschung: Das wissenschaftliche Vermächtnis Charles Darwins*. Stuttgart, 1960.

Hellwald, Friedrich. *Culturgeschichte in ihrer natürlichen Entwicklung bis zur Gegenwart*. 2d ed. 2 vols. Augsburg, 1876.

Hemleben, Johannes. *Ernst Haeckel in Selbstzeugnissen und Bilddokumenten*. Hamburg, 1964.

Henning, Max. *Handbuch der freigeistigen Bewegung Deutschlands, Österreichs und der Schweiz*. Frankfurt, 1914.

Hermes, Gertrud. *Die geistige Gestalt des marxistischen Arbeiters und die Arbeiterbildungsfrage*. Tübingen, 1926.

Hertling, Georg Friedrich. *Der Darwinismus, eine geistige Epidemie*. Frankfurt, 1880.

Hertwig, Oscar. *Zur Abwehr des ethischen, des sozialen, des politischen Darwinismus*. Jena, 1921.

Heuss, Theodor. *Justus von Liebig*. Hamburg, 1949.

Hiller, Helmut. *Zur Sozialgeschichte von Buch und Buchhandel*. Bonn, 1966.

Himmelfarb, Gertrude. *Darwin and the Darwinian Reovlution*. London, 1959.

Hirschberg, Susanne. "Das Bildungsschicksal des gewerblichen Proletariats im Lichte der Arbeiterbiographie." Ph.D. dissertation, Cologne, 1928.

Hitler, Adolf. *Mein Kampf*. Boston, 1971, originally published 1925–26.

Höffding, Harald. *Charles Darwin: Eine populäre Darstellung seines Lebens und seiner Lehre*. Berlin, 1895.

Hofstadter, Richard. *Social Darwinism in American Thought*. New York, 1944.

Holek, Wenzel. *Vom Handarbeiter zum Jugenderzieher*. Jena, 1921.

Holt, Niles R. "Ernst Haeckel's Monistic Religion." *Journal of the History of Ideas* 32 (1971):265–80.

———. "Monists and Nazis: A Question of Scientific Responsibility." *Hastings Center Report* 5 (April 1975):37–43.

Hughes, H. Stuart. *Consciousness and Society: The Reorientation of European Social Thought, 1890–1930*. New York, 1958.

Humboldt, Alexander von. *Ansichten der Natur*. 3d ed. Stuttgart and Tübingen, 1849, originally published 1807.

100 Jahre Reclams Universal Bibliothek, 1867–1967. Leipzig, 1967.

Jaeger, Dr. G. *Die Darwin'sche Theorie und ihre Stellung zu Moral und Religion*. Stuttgart, 1869.

Joos, Joseph. *Krisis in der Sozialdemokratie*. M. Gladbach, 1911.

Jordan, Pascal. *Der Naturwissenschaftler vor der religiösen Frage: Abbruch einer Mauer*. Oldenburg, 1963.

Kaufmann, Walter. *Nietzsche: Philosopher, Psychologist, Antichrist*. New York, 1950.

Kautsky, Karl. "Darwinismus und Marxismus." *Die Neue Zeit* 13, no. 1 (1894–95):709–16.

———. "Darwinismus und Marxismus." *Österreichischer Arbeiter-Kalender* 11 (1890):49–54.

———. *Erinnerungen und Erörterungen*. The Hague, 1960.

Keil, Wilhelm. *Erlebnisse eines Sozialdemokraten*. 2 vols. Stuttgart, 1947.

Kelly, Alfred. "Between Poetry and Science: Wilhelm Bölsche as Scientific Popularizer." Ph.D. dissertation, University of Wisconsin, 1975.

Kirschstein, Eva-Annemarie. *Die Familienzeitschrift: Ihre Entwicklung und Be-deutung für die deutsche Presse.* Berlin, 1937.

Klein, Peter. *Ernst Haeckel, Der Ketzer von Jena: Ein Leben in Berichten, Briefen und Bildern.* Leipzig, 1966.

Koch, Hannsjoachim. *Der Sozialdarwinismus: Seine Genese und sein Einfluss auf das imperialistische Denken.* Munich, 1973.

Köhler, Oswald. *Weltschöpfung und Weltuntergang: Die Entwicklung von Himmel und Erde auf Grund der Naturwissenschaften, populär dargestellt.* 2d ed. Stuttgart, 1890, originally published 1887.

Kölliker, Albert von. *Über die Darwin'sche Schöpfungstheorie.* Leipzig, 1864.

Kossman, H. "Darwinismus und Sozialdemokratie." *Die Deutsche Rundschau* 17 (1878):278–92.

Kraepelin, Karl. *Einführung in die Biologie zum Gebrauch an höheren Schulen und zum selbst Unterricht.* 3d ed. Leipzig and Berlin, 1912.

———. *Leitfaden für den biologischen Unterricht in den oberen Klassen der höheren Schulen.* Leipzig and Berlin, 1907.

Krause, Ernst. *Charles Darwin und sein Verhältnis zu Deutschland.* Leipzig, 1885.

Krille, Otto. *Unter dem Joch: Die Geschichte einer Jugend.* Edited by Ursula Münchow. Berlin, 1975, originally published 1911.

Kruck, Alfred. *Geschichte des Alldeutschen Verbandes, 1890–1939.* Wiesbaden, 1954.

Kuhl, Joseph. *Die Descendenzlehre und der Neue Glaube.* Munich, 1879.

Kupisch, Karl. "Bürgerliche Frommigkeit im Wilhelminischen Zeitalter." *Zeitschrift für Religions-und Geistesgeschichte* 14 (1962):123–43.

Langbehn, Julius. *Rembrandt als Erzieher.* 17th ed. Berlin, 1940, originally published 1890.

Langewiesche, Dieter, and Schönhoven, Klaus. "Arbeiterbibliotheken und Ar-beiterlektüre im Wilhelminischen Deutschland." *Archiv für Sozialgeschichte* 16 (1976):135–204.

Langkavel, Bernhard. *Der Mensch und seine Rassen.* Stuttgart, 1892.

Lehrpläne und Lehraufgaben für die höheren Schulen in Preussen. Berlin, 1901.

Leunis, Johannes. *Analytischer Leitfaden für den ersten wissenschaftlichen Unterricht in der Naturgeschichte.* 7th ed. Vol. 1, *Zoologie.* Hanover, 1877.

———. *Schul-Naturgeschichte: Eine analytische Darstellung der drei Naturreiche.* 8th ed. Part 1, *Zoologie.* Hanover, 1877.

———. *Synopsis der drei Naturreiche: Ein Handbuch für höhere Lehranstalten.* 3d ed. Part 1, *Zoologie.* Hanover, 1883.

Levenstein, Adolf. *Die Arbeiterfrage.* Munich, 1912.

———. *Arbeiter-Philosophen und -Dichter.* Berlin, 1909.

———. *Aus der Tiefe: Arbeiterbriefe: Beiträge zur Seelenanalyse moderner Arbeiter.* Berlin, 1909.

Lexikon Sozialistischer Deutscher Literatur. Leipzig, 1973.

Lichtheim, George. *Marxism: An Historical and Critical Study.* New York and Washington, 1961.

Lidtke, Vernon L. "Naturalism and Socialism in Germany." *American Historical Review* 79, no. 1 (Feb. 1974):14–37.

Lilge, Frederic. *The Abuse of Learning: The Failure of the German University.* New York, 1948.

Lilienfeld, Paul von. *Gedanken über die Sozialwissenschaft.* 5 vols. Mitau, 1873–81.

Lippert, Julius. *Kulturgeschichte der Menschheit in ihrem organischen Aufbau.*
    Stuttgart, 1886–87.
Lovejoy, Arthur. *The Great Chain of Being.* New York, 1960.
Lübbe, Hermann. *Politische Philosophie in Deutschland.* Basel and Stuttgart, 1963.
Lucas, Erhard, "Marx' und Engels' Auseinandersetzung mit Darwin: Zur
    Differenz zwischen Marx und Engels." *International Review of Social History* 9
    (1964):433–69.
Luft, Friedrich, ed. *Facsimile Querschnitt durch die Berliner Illustrierte Zeitung.*
    Munich, 1965.
Lukacs, Georg. *Die Zerstörung der Vernunft.* Berlin, 1954.
Magnus, Rudolf. *Wilhelm Bölsche: Ein biographisch-kritischer Beitrag zur modernen
    Weltanschauung.* Berlin, 1909.
Maser, Werner. *Adolf Hitler: Legende, Mythos, Wirklichkeit.* Munich, 1971.
Mason, Stephen F. *A History of the Sciences.* New York, 1962.
May, Walther. *Ernst Haeckel: Versuch einer Chronik seines Lebens und Wirkens.*
    Leipzig, 1909.
Mehring, Franz. "Die Welträtsel." *Die Neue Zeit* 18 (1899–1900):417–21.
Misteli, Hermann. *Carl Vogt: Seine Entwicklung vom angehenden naturwis-*
    senschaftlichen Materialisten zum idealen Politiker der Paulskirche, 1817–1849.
    Zurich, 1938.
Moleschott, Jakob. *Der Kreislauf des Lebens.* 5th ed. Giessen, 1875–87, originally
    published 1852.
Montgomery, William M. "Germany." In *The Comparative Reception of Darwinism.*
    Edited by Thomas F. Glick. Austin and London, 1972, pp. 81–116.
Moore, Barrington, Jr. *Injustice: The Social Basis of Obedience and Revolt.* White
    Plains, 1978.
Mosse, George L. *The Crisis of German Ideology: Intellectual Origins of the Third
    Reich.* New York, 1964.
————. *Toward the Final Solution: A History of European Racism.* New York, 1978.
Mühlberg, F. *Zweck und Umfang des Unterrichts in der Naturgeschichte an höheren
    Mittelschulen mit besonderer Berücksichtigung des Gymnasiums.* Leipzig and
    Berlin, 1903.
Mullen, Pierce C. "The Preconditions and Reception of Darwinian Biology in
    Germany, 1800–1870." Ph.D. dissertation, The University of California,
    Berkeley, 1964.
Münster, Hans A. *Geschichte der deutschen Presse in ihren Grundzügen dargestellt.*
    Leipzig, 1941.
Münzenberg, Willi. *Die Dritte Front: Aufzeichnungen aus 15 Jahren proletarischer
    Jugendbewegung.* Berlin, 1930.
Nitschke, Wilhelm. "Wie und nach welcher Richtung entwickelt sich das
    Lesebedürfnis der Arbeiterschaft?" *Sozialistische Monatshefte* 19, no. 1
    (1913):364–70.
Nordau, Max. *Die conventionellen Lügen der Kulturmenschheit.* Leipzig, 1883.
    Translated as *The Conventional Lies of Our Civilization.* Chicago, 1886.
Nordenskiöld, Erik. *The History of Biology.* New York, 1936.
Norrenberg, J. *Geschichte des naturwissenschaftlichen Unterrichts an den höheren
    Schulen Deutschlands.* Leipzig and Berlin, 1904.
Notestein, Wallace, and Stoll, Elmer. *Conquest and Kultur: Aims of the Germans in
    Their Own Words.* Washington, 1918.

Novalis. *Hymns to the Night and Other Selected Writings.* Translated by Charles Passage. Indianapolis, 1960.

———. *Schriften.* Edited by Paul Kluckhohn. 4 vols. Leipzig, 1928.

Osterroth, Nikolaus. *Vom Beter zum Kämpfer.* Berlin, 1920.

Ostwald, Wilhelm. *Monistische Sonntagspredigten.* Leipzig, 1911–13.

Pannekoek, Anton. *Marxismus und Darwinismus: Ein Vortrag.* 2d ed. Leipzig, 1914, originally published 1912.

Pascal, Roy. *From Naturalism to Expressionism: German Literature and Society, 1880–1918.* London, 1973.

Paulsen, Friedrich. "Die Biologie im Unterricht der höheren Schulen." *Natur und Schule* 1 (1902):20–29.

———. *Geschichte des gelehrten Unterrichts.* 2 vols. Berlin, 1921.

Penzig, Rudolf. *Ohne Kirche: Eine Lebensführung auf eigenem Wege.* Jena, 1907.

Petzold, Alfons. *Aus dem Leben und der Werkstätte eines Werdenden.* Vienna and Leipzig, 1913.

Pfannkuche, A. H. T. *Was liest der deutsche Arbeiter?* Tübingen, 1900.

Pfannstiel, G. "Zum entwicklungsgeschichtlichen Lehrplan." *Natur und Schule* 4 (1905):457–61.

Pfetsch, Frank R. *Entwicklung der Wissenschaftspolitik in Deutschland, 1750–1914.* Berlin, 1974.

Pick, Ad. Jos. "Die Darwinsche Weltanschauung und die Schule." *Paedagogium* 3 (1881):721–33.

Picker, Henry, ed. *Hitlers Tischgespräche im Führerhauptquartier, 1941–1942.* Stuttgart, 1965.

Piechowski, Paul. *Proletarischer Glaube: Die religiöse Gedankenwelt der organisierten deutschen Arbeiterschaft nach sozialistischen und kommunistischen Selbstzeugnissen.* Berlin, 1927.

Plate, Ludwig, ed. *Ultramontane Weltanschauung und moderne Lebenskunde, Orthodoxie und Monismus: Die Anschauungen des Jesuitenpaters Erich Wasmann und die gegen ihn in Berlin gehaltenen Reden.* Jena, 1907.

Ploetz, Alfred. *Die Tüchtigkeit unserer Rasse und der Schutz der Schwachen: Ein Versuch über Rassenhygiene und ihr Verhältnis zu den humanen Idealen, besonders zum Sozialismus.* Berlin, 1895.

Popp, Adelheid. *The Autobiography of a Working Woman.* Translated by F. C. Harvey. London, 1912.

Preyer, Wilhelm. *Der Kampf um das Dasein: Ein populärer Vortrag.* Bonn, 1869.

———. *Naturforschung und Schule.* Stuttgart, 1887.

Radl, Emmanuel. *Geschichte der biologischen Theorien.* 2 vols. Leipzig, 1909.

Ratzel, Friedrich. *Sein und Werden der organischen Welt: Eine populäre Schöpfungsgeschichte.* Leipzig, 1877, originally published 1869.

Rauschning, Hermann. *Gespräche mit Hitler.* Zurich, 1939.

Rehbein, Franz. *Gesinde und Gesindel: Aus dem Leben eines Landarbeiters im Wilhelmischen Deutschland.* Berlin, 1955, originally published 1911.

Reinke, J. *Haeckels Monismus und seine Freunde: Ein freies Wort für freie Wissenschaft.* Leipzig, 1907.

———. "Was heisst Biologie?" *Natur und Schule* 1 (1902):449–53.

Riehm, Gottfried. "Darwinismus und Christentum." *Göttinger Arbeiterbibliothek.* Edited by Friedrich Naumann. Göttingen, 1896, 1:127–44.

Ringer, Fritz. *The Decline of the German Mandarins: The German Academic Community, 1890–1933.* Cambridge, 1969.

Ritter, Gerhard A. "Workers' Culture in Imperial Germany: Problems and Points of Departure for Research." *Journal of Contemporary History* 13, no. 2 (April 1978):166–89.

Rolle, Friedrich. *Ch's Darwin's Lehre von der Entstehung der Arten im Pflanzen- und Thierreich in ihrer Anwendung auf die Schöpfungslehre.* Frankfurt, 1863.

Rossmässler, E. A. *Mein Leben und Streben.* Hanover, 1875.

Roth, Günther, "Die kulturellen Bestrebungen der Sozialdemokratie im kaiserlichen Deutschland." In Hans-Ulrich Wehler, ed., *Moderne deutsche Sozialgeschichte.* Cologne and Berlin, 1966.

————. *The Social Democrats in Imperial Germany: A Study in Working Class Isolation and National Integration.* Totowa, N.J., 1963.

Rubinstein, Friedrich. "Darwinismus in der Moral." *Nord und Süd* 76 (1896):196–203.

Ruse, Michael. *The Darwinian Revolution.* Chicago and London, 1979.

Ryder, A. J. *Twentieth Century Germany: From Bismarck to Brandt.* New York, 1973.

J. S. and E. F. "Was lesen die organisierten Arbeiter in Deutschland?" *Die Neue Zeit* 13, no. 1 (1894–95):153–55.

Sagarra, Eda. *Tradition and Revolution: German Literature and Society, 1830–1890.* New York, 1971.

Schäffle, Albert. *Bau und Leben des Socialien Körpers.* 4 vols. Tübingen, 1875–78.

————. "Darwinismus und Socialwissenschaft." In *Gesammelte Aufsätze.* Tübingen, 1885, 1:1–36.

Schallmeyer, Wilhelm. *Vererbung und Auslese im Lebenslauf der Völker: Eine staatswissenschaftliche Studie auf Grund der neueren Biologie.* Jena, 1903.

Schatzberg, Walter. *The Scientific Themes in the Popular Literature and the Poetry of the German Enlightenment, 1720–1760.* Berne, 1973.

Schelling, Samuel. *Grundriss der Naturgeschichte des Thier-Pflanzen-und-Mineralreichs.* 14th ed., Breslau, 1874; 20th ed., Breslau, 1893; 22d ed., Breslau, 1909.

Schenda, Rudolf. *Volk ohne Buch: Studien zur Sozialgeschichte der populären Lesestoffe, 1770–1910.* Frankfurt, 1970.

Scherer, H. *Bürgerlich- oppositionelle Literaten und sozialdemokratische Arbeiter Bewegung nach 1890: Die 'Friedrichshagener' und ihr Einfluss auf die sozialdemokratische Kulturpolitik.* Stuttgart, 1974.

Schleiden, M. J. *Das Alter des Menschengeschlechts, die Entstehung und die Stellung des Menschen in der Natur: Drei Vorträge für gebildete Laien.* Leipzig, 1863.

Schmeil, Otto. *Der Mensch: Ein Leitfaden für den Unterricht.* 3d ed. Stuttgart and Leipzig, 1903.

————. *Über die Reformbestrebungen auf dem Gebiete des naturgeschichtlichen Unterrichts.* 10th ed. Leipzig, 1910, originally published 1896.

Schmid, Bastian. "Darwin und die Schule." *Monatshefte für den naturwissenschaftlichen Unterricht (aller Schulgattungen)* 2 (1909):220–13.

————. "Dringen durch die modernen Naturwissenschaften materialistische Ideen in die Schulen?" *Natur und Schule* 3 (1904):1–6.

Schmid, Karl Adolf. *Geschichte der Erziehung vom Anfang an bis auf unsere Zeit.* 5 vols. Stuttgart, 1901.

Schmidt, Günter. *Die literarische Rezeption des Darwinismus: Das Problem der Vererbung bei Emile Zola und im Drama des Deutschen Naturalismus*. Berlin, 1974.

Schmidt, Heinrich. *Ernst Haeckel: Leben und Werke*. Berlin, 1926.

―――. *Was wir Ernst Haeckel verdanken*. Leipzig, 1914.

Schmidt, Oscar. *Die Anwendung der Descendenzlehre auf den Menschen*. Leipzig, 1873.

―――. *Thierkunde*. Strassburg, 1878.

Schmidts, Rolf. "Die Aufassung der Sinnlichkeit und die Einstellung zur Sexualität bei Wilhelm Bölsche." Ph.D. dissertation, Munich, 1964.

Schmucker, Theodor. *Geschichte der Biologie: Forschung und Lehre*. Göttingen, 1936.

Schoenichen, Walther. *Die Abstammungslehre im Unterrichte der Schule*. Leipzig and Berlin, 1903.

Schönke, K. A. *Naturgeschichte*. 2d ed. Part 1, *Das Thierreich*. Berlin, 1866.

Schottenloher, Karl. *Bücher bewegten die Welt: Eine Kulturgeschichte des Buches*. 2 vols. Stuttgart, 1952.

Schulte-Tigges, A. "Biologie und Entwicklungslehre im Rahmen der neuen preussischen Lehrpläne für höhere Schulen." *Natur und Schule* 1 (1902):337–42.

Seidlitz, Georg. *Die Darwin'sche Theorie*. Dorpat, 1871.

―――. "Erfolge des Darwinismus." *Ausland* 47 (1874):709–14, 727–32, 748–52.

Sendel, Rudolf. "Zur Aussöhnung mit dem Darwinismus." *Nord und Süd* 36 (1896):360–77.

Severing, Carl. *Mein Lebensgang: Vom Schlosser zum Minister*. Cologne, 1950.

Smalian, Karl. *Grundzüge der Pflanzenkunde für höhere Lehranstalten*. Leipzig, 1903.

―――. *Kleine Naturgeschichte der drei Reiche für Mittelschulen*. Leipzig, 1912.

Springer, August. *Der Andere das bist Du: Lebensgeschichte eines reichen armen Mannes*. Tübingen, 1954.

Stampfer, Friedrich. *Erfahrungen und Erkenntnisse: Aufzeichnungen aus meinem Leben*. Cologne, 1957.

"Statistisches über die Bildung Berliner Arbeiter." *Der Bibliothekar* 2 (1910):168–69.

Steinberg, Hans-Josef. *Sozialismus und deutsche Sozialdemokratie: Zur Ideologie der Partei vor dem I. Weltkrieg*. 3d ed. Hanover, 1972.

Stenbock-Fermor, Count. *My Experiences as a Miner*. Translated by Frances, Countess of Warwick. London and New York, 1930.

Stenographische Berichte über die Verhandlungen der durch die Allerhöchste Verordnung vom 3. November 1878 einberufenen beiden Häuser des Landtages, Haus der Abgeordneten. Vol. 1. Berlin, 1879.

Stenographische Berichte über die Verhandlungen der durch die Allerhöchste Verordnung vom 2. November 1882 einberufenen beiden Häuser des Landtages, Haus der Abgeordneten. Vol 2. Berlin, 1883.

Stern, Fritz. *The Politics of Cultural Despair: A Study in the Rise of Germanic Ideology*. Berkeley, 1961.

Sternberger, Dolf. *Panorama, oder Ansichten vom 19. Jahrhundert*. Hamburg, 1946.

Sterne, Carus. "Menschliche Erbschaften aus dem Tierreiche." *Die Gartenlaube* 23 (1875):266–68.

———. *Werden und Vergehen: Eine Entwicklungsgeschichte der Naturganzen in gemeinverständlichster Fassung.* 4th ed. 2 vols. Berlin, 1901.

Strauss, David Friedrich. *Der alte und der neue Glaube.* Leipzig, 1872. Translated as *The Old Faith and the New.* 2 vols. New York, 1873.

Strauss, Emil. *Die Hypothese in der Schule und der naturwissenschaftliche Unterricht in der Realschule zu Lippstadt: Ein Wort zur Abwehr und Rechtfertigung von Dr. Hermann Müller, Oberlehrer.* Bonn, 1879.

Strauss, Victor von. "Die Darwinische Hypothese, Ein Gespräch." *Daheim* 1 (1865):630–32.

Strothmann, Dietrich. *Nationalsozialistische Literaturpolitik: Ein Beitrag zur Publizistik im Dritten Reich.* Bonn, 1963.

Südekum, Albert. *Darwin: Sein Leben, seine Lehre und seine Bedeutung.* Leipzig, 1893.

Tille, Alexander. *Von Darwin bis Nietzsche.* Leipzig, 1895.

Treitschke, Heinrich von. *Politics.* Translated by Blanche Dugdale and Torben de Bille. London, 1916.

Trümpelmann, August. "Seelenverwandtschaft der Monisten und Socialisten." *Deutsch-evangelische Blätter* 1 (1876):208–21, 282–98.

Tschulok, Dr. S. *Entwicklungstheorie (Darwins Lehre): Gemeinverständlich dargestellt.* Stuttgart, 1912.

Turek, Ludwig. *Ein Prolet erzählt.* Berlin, 1957.

Unger-Winkelried, Emil. *Von Bebel zu Hitler: Vom Zukunftsstaat zur Dritten Reich: Aus dem Leben eines sozialdemokratischen Arbeiters.* Berlin, 1934.

Uschmann, Georg. *Ernst Haeckel: Forscher, Künstler, Mensch: Briefe.* Leipzig, 1962.

"Die Verbreitung der naturwissenschaftlichen Literatur." *Kosmos* 18 (1921):162–64.

"Verhandlungen über den biologischen Unterricht an höheren Schulen." In *Verhandlungen der Gesellschaft deutscher Naturforscher und Aerzte, 75. Versammlung zu Cassel 20.–26. September 1903.* Leipzig, 1904, pp. 145–60.

Verhandlungen über Fragen des höheren Unterrichts, Berlin 4. bis 17. Dezember 1890.

Verlag der Frankfurter Zeitung. *Geschichte der Frankfurter Zeitung, 1856–1906.* Frankfurt, 1906.

Vetter, J. *Darwinismus oder Christentum.* Geisweid, 1909.

Virchow, Rudolf. "Die Freiheit der Wissenschaft im modernen Staat." In *Amtlicher Bericht der 50. Versammlung deutscher Naturforscher und Aerzte in München vom 17. bis 22. September 1877.* Munich, 1877, pp. 65–77.

Vogt, Carl. "Einige Darwinistische Ketzereien." *Westermanns Monatshefte* 61 (1887):481–91.

———. "Pope and Anti-Pope." *The Popular Science Monthly* 14 (1878–79):320–25.

———. *Vorlesungen über den Menschen, seine Stellung in der Schöpfung und in der Geschichte der Erde.* 2 vols. Giessen, 1863. Translated as *Lectures on Man* by James Hunt. London, 1864.

Wächter, Christian. *Methodischer Leitfaden für den Unterricht in der Thierkunde.* 3d ed. Part 1, *Die Wirbelthiere.* Braunschweig, 1892

Wagner, Mortiz. "Darwinistische Streitfragen." *Westermanns Monatshefte* 51 (1881):45–53.

"Was macht Darwin populär?" *Das Ausland* 44 (1871):813–15.

Wasmann, Erich. *Haeckels Monismus: Eine Kulturgefahr.* Freiburg, 1919.

Wehler, Hans-Ulrich. "Sozialdarwinismus im expandierenden Industriestaat." In Imanuel Geiss and Bernd Jürgen Wendt, eds., *Deutschland in der Weltpolitik des 19. und 20. Jahrhunderts*. Düsseldorf, 1973, pp. 133–42.

Wettstein, H. *Leitfaden für den Unterricht in der Naturkunde an Sekundär-und Bezirksschulen, sowie unteren Gymnasien*. 7th ed. Part 1. Zurich, 1902.

Wetzels, Walter D. "Versuch einer Beschreibung populärwissenschaftlicher Prosa in den Naturwissenschaften." *Jahrbuch für Internationale Germanistik* 3 (1971):76–95.

Weygoldt, G. P. *Darwinismus, Religion, Sittlichkeit*. Leiden, 1878.

Wigand, Albert. *Der Darwinismus, ein Zeichen der Zeit*. Heilbronn, 1878.

Wille, Bruno, ed. *Darwins Weltanschauung*. Heilbronn, 1906.

———, ed. *Lehrbuch für den Jugendunterricht freier Gemeinden*. 2 parts. Berlin, 1891, 1893.

Winnig, August. *Frührot: Ein Buch von Heimat und Jugend*. Stuttgart, 1924.

Wittich, Dieter. *Vogt, Moleschott, Büchner: Schriften zum kleinbürgerlichen Materialismus in Deutschland*. 2 vols. Berlin, 1971.

Woltmann, Ludwig. *Die Darwinsche Theorie und der Sozialismus*. Düsseldorf, 1899.

Wuttke, Heinrich. *Die deutschen Zeitschriften und die Entstehung der öffentlichen Meinung*. Leipzig, 1875.

Zacharias, Otto. "Charles R. Darwin, der wissenschaftliche Begründer der Descendenzlehre." *Westermanns Monatshefte* 54 (1883):341–67.

———. *Katechismus des Darwinismus*. Leipzig, 1892.

———. "Die Popularisierung der Naturwissenschaft." *Die Gegenwart* 13 (1878):380–82.

Zentralblatt für die gesammte Unterrichts-Verwaltung in Preussen, 1882. Berlin, 1882.

Zevenhuizen, Erika. *Politische und weltanschauliche Strömungen auf den Versammlungen deutscher Naturforscher und Ärzte von 1848–1871*. Berlin, 1937.

Ziegler, Heinrich Ernst. *Einleitung zu dem Sammelwerke Natur und Staat: Beiträge zur naturwissenschaftlichen Gesellschaftslehre*. Jena, 1903.

———. *Die Naturwissenschaft und die Socialdemokratische Theorie*. Stuttgart, 1893.

———. "Verhältnis der Sozialdemokratie zu Darwinismus." *Zeitschrift für Sozialwissenschaft* 2 (1899):424–32.

Zimmermann, Magdelene. *Die Gartenlaube als Dokument ihrer Zeit*. Munich, 1963.

Zmarzlik, Hans-Günter. "Social Darwinism in Germany, Seen as a Historical Problem." In Hajo Holborn, ed. *Republic to Reich: The Making of the Nazi Revolution: Ten Essays*. Translated by Ralph Manheim. New York, 1972, pp. 435–74.

Zola, Émile. *Germinal*. Translated by L. W. Tancock. Baltimore, 1954, originally published 1885.

Index